The Christian Hebraism of John Donne

Medieval & Renaissance Literary Studies

The
Christian Hebraism
of John Donne

*written with the
fingers of man's hand*

Chanita Goodblatt

DUQUESNE UNIVERSITY PRESS
PITTSBURGH, PENNSYLVANIA

Copyright © 2010 Duquesne University Press
All rights reserved

Published in the United States of America by
DUQUESNE UNIVERSITY PRESS
600 Forbes Avenue
Pittsburgh, Pennsylvania 15282

Library of Congress Cataloging-in-Publication Data

Goodblatt, Chanita.
    The Christian Hebraism of John Donne : written with the fingers of man's
hand / Chanita Goodblatt.
        p. cm. — (Medieval & Renaissance literary studies)
    Includes bibliographical references and index.
    Summary: "During the Reformation, as Christian scholars demonstrated
more interest in Hebrew language and the Jewish roots of European civilization, John Donne's prose works highlight this intellectual trend as Donne
draws on specific exegetical, lexical, rhetorical, and thematic strategies tied
to Hebrew traditions. Goodblatt also includes reproductions of the Hebrew
Rabbinic and Geneva Bibles for reference"—Provided by publisher.
    ISBN 978-0-8207-0431-9 (cloth : alk. paper)
    1. Donne, John, 1572–1631—Prose. 2. Donne, John, 1572–1631—Religion.
3. Christian Hebraists—England—History—16th century. 4. Christian
Hebraists—England—History—17th century. 5. Jewish learning and
scholarship—England—History—16th century. 6. Jewish learning and
scholarship—England—History—17th century. I. Title.

    PR2248.G66 2010
    828'.308—dc22
                                                        2010003065

∞ Printed on acid-free paper.

In appreciation of the present
Joseph Glicksohn

With confidence in the future
Arit Goodblatt Glicksohn
Ofer Goodblatt Glicksohn

CONTENTS

Acknowledgments

Research for this book was supported by the following sources: a grant from the Office of the Dean, Faculty of Humanities & Social Sciences, Ben-Gurion University in 1998; a fellowship from the Center for Advanced Judaic Studies (CAJS) at the University of Pennsylvania in January–February 2000; two grants from the Israel Science Foundation (grants no. 846/02 and 1538/04) in 2002–2005; and a James. M. Osborn Fellowship in English Literature and History at the Beinecke Library, Yale University in January–February 2005.

I would like to thank: my many colleagues from the John Donne Society, for a stimulating intellectual and collegial environment; my colleagues from Ben-Gurion University—Chaim Cohen, Mayer I. Gruber, Howard Kreisel, Daniel Lasker and Yishai Tobin—with whom I consulted in my study of the intellectual and linguistic background of the medieval Jewish exegetes; Father David Nyhouse from the Pontifical Biblical Institute in Jerusalem for his assistance in locating Latin material; Seth Jerchower from CAJS for his assistance with the Complutensian Polyglot; the editor of this series, Albert C. Labriola, and Duquesne University Press Director Susan Wadsworth-Booth for their generous encouragement and editorial expertise throughout the preparation of the manuscript. Sadly, during the preparation of this book for publication, Professor Labriola passed away. He was to the utmost a gentleman and a scholar, and will be greatly missed. May his memory be blessed. I would also like to thank an anonymous reviewer of my manuscript, who realized the image of the "ideal reader" in an invaluable response to my work.

I would like to thank the Beneicke Library of Yale University for access to the Evelyn Simpson Papers, in the James Marshall and Marie-Louise Osborn Collection, Beinecke Rare Book and Manuscript Library, Yale University (OSB MSS 90). Simpson's daughter, Mary Fleay, has graciously given me permission to quote extensively from her mother's correspondence and papers. I have not been able to locate the holders of copyright for the letters of various scholars with whom Evelyn Simpson corresponded: David Capell Simpson, George Reuben Potter, Don Cameron Allen and Otto Lehman. If these heirs are located, future editions of this book will be corrected. Lastly, I would like to thank Cathy Keating, First Lady of the State of Oklahoma in 1995, for her help in obtaining copies of the various speeches made during the "A Time of Healing" prayer service, as well as Rabbi David Packman for a printed copy of his remarks.

Diverse material from earlier essays have been included in several places: portions of the discussion of Christian Hebraism (introduction and chapter 1) and the discussion of the sermons on the Penitential Psalm 6:1 and 6:6–7 (chapter 2) are from "From 'Tav' to the Cross: John Donne's Protestant Exegesis," in *John Donne and the Protestant Reformation: New Perspectives,* ed. Mary Arshagouni Papazian, copyright © 2003, Wayne State University Press, with the permission of Wayne State University Press; portions of my essay "High Holy Muse" appear in a further discussion of the sermon in the Penitential Psalm 6:6–7 (chapter 2); and portions of my essay "The Presence of Abraham Ibn Ezra in Seventeenth-Century England" appear in the discussion of "The Literal Sense: Moralized Grammar" (chapter 4). I would like to thank Wayne State University Press, Ben-Gurion University Press ("High Holy Muse") and Heldref Publications ("The Presence of Abraham Ibn Ezra") for permission to include passages from these essays. The "Appendix: Hebrew and Aramaic Texts" cites passages from the Hebrew Bible, the Talmud and medieval Jewish exegetes; all of these texts are considered to be in the public domain.

Finally, I would like to thank the following for their generous assistance in providing funding for the research and publication of this book: Professor Avishai Henik, former dean of the Faculty of Humanities and Social Sciences, Ben-Gurion University; Professor Mark Gelber, as department chair, and the Conrad and Chinita Abrahams-Curiel Fund of the Department of Foreign Literatures and Linguistics, Ben-Gurion University; Professor Moshe Justman, dean of the Faculty of the Humanities and Social Sciences, Ben-Gurion University; and Professor Rivkah Carmi, president, Ben-Gurion University.

A Note on the Texts

The present discussion of the commentaries written by the medieval Jewish exegetes Rashi, Ibn Ezra, and Kimhi is based upon the original Hebrew texts, whenever possible taken from the 1525 *Biblia Rabbinica* (cited by volume and page numbers). For translations of these commentaries, I have either produced my own or have turned to modern, accessible translations when they are available—making emendations, however, based upon my own readings of the Hebrew originals. I have produced my own translations of passages from the Aramaic *Targum;* translations from the Talmud have been adapted from the Soncino edition.

All translations from critical essays in Hebrew are my own. Translations from Latin and Greek were provided by Mayer I. Gruber, Ilaria Stiller-Timor, Georges Salma, Pau Figeuras and Michele Horowitz. English translations of the Hebrew Bible are cited from the following sources: the 1850 edition of *The Holy [Wycliffe] Bible,* originally completed in 1395 by John Wycliffe and his followers; the 1530 edition of the *Tyndale Bible;* the 1535 edition of the *Biblia the Byble,* created by Miles Coverdale; the 1560 edition of *The [Geneva] Bible and Holy Scriptures;* the 1572 edition of *The Holie [Bishops'] Bible;* the 1609–10 edition of the Catholic *The Holie [Doway] Bible;* and the 1611 edition of *The Holy [King James] Bible.* In addition, a modern Jewish source was consulted: *Tanakh: The Holy Scriptures,* published by the Jewish Publication Society. The *Vulgate Bible* is cited from either of two sources: Jerome's 405 Latin translation, retrieved from http://www.speedbible.com/vulgate; and the *Biblia Sacra: Juxta Vulgatam Clementinam*. Unless otherwise noted, biblical verses throughout the book will be cited from the 1611 *Holy [King James] Bible*, sanctioned by liturgical use in St. Paul's Cathedral (*Sermons* 10:328). In relating, however, to Jewish exegetical sources in the Tables, biblical verses are cited from the *Tanakh*.

All quotations from John Donne's sermons are taken from the Simpson and Potter edition, and cited as *Sermons*, followed by volume and page numbers. Citations of material from the James M. and Marie-Louise Osborn Collection, at the Beinecke Rare Book and Manuscript Library, Yale University, are marked in the following manner: OSB MSS Number, Box Number, Folder Number.

Sixteenth and seventeenth century spelling and punctuation of texts have been preserved in all quotations cited here. Exceptions are the modernization in the use of: long "s" ["f"] as modern "s"; "i" as "j"; "u" as "v"; replacing the vowel-macron with the succeeding "n" or "m"; replacing letters superscripted over "y" ("e" with "ye"/"the"; "t" with "that"); and replacing the superscripted "c" over "w" with "which."

Introduction

The second part of this book's title is cited from Donne's 1621 Lenten sermon, preached on February 16 before King James at Whitehall. Donne turns to the *Book of Daniel* in order to substantiate his argument about the integrity and authority of the biblical text as "a sufficient Instruction to *Timothy*" (*Sermons* 3:207). He explains:

> It is the Text that saves us; the interlineary glosses, and the marginal notes, and the *variæ lectiones*, controversies and perplexities, undo us: the Will, the Testament of God, enriches us. . . . The Word of God is *Biblia*, it is not *Bibliotheca*; a Book, a Bible, not a Library. And all that book is not written in *Balthazars* character, in a *Mene, Tekel, Upharsim* [marginal note: Dan. 5:25] that we must call in Astrologers, and Chaldeans,[1] and Southsayers, to interpret it. That which was written so, as that it could not be understood, was written, sayes the text there [marginal note: v. 5], with the fingers of mans hand; It is the hand of man that induces obscurities; the hand of God hath written so, as a man may runne, and read; walk in the duties of his calling here, and attend the salvation of his soul too. (*Sermons* 3:208)

Jeanne Shami has placed this sermon against the backdrop of the attempt by church and state to introduce conformity into the English pulpit, particularly in Donne's "opposition to controversial handling of scriptural mysteries" (*John Donne and Conformity in Crisis* 94). To do so, the preacher epitomizes the crucial difference between the text written on the wall by "man's hand" (*Daniel*)

1

and that written by "the hand of God" (*Habakkuk*); whereas the Aramaic phrase from *Daniel*, "MENE, MENE, TEKEL UPHARSIN" (i.e., "Numbered, numbered, weighed and divided")[2] is enigmatic and "induces obscurities,"[2] the prophetic text from *Habakkuk* 2:2 ("And the LORD answered me and said, Write the vision, and make it plaine upon tables, that he may runne that readeth it") provides clear instruction for "duties" and "salvation." Donne thus cleverly juxtaposes two instances of inscription, at once emphasizing the significance of a written text and distinguishing between its status as human or divine authority.

Yet notwithstanding this lesson, which was specifically designed to suit the particular historical and homiletic circumstances of his preaching, Donne himself is an inveterate user of just those "interlineary glosses, and the marginal notes, and the *variae lectiones*"—which are themselves very much "written with the fingers of man's hand." Thus inserted into the written record of Donne's response to the biblical text are marginal notes—references to the cited biblical passages. By thus interweaving these citations from the books of *Daniel* and *Habakkuk*[3] into his sermonic lesson on 1 Timothy 3:16,[4] Donne conceives of the biblical text as one vast interpretive panorama in which each biblical verse bespeaks the meaning of another. In addition, Donne's citing of the Latin and Aramaic phrases indicates what Mikhail Bakhtin has termed a "heteroglot conception of the world" ("Discourse" 293), a description that is highly appropriate for encounters in Donne's sermons among the various languages of the Christian (Latin, Greek) and Jewish (Hebrew, Aramaic) exegetical traditions.

Bakhtin's words also elucidate in a more general way Donne's participation in the multilingual, intertextual endeavor of Christian Hebraism in Reformation England. My purpose in this book is therefore to authenticate Donne as a Christian Hebraist by elucidating the exegetical strategies that make him a participant in this intellectual and religious movement. Four major points distinguish this effort. First, that the discussion of Donne's study of the Hebrew Bible must include an investigation into the complex Jewish exegetical tradition, as well as into its direct and indirect Christian transmission. Second, that any discussion of Donne's biblical hermeneutics must also address the textual and religious polemic, both intra-Christian and Jewish-Christian, which is foregrounded in biblical exegesis. Third, that a flexible understanding of exegetical connections should be maintained, reflecting the intertwined character of both Jewish and Christian exegetical projects. Fourth and finally, that this book itself demonstrates that Bakhtinian "heteroglot conception" by juxtaposing, confronting and comparing various exegetical and scholarly voices.

These voices are most distinctly apparent in Donne's four sermon series on the Penitential and Prebend Psalms (table 1):[5] an undated series on the Penitential Psalm 6, possibly preached at Lincoln's Inn during the Lenten seasons of 1616–1621 and re-preached in parochial situations;[6] the series on the Penitential Psalm 38, listed in *Fifty Sermons* under the title "Sermons Preached at *Lincolns-Inne*" and primarily preached during the spring of 1618;[7] an undated series on the Penitential Psalm 32, probably preached at St. Paul's Cathedral, very possibly during the Lenten seasons of 1626–1627;[8] and the Prebend Sermons, preached at St. Paul's Cathedral and dated in the years 1625–1627.[9] These series conjointly link him to the scholarly tradition of Christian Hebraism. For one can conjecture, as does David Edwards, that Donne's "love of the psalms may well have been the main reason why he began to study Hebrew seriously amid all the problems of his life in 1613" (313). Furthermore, D. C. Allen attests to the fact that Donne's series of sermons on the Penitential Psalms "seem to be the high point of his use of the Hebrew" (Allen, "Dean Donne" 214), while Evelyn Simpson confirms that these sermons "contain the most careful and detailed of his Hebrew expositions" (*Sermons* 10:308). Finally, Janel Mueller's edition of the Prebend sermons clearly demonstrates that (what she aptly terms) Donne's "showy but demonstrably genuine erudition" ("Preface" viii) includes his use of Christian Hebraist sources.[10]

Table 1. Donne's Sermon Series on the Penitential and Prebend Psalms

Biblical Verse	Venue	Date
Psalm 6:1–10	[Inns of Court]	[1616–21]
LXXX Sermons 50–55	Parochial	1625
Psalm 38:2–5	Inns of Court	
Fifty Sermons 19–23		Spring 1618
Psalm 38:9		Winter 1620
Circulated in manuscript		
Psalm 32:1–11	St. Paul's Cathedral	January–June 1626
LXXX Sermons 56–63		January–March (Hilary Term) 1627
Prebend Sermons	St. Paul's Cathedral	
LXXX Sermons 65–69		
Psalm 62:9		May 8, 1625
Psalm 63:7		January 29, 1626
Psalm 64:10		November 5, 1626
Psalm 65:5		January 28, 1627
Psalm 66:3		[May–December] 1627

What is more, these sermon series also comprise a point of confluence for several central issues in the study of Donne's sermons. Mueller's assertion in her preface to *Donne's Prebend Sermons* comprises a fruitful starting point for the present discussion. She writes,

> It need not be argued that a sermon of Donne's, like any other work, is best read and certainly best understood whole. But I do wish to claim that the advantage of wholeness extends to an entire series in the case of the five Prebend sermons, and that as a unit they rank high among Donne's best and most representative produc-

tions. (This unit, as originally designed, was preserved in its first printing in *LXXX Sermons*—and in Alford's otherwise highhanded edition—but is broken in the chronological ordering of Potter and Mrs. Simpson). ("Preface" x)

Mueller's reference to Simpson and Potter's *The Sermons of John Donne* forefronts two different approaches to editing. In her early essay, Simpson argued for the overriding importance of a chronological organization of Donne's sermons, supporting her expressed (though somewhat elusive) purposes of illustrating "the course of Donne's life by reference to his sermons" and of tracing "any development in his theology and his inward experience during the sixteen years of his ministry" (Spearing "Chronological Arrangement" 468).[11] This biographical, historical approach supports a chronological divide between Donne's early and later preaching career, which was effectively brought about by his move at the end of 1621 from the Readership at Lincoln's Inn to the position as Dean of St. Paul's Cathedral.[12] Yet Janel Mueller's assertion of the "advantage of wholeness" invites attention to another, more synchronic, generic approach to editing, which gives "an aesthetic orientation precedence over the strictly historical" (Shillingsburg 19). This approach is very much in evidence throughout Donne's three seventeenth century Folios, three collections of his sermons that were published posthumously in 1640, 1649 and 1661. For these collections particularly forefront groups of sermons attuned to the Church calendar—for example, Christmas, Candlemas, and Whitsunday—and Church ritual—for example, marriages and churching. Not only have these varied groups attracted considerable scholarly attention,[13] but Simpson also gives credence to this original editorial intent by editing a selection entitled *John Donne's Sermons on the Psalms and Gospels*. This latter approach thus corroborates Donne's use of his sermon series on the Psalms throughout his ecclesiastical career, whether before what I. A. Shapiro has described as "the smaller, homogeneous congregation of lawyers and other learned men who heard him preach at Lincoln's Inn" or before the "heterogeneous congregations

Donne would ordinarily preach to in his parish churches or at St. Paul's" ("Sermon Dates" 55).

Taking a cue, therefore, from Janel Mueller's acknowledgment that her edition, which "follows so closely in the wake of George Potter's and Evelyn Simpson's monumental, ten-volume *Sermons of John Donne* requires some explanation" ("Preface" vii), this introduction must address the question: "Why include in one study Donne's sermons on the Penitential and Prebend Psalms?"—particularly as Mueller's well-annotated edition of the Prebend sermons is complemented by the full-length studies of Timothy Stevens and Philip George on the sermons on the Penitential Psalms. It is the presence of both sermon types together as a significant, sequential group in the 1640 *LXXX Sermons* that first raises the potential for such a study. For following the "Sermons Preached upon The Conversion of S. Paul" and preceding those "Preached at Court, and Else-Where upon Severall Occasions," the "Sermons Preached upon the Penitentiall Psalmes" (6, 32, 51) and the "Prebend Sermons Preached at S. Pauls [Cathedral]" (62–66) are positioned between the ecclesiastical celebration of revelation and conversion on the one hand, and the variable determinants of venue, occasion and auditory on the other. It can well be said that the sermons on the Psalms reflect these concerns, marking a personal, religious experience (penitence) that is encompassed within a liturgical context of confession and penitence—specifically within the ecclesiastical season of Lent (*Sermons* 9:34–38)—as well as a personal, homiletic commitment entailed by liturgical place and duty (the recitation of Prebend Psalms at St. Paul's Cathedral). As such, this group as a whole also aligns itself with the series on the Penitential Psalm 38, most especially because the two Folios, as Evelyn Simpson argues, "should be regarded as essentially one volume" (*Sermons* 1:46).

Donne's series of sermons on the Psalms thereby continues the liturgical traditions appointed by both the Catholic and Protestant churches. Thus the sermons on the Penitential Psalms are most notably participants in what Stanwood has discussed as "a literary and devotional tradition" ("Earliest Sermons" 366) extending back to the medieval church: the belief that these Psalms were composed by David "in his remorse for his unlawful passion for Bathsheba, the murder of her husband Uriah, and the subsequent judgment of God in the death of their child" (Duffy 226); the creation of the group of Penitential Psalms by the sixth century CE Roman writer, statesman and monk Cassiodorus; its regular use in the Divine Office; and its presence in pre-Reformation and post-Reformation primers.[14] There is in addition a strong tradition of homiletic responses to these biblical texts; one needs only to cite Luther's *The Seven Penitential Psalms* (14:137–205) or Lancelot Andrewes's paraphrase of *The 7 Penitential Psalms* (included in the *Holy Devotions* 318–61). Similarly, the Prebend sermons are associated with, and transform, the daily obligation for psalm recitation by the church canons that was prescribed by an "ancient statute, believed to transmit apostolic practice" (Janel Mueller, "Introduction" 5). They thus particularly demonstrate—as Eiléan Ní Chuilleanáin argues—"the Protestant habit of substituting sermons for other more traditional proceedings.... The sermon, then, may be simultaneously a continuation of the perennial Christian tradition of preaching, a substitute for a medieval ritual rejected by Protestantism and a commentary on the reasons for rejection or acceptance of medieval practices" (198–99).[15]

This essentially generic concept of Donne's sermons on the Penitential and Prebend Psalms is complemented by the conception of a series united by a biblical text: either in reflection upon a single biblical verse; or called forth (in two pairs: John 5:22 and John 8:15; Job 19:26 and 1 Corinthians 15:30)[16] by the attempt to "reconcile some such places of Scripture, as may at first sight seem to differ from one another" (*Sermons* 2:325). Table 2 lists 13 such series,[17] also preached continuously throughout

Donne's ecclesiastical career. In this context, the sermons on the Penitential and Prebend Psalms not only sustain the larger, generic groups of the Folios, but also enlarge as well upon the relatively restrained scope determined by individual biblical verses. Thus Donne makes explicit the integral rhetorical strategy within each series of his sermons on the Penitential Psalms 6, 32 and 38; whether it is his amplification of the psalmic speech acts (6 and 38) into rhetorical devices for prayer and penitence,[18] or whether it is his amplification of the psalmic title (32) into the "way of Catechisme, of instruction in fundamentall things, and Doctrines of edification" (*Sermons* 9:251).[19] In a similar manner, he introduces the Prebend sermons by saying (in his first Prebend sermon, on verse 62:9): "And of those five Psalmes, which belong to mee, this out of which I have read you this Text, is the first. And by God's grace, (upon like occasions) I shall handle here some part of every one of the other foure Psalmes, for some testimony, that those my five Psalmes returned often into my meditation" (*Sermons* 6:293).[20] In doing so, they provide Donne not only with an opportunity to fully develop an integrated method of preaching on the biblical text, but also with the means by which to continue liturgical traditions.

Table 2. Donne's Sermon Series on Biblical Verses

Biblical Verse	**Venue**	**Date**
1 Timothy 1:15 *XXVI Sermons* 13–14	Whitehall	April 19, 1618 April 21 or 26, 1618
Matthew 4:18–20 *LXXX Sermons* 71–72	The Hague	December 19, 1619
John 5:22 / John 8:15 *Fifty Sermons* 12–13	Inns of Court	January 30, 1620
Ecclesiastes 5:13–14 *XXVI Sermons* 10	Whitehall	April 2, 1620

Table 2 (*cont.*)

Biblical Verse	Venue	Date
Job 19:26 *1 Corinthians 15:50* *Fifty Sermons* 14–15	Inns of Court	[Easter Term 1620]
Matthew 18:7 Fifty Sermons *17–18*	Inns of Court	[November] 1620
John 1:8 Fifty Sermons *36–38*	St. Paul's Cathedral	December 25, 1621 June 24, 1622 October 13, 1622
Micah 2:10 Fifty Sermons *9–10*	[Bridgewater House]	[1621/1623]
Ezekiel 34:19 Fifty Sermons *24–25*	Whitehall	1622–1625
John 16:8–11 LXXX Sermons *36–37*	St. Paul's Cathedral	Whitsunday [1624] Whitsunday [1625]
1 Corinthians 15:29 *LXXX Sermons* 21	St. Paul's Cathedral	Easter April 12, 1626 May 21, 1626 June 21, 1626
John 14:26 *LXXX Sermons* 28–29	St. Paul's Cathedral	Whitsunday May 13, 1627 Whitsunday June 1, 1628
Genesis 1:26 *Fifty Sermons* 28–29	Whitehall	April 1629

Certainly then, as homiletic, liturgical and exegetical texts, the sermons on the Penitential and Prebend Psalms provide a remarkable opportunity for studying Donne's utilization of biblical and interpretive sources within a specific ecclesiastical context. The present study of Donne's sermon series on the Psalms thus takes up the challenge posed by Jeanne Shami, when she writes that "rarely are the sermons seen as issuing from any specific context—generic, historical, theological, political, or cultural" ("Donne's Sermons and the Absolutist Politics of Quotation" 383). The goal of the subsequent chapters is therefore to discern, in the four different sermon series on the Penitential (6, 32, 38) and Prebend psalms (62–66), Donne's attention to the original, Hebrew biblical text from within a concept central to his preaching on these psalms. This is quite different from the indexical approach that has characterized previous discussions of Donne's knowledge of Hebrew. For the emphasis is not on ascertaining the lexical extent of such knowledge; as such, individual Hebrew terms in each sermon will not be indexed. Rather, the emphasis is on Donne's interpretive and homiletic use of Hebrew terms as an essential part of his development of a clearly defined, integrated sermon series, most particularly focusing on those terms clustered around a central meaning. This generic concept therefore provides a most fruitful way in which to understand how Donne as preacher participated in the Christian Hebraism of Reformation England, and how he utilized it for his own singular religious and theological purposes. It is my hope that in this manner the various exegetical and scholarly voices—inscribed with the "fingers of man's hand" as commentaries on and readings of a variety of texts (biblical verses, sermons, critical essays)—will provide a fascinating encounter for the reader with an enduring tradition focused not only on the study of language, philology and text, but also on an intellectual dialogue spanning religions, languages and centuries.

ONE

Christian Hebraism

Sources and Strategies

[Philology] is precisely what the etymology of the word declares, "love of the word": an appreciative attraction to verbal documents that seeks to understand their meaning, starting with the surface and penetrating to whatever depths are possible, but also alert to the fact that a given text comes from and is shaped by a specific time and place that usually is significantly different from that of the observer.
— Siegfried Wenzel, "Reflections on (New) Philology"

Reading the Biblical Text

As one of the most prominent preachers of the early seventeenth century, John Donne was a participant in the intellectual and religious movement of Christian Hebraism in Reformation England. Hebraic scholarship asserted itself in the creation of the English Reformation Bibles—particularly the Geneva and the King James versions[1]—as well as in contemporary (Sidneian) psalm translations and sermons (such as those by Lancelot Andrewes).[2] This was the period (extending until the outbreak of the English civil war) in which, as David Katz writes, "the interest of these early scholars was biblical alone" ("Abendana Brothers" 30), and this interest encouraged the creation of complex, multilingual systems of biblical and interpretive texts: the original source text, the Hebrew Bible, with its inimitable matrix of hermeneutic gaps; the *Targum,* the Aramaic interpretative translation of the Hebrew Bible, published (in the original and in Latin translation) in the sixteenth century Complutensian and (Royal) Antwerp Polyglots;[3] the medieval Jewish exegetical sources consulted, for example, by the translators of the Geneva and King James Bibles; and the many dictionaries, biblical translations and commentaries—such as the *Biblia Rabbinica* (see fig. 1),[4] Nicholas of Lyre's *Postillae Perpetuae,* the Wycliffe and Coverdale Bibles, and John Minsheu's *Ductor in Linguas.*

There is no more fascinating paradigm of this Hebraic scholarship in England than the "King's Great Matter," the protracted annulment of Henry VIII's marriage to Catherine of Aragon during the years 1527–1533, which prefigures and encourages Christian Hebraism in its interconnected exegetical, religious and political aspects. Embroiled in this crisis, the "king-theologian,"[5] as Guy Bedouelle writes, "chose to fight the battle in a different [not legal or ecclesiastical] arena, one in which theology and exegesis had a part to play" (22–23).[6] The King did so by pitting the Levitical prohibition of marriage to a sister-in-law against the Deuteronomic obligation of a Levirate marriage; as William Tyndale summarizes in his 1530 tract *The Practice of Prelates,* these" "two texts seem contrary, the one [Lev. 18:16] forbidding, the other [Deut. 25:5] commanding, a man to take his brother's wife" (323–24). This contradiction seems apparent in Tyndale's contemporary translation of the Pentateuch. For while Leviticus 18:16 reads: "Thou shalt not unheale [uncover] the secrettes of thy brothers

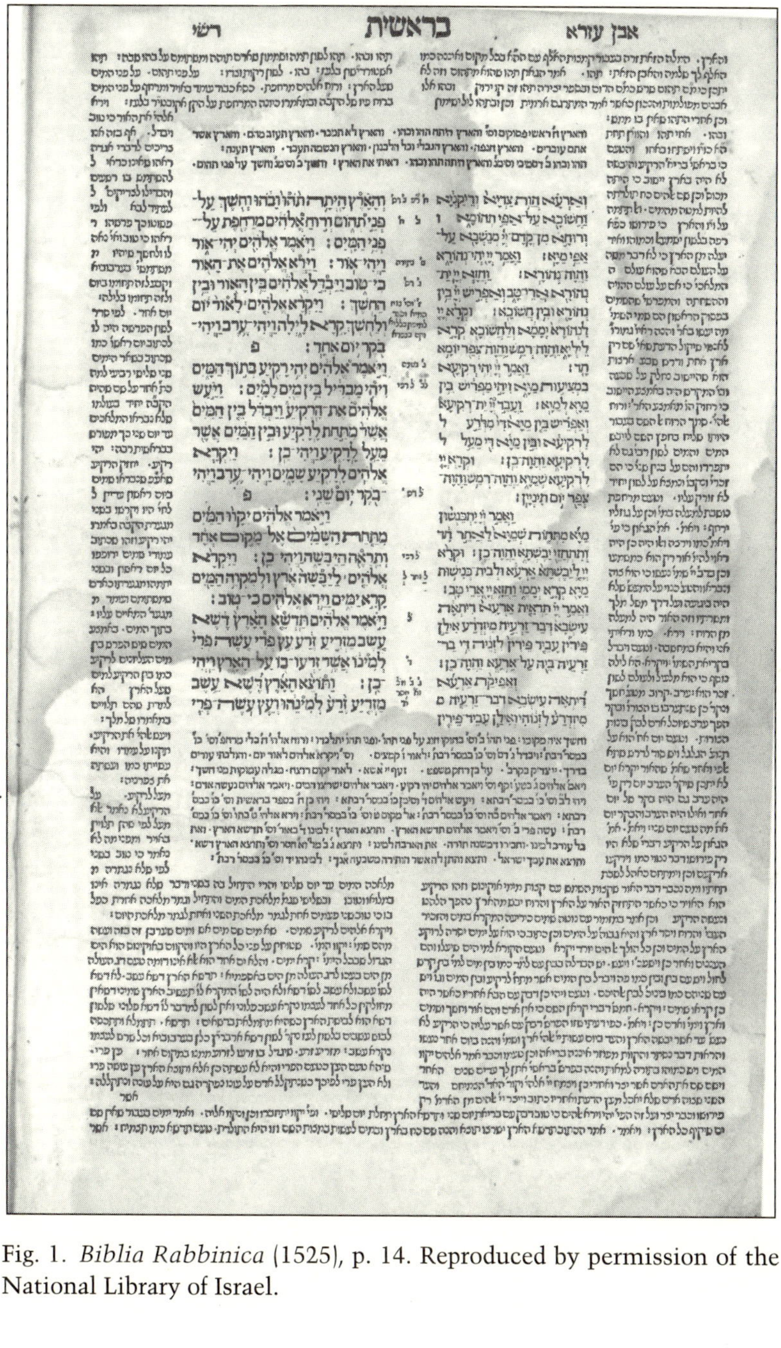

Fig. 1. *Biblia Rabbinica* (1525), p. 14. Reproduced by permission of the National Library of Israel.

wife [*eishet-aḥikha*], for that is thy brothers [*aḥikha*] prevyte" ("Leviticus" xxxiii[r]), Deuteronomy 25:5 reads: "When brethren [*aḥim*] dwell together and one of them dye and have no childe, the wyfe of the deed shall not be geven out unto a stranger: but hir brotherlawe [*yevamah*] shall goo in unto her and take her to wife and marie her [*ve-yibmah*]" ("Deuteronomye" xliii[v]).

Yet Tyndale's translations elide the semantic crux involving the opaque Hebrew biblical word יָבָם *yevam*, which could contextually be read as either "brother-in-law" or "kinsman;" this as a result of its juxtaposition to the Hebrew term *aḥim*, which can itself be explained as either "biological brothers" who naturally live together, or as the more general, alternative meaning of "kinsman, son of the same family or nation" (Even-Shoshan 1:43). This is readily evident in the various English biblical translations and commentaries (tables 3 and 4), as well as accurately set out in the Genevan scholia (see fig. 2), which note that "the Ebrewe worde [*yevam*] signifieth not the natural brother, and the worde, that signifieth a brother [*aḥ*], is taken also for a kinseman." Indeed, this semantic confusion is highlighted by the lengthy explanation proposed by the medieval Jewish exegete Abraham Ibn Ezra, who draws on an intertextual reading of three books of the Hebrew Bible (containing the only occurrences of the word *yevam*) to make his own argument that this term does indeed mean "brother-in-law" (table 5)."[7]

Table 3. Deuteronomy 25:5: "Yevam" as Kinsman

A Glasse of the Truthe	Biblia the [Coverdale] Byble	The [Geneva] Bible and Holy Scriptures
THE DIVINE. Ye forsoth, for in the levitike it [*ahikha*] can nor may be taken for other than for the very brother, the texts	When brethren dwell together, and one of them dye without children, then shall not ye wife of the deed take a strange	If brethren dwel together, and one of them dye and have no childe, the wife of the dead shal not mary without: *that is*, unto a

Table 3 (*cont.*)

A Glasse of the Truthe	Biblia the [Coverdale] Byble	The [Geneva] Bible and Holy Scriptures
beynge judge it selfe. But by the Deuteronomyke, as many taketh it: is ment the nexte of the bloode after the degrees prohibite, tho he be but kynseman. And so it might well stand with the Leviticall emongest the Jewes. The whiche interpretation is well approved also by the playne history of Ruth (n. pag.).	man with out, but hir kinsman shal go in unto her, and take her to wyfe: and the first sonne that she beareth, shal be set up after the name of his brother which is deed, that his name be not put out of Israel (Fyrst Parte. lxxxv[r]).	stranger, but his [d] kinseman shal go in unto her, and take her to wife, and do the kinsman's office to her (91v). [d] Because the Ebrewe worde [*yevam*] signifieth not the natural brother, and the worde, that signifieth a brother [*aḥ*], is taken also for a kinseman; it semeth that it is not ment that the natural brother shuld mary his brothers wife, but some other of the kinred, that was in that degree which might marry.

Table 4. Deuteronomy 25:5: "Yevam" as Brother

The Vulgate Bible	The Holy [Wycliffe] Bible	The Holy [King James] Bible
Quando habitaverint fraters simul et unus ex eis absque liberis mortuus fuerit uxor defuncti non nubet alteri sed accipiet eam frater eius et suscitabit semen	Whanne britheren dwellen to gidere, and oon of hem is deed with out fre children, the wijf of the deed brother schal not be weddid to anothir man, but his brothir	If brethren dwell together, and one of them die, and have no child, the wife of the dead shall not marrie without, unto a stranger: her [ll] husbands brother shall go in unto her, and take her to him to wife,

Table 4 (*cont.*)

The Vulgate Bible	The Holy [Wycliffe] Bible	The Holy [King James] Bible
fratris sui (*Vulgate Bible* n.p.).	schal take hir, and schal reise seed of his brother (n.p.).	and performe the duetie of an husbands brother unto her ("The Old Testament" n.p.).
When brethren shal dwel together, & one of them die without children, the wife of the deceased shal not marie to another: but his brother shal take her, and rayse up the seede of his brother (*The Holie* [*Doway*] *Bible* 1:447).		‖ Or, next kinseman

Yet even more significant is the interpretive purpose to which this exegetical dispute is put, for the philological aspect is ultimately used to set the inclusive authority of the Levitical concern with incest and familial purity against the Deuteronomic concern with dynasty and familial continuity. The earlier medieval Jewish dispute over the literal meaning of the biblical text is evident in Ibn Ezra's argument against the Karaite (or "Scripturalist") reading,[8] while this dispute over marriage rules resonates with particular meaning for the Henrician debate. Desiring to extricate himself from his marriage with Catherine, Henry argued against Tyndale's reading of the Deuteronomic obligation and claimed that the literal meaning of *yevam* is actually "kynseman" (*A Glasse of the Truthe*; table 3),[9] thereby concerning himself with the sin of incest involved in marriage to a brother's widow rather than with the maintenance of a Catholic dynasty in England.[10] Jason Rosenblatt has astutely noted that those Bibles contemporary neficial vnto others.

3 The beating of the offenders. 5 To raise vp sede to the kinseman. 11 In what case a womans hand must be cut of. 13 Of iust weights,and measures. 19 To destroy the Amalekites.

1 WHen there shal be strife betwene men, & they shal come vnto iudgement, a and sentéce shalbe giuen vpon them, and the righteous shalbe iustified, and the wicked condemned,

a Whether there be a plaintife or none, y magistrates oght to trie out fautes and punishe according to the crime.

2 Then if so be the wicked be worthy to be beaten, the iudge shal cause him to lye downe, b and to be beaten before his face, according to his trespas, vnto a certeine nomber.

b When the crime deserueth not death.

3 c Forty *stripes* shal he cause him to haue and not past, lest if he shulde excede and beat him aboue that with manie stripes, thy brother shulde appeare despised in thy sight.

c The iewes of superstition afterward take one awaie, 2.Cor.11.24.

4 ¶ *Thou shalt not mosel the oxe that treadeth out the corne.

1.Cor.9.9.
1.tim.5.18.

5 ¶ *If brethren dwel together, and one of thé dye & haue no childe, the wife of the dead shal not mary without: *that is*, vnto a stranger, but his d kinseman shal go in vnto her, and take her to wife, and do the kinsmans office to her.

Ruth 4.3.
matt.22.24.
mar.12.19.
luk.20.27.
d Because the Ebrewe worde signifieth not y natural brother, & the worde, that signifieth a brother, is take also for a kinseman: it semeth that it is not ment that the natural brother shuld mary his brothers wife, but some other of y kinred, y was in that degre w might mary.

6 And the first borne which she beareth, shal succede in the name of his brother which is dead, that his name be not put out of Israél.

7 And if the man wil not take his kinsewoman, then let his kinswoman go vp to the gate vnto the Elders, and say, My kinsmã refuseth to raise vp. vnto his brother a name in Israél: he wil not do the office of a kinsman vnto me.

8 Thé the Elders of his citie shal call him, and comen with him: if he stand and say, I wil not take her,

Fig. 2. *The [Geneva] Bible and Holy Scriptures* (1560), leaf 91v. Reproduced by permission of The Huntington Library, San Marino, California. Manuscript call no. RB 55362.

with the "Great Matter"—such as the Coverdale and Geneva
Bibles (table 3)—"distorted this verse [Deuteronomy 25:5] into
compliance with a Henrician emphasis on the unacceptability of
the levirate" ("*Hamlet*" 23). It is also significant that the earlier
Vulgate and Wycliffe Bibles as well as the later King James Bible
adhere to the Deuteronomic concern with familial continuity (by
translating *yevam* as "husbands brother"; table 4). The historical
fault line running between the two groups of texts thus exposes
the way in which an exegetical crux is attuned to a specific political and theological agenda, "shaped," in Siegfried Wenzel's terms
cited above, "by a specific time and place."

Table 5. Ibn Ezra

Genesis 38:8	Deuteronomy 25:5	Ruth 1:15
The duty of a husband's brother [ve-yabbem otah]: This means, since you are her husband's brother, act as the husband's brother by going unto thy brother's wife (*Biblia Rabbinica* 1:92).	*When brothers dwell together:* When brothers dwell together: [The Karaites] also said that these are not actually brothers, but rather relatives, and they brought proof from [the matter of] Boaz. But they have no case because *yibbum* [Levirate marriage] does not occur there [in the matter of Boaz], but rather redemption [is the custom at hand]. And what is the reason for mentioning [the word] *yaḥdav* ["together"]? That they live in one country or one courtyard? Or that they loved one another? And they [the Karaites] said that the text clearly states *ve-yibmah* ["and he will perform on her the duty of the *yevam*"] and this is an indication that a woman may only be called a *yevamah* with reference to the act of *yibbum*, as is also the case in *shavah yevimtekh* [your *yevamah* has returned; Ruth 1:15]. But [their case] is completely	*Thy brother's wife [yevimteikh] is gone back:* From the word *yevamah* [brother's wife], as already explained in the Pentateuch (*Biblia Rabbinica* 4:282).

Table 5 (*cont.*)

Genesis 38:8	Deuteronomy 25:5	Ruth 1:15
	frustrated, for the text specifically states with respect to the sons of Judah *ve-yabeim otah* ["and he will perform on her the duty of the *yevam*"; Genesis 38:8], and he [Onan] was in fact her [Tamar's] brother-in-law; also in the case of *yevimteikh* [Orpah is called by that title, i.e., "your sister-in-law"] due to their being married to two brothers [and not due to the possibility of Levirate marriage].... we rely on the tradition that they were actual brothers" (*Biblia Rabbinica* 1:440. Trans. Chaim Cohen, "Biblical Institution").	

While Guy Bedouelle, a church historian, has recognized the relationship between exegesis and theology that characterized Henry's "Great Matter," the biblical scholar Moshe Goshen-Gottstein distinguishes several other ramifications of such a Christian Hebraist enterprise:

> The Hebraic revival presents perforce an inbuilt ambivalence. That very same text [the Bible] had been taught for centuries by authority of the church—now the *ad fontes* ideal becomes equated with the *Hebraica Veritas* claim, which in turn links up with the *sensus literalis* claim—to be satisfied, as it were, solely by the "tradition" of Jewish exegesis. The Jewish Bible text, complete with its exegetical tradition, is made to usurp the place held for centuries by the text sacred to the church. Church tradition is being discarded—only to be supplanted by the tradition of Rabbis. This is just to hint at the almost impossible tension created right from the beginning. How can one accept the Bible of the Jews without Judaizing? How can one prefer Ibn Ezra or Radak to the Church fathers? How can one claim superiority of the Jewish text over the text sanctified in the church for centuries? This is such a basic dilemma that it

had to arise—especially in the light of the "sola scriptura" slogan. ("Foundations" 79–80)

Immediately noticeable is Goshen-Gottstein's cataloging of the various Latin terms of Christian Hebraist scholarship: the humanists' *ad fontes* ("to the sources"); Jerome's *Hebraica veritas* ("Hebrew truth"), the medieval *sensus literalis* or *sensus historicus* ("literal or historical sense"), the Reformation's *sola Scriptura* ("sole [authority of] Scripture"). What is more, his various typographic markings of these Latin terms demonstrate the Jewish scholar's recognition of them as what Yury Lotman has called "the alien word" (107); in this instance indicating not simply Goshen-Gottstein's own scholarly distance, but also his qualification of their distinctive imports as Christian scholarship moves toward a new conception of exegesis and theological authority. Through such rhetorical strategies, this passage itself exposes the uncomfortable attitude toward Jewish authority held by those Christian Hebraist scholars who, belonging to that timeless *Respublica Litterarum Sacrarum* ("Republic of Sacred Letters") extending from Jerome's creation of the Vulgate to Luther's insistence on the sole authority of the biblical text, "explored the Jewish roots of European civilization" (Goodblatt, "Christian Hebraists," 110).[11]

Finally, Goshen-Gottstein sets out the importance to Christian Hebraism of two medieval Jewish exegetes: the Spanish Abraham Ibn Ezra (1089–1164) and the Provençal Radak or **Rabbi David Ki**mhi (c. 1160–c. 1235). These Jewish grammarians became, as Frank Manuel has written, "living presences among Christian Hebraists" (59): Ibn Ezra because he translated into Hebrew the work of early Spanish-Jewish philologists writing in Arabic, composed several books on grammar (*Moznei Leshon Ha-Kodesh, Sefer Tzaḥut, Yesod Ha-Dikduk*), and in his biblical commentaries stressed literal readings and grammatical explanations; Kimhi because of his Hebrew philological treatise, the *Mikhlol* (comprising a grammatical section and a lexicon, known as the

Sefer Ha-Shorashim, "The Book of Roots"), and his biblical commentaries that continued the philological analysis introduced by Ibn Ezra. To these two Jewish exegetes should be added the Northern-French Rashi or **Rabbi Shlomo** (Solomon) ben **Isaac** (1030/1040–1105) whose commentaries on the Hebrew Bible, which integrated both literal and midrashic (homiletic) interpretations, were not only consistently used by both Ibn Ezra and Kimhi, but also influenced Christian exegetes such as Hugh of St. Victor, Nicholas of Lyre, and Martin Luther.[12]

The significance of these Jewish exegetes from the eleventh to thirteenth century[13] for sixteenth and seventeenth century Christian readers of the Hebrew Bible is accessible through a discussion of that beleaguered term "Renaissance." Applied to both of these historical periods, this term emphasizes their Janus-like quality; facing both ways, like the Roman god of portals and beginnings, it designates a time of "conspicuous cultural progress in relation to the previous, adjacent period...[and] a conscious relation to ancient sources which are perceived as classic" (Touito 54). Yet it is Leah Marcus's deliberation on the alternative term "early modern" that bears a central import for a discussion of exegetical strategy. For, as she writes, "to look at the Renaissance through a lens called early modern is to see the concern of modernism and postmodernism in embryo...[among other things] an emphasis on textual indeterminacy as opposed to textual closure and stability, and an interest in intertextuality instead of filiation" (43). This statement confirms the implication of intertextuality drawn out from Goshen-Gottstein's passage. What is more, it enables one to perceive commonalities in different centuries and religious cultures as well as appreciate a shared exegetical strategy for reading the Hebrew Bible, one that employs an innovative—and for the Christian Hebraists, often overwhelming and subversive—use of grammar, syntax, logic, and semantic juxtaposition, as well as a reliance on intertextual sources.

Donne as Christian Hebraist

A discussion of Donne's use of such an exegetical strategy necessarily presumes a definition of his standing as a Christian Hebraist. Matt Goldish's cogent distinction among the different gradations of Hebrew knowledge in Reformation England is valuable here, according to which Donne can be designated as a third-order Hebraist, one "who could read *some* Hebrew, but who knew and used significant amounts of Jewish literature in Latin and vernacular translation" (18). Evident in Goldish's discussion is an issue that will be termed *linguistic knowledge*, or *how much* Hebrew is known; he further argues,

> Nevertheless, it is fairly clear that almost no Englishman before the seventeenth century achieved a really thorough fluency in Hebraic learning. G. Lloyd Jones has reproduced lists of the Hebrew and Aramaic works owned by John Dee at the end of the sixteenth century, and those owned by dons and booksellers of sixteenth-century Oxford and Cambridge.[14] These indicate clearly what the level and nature of Hebrew learning were like even at the highest academic spheres—the vast majority consisted of grammars, dictionaries, and Bibles.... Neither Jews nor university teaching, then, were driving forces in the peak of high-level English Hebraism. Most English Hebraists of the seventeenth century either learned only the rudiments of the language in grammar school or university and studied further on their own or were complete autodidacts. (20–21)

Donne's linguistic knowledge of Hebrew follows this paradigm; as Judith Herz has most recently pointed out (Raspa and Herz 98), biographical sources substantiate his study of Hebrew in the years immediately preceding his ordination in January 1615. Thus Izaak Walton writes that during that time Donne "applied himself to an incessant study of Textuall Divinity, and to the attainment of a greater perfection in the learned Languages, *Greek* and *Hebrew*" (40). This information is supported by a letter written by Donne himself (dated July 17, 1613), in which he explains (to an unknown addressee) that "[I am] busying myself a little

in search of the Eastern tongues, where a perpetual perplexity in
the words cannot choose but cast a perplexity upon the things"
(Gosse 2:16). Relying on these sources, R. C. Bald speculates that
"Donne's interests in these studies suggests that he must have
kept in touch with the learned ecclesiastics of his acquaintance"
(281). Bald finds confirmation of this suggestion in yet another letter (addressed to Sir Henry Goodyer and dated March 14, 1614), in
which Donne mentions both Dr. John Layfield, one of the translators of the King James Bible,[15] and William Alabaster, editor of
the *Schindleri Lexicon Pentaglotton* (an abridgement of Valentin
Schindler's 1612 Hebrew lexicon, which included Hebrew and
Aramaic).[16]

Donne's focus on essentially lexical and grammatical aspects
of the language is supported by Evelyn Simpson's "List of Hebrew
Words on Which Donne Comments in the Sermons" (*Sermons*
10:329–44), itself complemented by Troy Reeves's *Index to the
Sermons of John Donne.* Yet this important indexical work often
has significant limitations, as is suggested both by D. C. Allen's
colorful description of it as a wearying *fingerfertigkeit* ("finger
dexterity")[17] and by Jeanne Shami's words as a "power to perpetuate
misleading definitions" ("Troy D. Reeves" 62).[18] For indexers
may overlook transliterated Hebrew terms, as well as English
words that allude to the original Hebrew terms but which would
not be recognized as such by one not proficient in Hebrew.[19] A
discussion of linguistic knowledge alone cannot, therefore, defin-
itively establish Donne's competence as a Christian Hebraist.
David Capell Simpson—the twentieth century Oxford biblical
scholar and Christian Hebraist[20] to whom Evelyn Simpson turned
for assistance—provides important contextual information for
evaluating Donne's Hebraic knowledge. In a letter (dated January
30, 1949), D. C. Simpson writes:

> I am the more conscious of my uselessness to you the more I
> realize that what is needed is *not* a comparison of Donne's treat-
> ment of the Hebrew text of the Old Testament with the *treatment
> of it to-day* but with that of contemporaries of his who, within the

limits of their age, could be called Hebraists. On the other hand, on this very account (i.e. my ignorance of the period etc.) I am far less prejudiced than Don Cameron Allen in regard to Donne and his scholarship....According to Allen[,] Donne, if a scholar himself, *must* have quoted every version, translation good or bad available in his day. But after all, having quoted them[,] all Donne could do in his day was to try to *reconcile* the differences and comment on them—*to-day* of course one would propose emendations & so on on the basis of the differences—in Donne's day it was fairly axiomatic that the *Hebrew* was the original and at worst the version had made a mistake, at best that it could used to elucidate the meaning of the Hebrew....But, after 40 years' experience of teaching Hebrew, I can assure you that the *beginner* has the utmost difficulty in finding his way intelligently through the intricacies of a *Hebrew* Dictionary or a commentary on the *Hebrew* Text. To manipulate and quote intelligently from Dictionaries, Commentaries, Polyglott Bible etc. as Donne suggests Donne [*sic*] did (to the exclusion of having any working knowledge of his own of the Hebrew Bible), I maintain ~~really~~ would seem to presuposes [*sic*] and demands [*sic*] that very working knowledge of the Hebrew Bible which ~~Donne~~ Allen would wish to deny to Donne! (OSB MSS 90, Box 2, Folder 69)

D. C. Simpson is responding to D. C. Allen's pivotal 1943 essay, "Dean Donne Sets his Text,"[21] in which he examines "every biblical reference in the *LXXX Sermons* of 1640" (209),[22] as well as tracking down the many biblical translations Donne consulted, re-creating for this purpose that world "filled with Bibles" (209) in which Donne preached. Allen's credentials as a literary historian and Hebrew scholar[23] cause him, however, to look askance at Donne's more eclectic knowledge. It is here that D. C. Simpson provides a balance to what he sees as Allen's "prejudice." For Simpson stipulates that attention must be paid to the contextual, historical dimension of Christian Hebraist studies contemporary to Donne. Though admitting less knowledge of this period than Allen, Simpson, in discussing the primal status of the Hebrew Bible, fairly points to what Allen himself has elsewhere acknowledged as a dominant linguistic theory about Hebrew being "the innate and Original Language" ("Some Theories" 6).[24] What is of even more importance is Simpson's advocacy of what will be termed the issue of *transmitted knowledge,* or *which translated texts* comprise the intermediate source. In this instance he points to Donne's use of the various tools of Christian Hebraist scholarship, those "Dictionaries, Commentaries, Polyglott Bible[s]," supported by Anthony Raspa's recent comment about Donne's knowledge of "his Hebrew authorities either in their original Latin or in their Latin translations from the Hebrew and sometimes from other European languages" ("Introduction" xxx).

Louis Newman clearly describes this circuitous route of transmission when he writes,

> The works of Rashi, David Kimchi, Ibn Ezra and other medieval Rabbis were made available to Christian scholars, not so much through the original Hebrew texts, which few Christians, even though well versed in Hebrew, were able to consult, as through the writings of medieval Latinists, among them Nicholas of Lyra, who revealed to the Christian world the commentaries of Rashi; moreover, the editions of Christian Hebraists, such as Muenster, Pagninus, Reuchlin and others who compiled dictionaries, grammars, and material from the commentaries placed the works of medieval Jewish exegetes at the command of non-Jewish scholars. (99)

Newman raises an intriguing point regarding the transmission of medieval Jewish exegetical texts within the world of Christian Hebraism, namely, that "few Christians, though well versed in Hebrew" were able to consult these texts. Indeed, Newman's explanation ultimately undercuts Allen's assertion that "the best way to judge the proficiency of a seventeenth century divine in Hebrew is to see what he does with the rabbinical commentaries" (219 n. 5). For the difficulty in understanding medieval Jewish exegetical commentary is not only that, as Allen subsequently explains, the "Hebrew of the rabbis is difficult, wants vocalics, and can usually not be checked by translations" ("Dean Donne" 219–20 n. 5). The difficulty also resides in the commentary's use of a technical and often idiosyncratic Hebrew terminology, and in its highly intertextual nature. Rashi, Ibn Ezra and Kimhi all rely heavily on nonreferenced rabbinic sources, creating an exegetical discourse that is most intelligible to a reader conversant with this milieu.[25]

Newman's remark is therefore particularly relevant for the present study, since it serves to embed Donne within the multilingual, intertextual tradition of Christian Hebraism.[26] For throughout his prose works Donne demonstrates knowledge of these very Christian Hebraist sources: he owned a copy of the Vulgate Bible with Nicholas of Lyre's biblical commentary *Postillae Perpetuae* (originally written between 1322 and 1330);[27] and he cites the Latin translations of the Bible produced by the two sixteenth century Christian Hebraists Sebastian Münster and Santes Pagnino,[28] as well as Johannes Reuchlin's two books on the Kabbalah, *De Verbo Mirifico* ("On the wonder-working word," 1494) and *De Arte Cabalistica* ("On the art of the Kabbalah," 1517). The most productive strategy, therefore, in the study of Donne's Christian Hebraism is to realign the debate so as to include the two issues of *linguistic knowledge* and *transmitted knowledge;* there is nothing unusual, after all, about Donne possessing a basic, lexical grasp of the Hebrew language while learning the more sophisticated semantic nuances of Jewish medieval exegesis from the intermediate Christian Hebraist sources cited so abundantly throughout his sermons.[29]

Donne's Exegetical Strategies

In order to facilitate such a study, this chapter will look closely at four paradigmatic sermon passages, chosen so as to trace Donne's developing use of exegetical sources—from the negligible citation of such sources to their explicit use within a complex, multilingual system of intertextuality. Yet a word of caution. The essentially chronological arrangement of these particular sermons—from the two quite possibly preached at Lincoln's Inn (on Penitential Psalms) to the two preached at St. Paul's

Cathedral and before the King at Whitehall—does not point to a corresponding chronological development in the utilization of exegetical sources. Rather, it emphasizes Donne's varied use of Christian Hebraist texts throughout his ecclesiastical career and before his different auditories, adapting the biblical text and its lesson to the season and circumstance of his preaching.

Psalm 51:7: Purge me with hyssope, and I shalbe cleane

The first passage to be discussed is taken from Donne's single sermon preached upon the Penitential Psalm 51:7.[30] In a section entitled *Hyssopo*, Donne displays his fascination with words:

> All the sacrifices of Expiation of sin, in the Old Law, were done by blood, and that blood was sprinckled upon the people, by an instrument made of a certain plant, which because the word in Hebrew is *Ezob*, for the nearnesse of the sound, and for the indifferency of the matter, (for it imports us nothing to know, of what plant that *Aspergillum*, that Blood-sprinckler was made) the Interpreters have ever used in all languages to call this word Hyssop. And though we know no proper word for Hyssop in Hebrew, (for when they finde not a word in the Bible the Hebrew Rabbins will acknowledge no Hebrew word for any thing) yet the other languages deduced from the Hebrew, Syriaque, and Arabique, have clearly another word for Hyssop, *Zuf*; And the Hebrew Rabbins think this word of our text, *Ezob*, to signifie any of three or four plants, rather then our Hyssop. (*Sermons* 5:309)

The hyssop was used in the Hebrew Bible as part of purification rites, in which an unclean person or object was sprinkled (using the hyssop) with either water or blood (Delitzsch 2:138; Feliks). Donne's citation of the Latin term *Aspergillum* evokes the Church service of *Asperges*—from the Vulgate version of Psalm 51:7, *Asparges me hysopo* ("Thou shalt sprinkle me with Hyssope")—which has been traced back to this biblical rite; in it, water is sprinkled on the altar and congregation with an *Aspergillum* or holy water sprinkler while these words are sung (George 14–16; Wynne).[31] Accordingly, in subsequent lines Donne transforms the Jewish instrument of purification into one of Christian redemption, writing that "This then was *Davids* petition here; first, That hee might have the blood of Christ Jesus applied and sprinkled upon him.... And then he desired this blood to be applied to him, by that Hyssope, by that Blood-sprinkler, which was ordained by God for the use of the Church" (*Sermons* 5:310). Donne's statement is not at all unique; Henry Ainsworth, for example (considered to be "one of the finest Hebrew scholars of his day"; Michael Moody, "Ainsworth"), explains in his 1612 *The Book of Psalmes* that this sprinkling was "here used to signify the ful clensing from syn by the bloud of Christ" (137).

This passage from Donne's sermon thus demonstrates in a somewhat minor chord what Hannibal Hamlin has remarked upon as "the imaginative lengths to which Christian readers would go in order to interpret the Hebrew psalms in Christian terms" (187). Donne takes a philological respite from his Christian exposition of the psalm to instruct his auditory and his reader on the etymology and meaning of the Hebrew word אֵזוֹב *eizov*—translated as "hyssop." Both auditory and reader might well inquire as to the reasons for such a respite. In answer, one can first point to Donne's use of his philological discussion to abrogate Jewish exegetical authority, remarking somewhat facetiously that when the "Hebrew Rabbins" "finde not a word in the Bible" they will not acknowledge its existence. Though his reference to the general, obscure source "Hebrew Rabbins"[32] is indeed problematic, it is not at all unique in his citation of exegetical sources. For Mark Vessey has duly observed regarding Donne's use of Patristic sources in this sermon that "the consensus [Donne cites] of the three great Latin Fathers [Ambrose, Augustine, Jerome] on the allegorical meaning of hyssop smacks of a secondary source" (104).[33] Donne's statement about the Rabbis' confusion regarding the identity of the biblical plant *eizov* is, moreover, quite correct, and is confirmed in Ibn Ezra's commentary on the problems of such identification when he writes that "I do not know what it [*eizov*] is" (table 6).[34]

Table 6. Psalm 51:7: Purge me with hyssope, and I shalbe cleane

Ibn Ezra. Exodus 12:22	Minsheu. *Ductor in Linguas*	Even-Shoshan
Eizov: Rabbi Sa`adiah Ga'on says that *eizov* in Arabic is *zatr* and in the vernacular is oregano. It is an herb distinguished by various kinds of flavors. This is not possible, because Scripture states: "even unto the Hyssope that springeth out of the wall" [1 Kings 5:13]. I do not know what it [*eizov*] is (*Biblia Rabbinica* 1:151; Ibn Ezra's *Commentary on the Pentateuch, Exod.* 240).	6007. *Hysope*: G[allicum]. Hyssópe. T[eutonick]. Ysop, Hyssop, Hisop. B[Belgicum]. Ysop. I[talicum]. Hisopo. H[ispanicum]. Hysòpo, Ysòpo, Hisòpo, Isòpo. P[ortugallicum]. Isòpo. L[atinum]. Hyssòpus, Hyssòpum. Gr[ecum] ὕσσωπος vel ὕσσωπον, ab Heb[raicum]: ezob, *idem*: vel dici volunt quasi ὕομενον, pro χευόμενον, ἐπὶ τὸν ὦπα. Auxiliatur oculis. *Incidit, attenuat, aperit, & aspergit.* Adversatur serpentium ictibus, *si cum sale & cumino tritum ex melle vulneri imponatur.* Ex olco inunctum pediculos necat, *& capitis prurug-inem tollit.* ¶ Matthiol: (242).

Hysope: F[rench]. Hyssópe. G[erman]. Ysop. Hyssop, Hisop. B[elgian]. Ysop. I[talian]. Hisopo. S[panish]. Hysòpo, Ysòpo, Hisòpo, Isòpo. P[ortuguese]. Isòpo. L[atin]. Hyssòpus, Hyssòpum. Gr[eek] *hyssopos* or *hyssopon*, from Heb[rew]: ezob, *same*: or they want to say something like *the thing that rains [hyomenon]*, meaning *poured upon his face [cheuomenon, epi ton opa]*. It cures the eyes. *It cuts, weakens, opens and spreads.* It is used as an antidote for snake bites, *sometimes with salt and minced with cumin and honey, it is put on a wound.* Greased with oil, it kills lice, *and takes away an itch from the head.* ¶ Matthiolus. | *Eizov*: Akkadian: zûpu; Aramaic: ezova; Arabic: zufa; Greek: hyssopos (1:40). |

Secondly, within the sermonic genre Donne is reproducing the etymological concern of John Minsheu's "monumental" (Schäfer 23) seventeenth century dictionary, *Ductor in Linguas* (see fig. 3). Donne is once again correct in his citation of the etymology of the word *eizov* as being related to the word *zuf*, which exists in various Semitic languages; this is confirmed by Even-Shoshan's twenty-first century Hebrew dictionary (table 6). Judith Anderson's discussion of the consequences of Minsheu's "lexical presentation of etymological data" (73) throws light on Donne's search for meaning. She writes:

> Any decontextualization of words is simultaneously a recontextualization, and the radically methodical form of Minsheu's dictionary strives to decontextualize language in order to recontextualize it as linguistic science. Like the effect of Cooper's *Thesaurus* [*Linguae Romanae et Britannicae*] that of the *Ductor* is finally and doubly two-sided, at once to freeze language and to display its irrational if productive mutability, and at once to substantiate its referentiality and its own thingness, its objectivity as a self-contained system or an entity in a world of things (80).

Minsheu's entry (table 6) reveals itself as linguistic science, specifically through the vernacular parallels that he is so careful to list. Such a list does indeed "freeze" the meaning of the Hebrew term *eizov*, particularly in its insistent attempt to secure phonetic transliteration of the word (as Donne himself has explained) into the multilingual term "hyssop." Furthermore, by citing the sixteenth century botanist Pier Andrea Matthiolus[35] as his authority, Minsheu takes care to substantiate this term's reference to a well-known medicinal plant. In a similar manner, Donne also recontextualizes the word "hyssop," though not surprisingly he bases his interest in linguistic science on the Semitic parallels to biblical Hebrew. By doing so, he supersedes the authority of the "Hebrew Rabbins," filling their linguistic lacuna with the knowledge he considers valuable for a seventeenth century educated reader of the Bible. Consequently, while Minsheu vividly explains the various medicinal uses for the hyssop plant, Donne

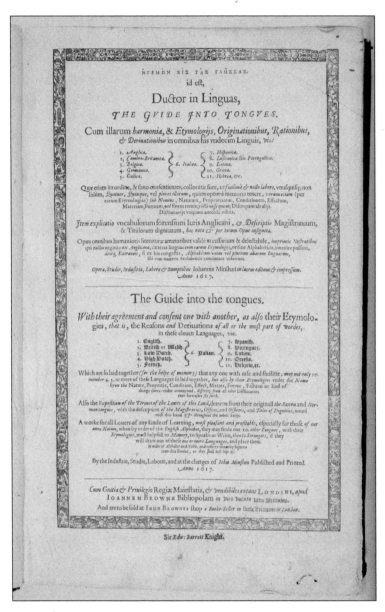

Fig. 3. Title page of John Minsheu, Ductor in Linguas, *The Guide into Tongues* (1617). Reproduced by permission of The Huntington Library, San Marino, California. Manuscript call no. RB 357181.

emphasizes its "thingness" as an *Aspergillum*, that horsehair brush or metal wand used in the Church service (George 15). Minsheu is of course first and foremost a lexicographer, attuned to providing a contemporary scientific account of language, embedded in this instance within a medical discourse. As preacher and priest, Donne draws instead on the discourse of biblical philology; though unfortunately his exact sources are not cited, they clearly demonstrate a primary concern with explanation of the Hebrew language. Donne himself is counted among the audience for Minsheu's dictionary,[36] but concerned as he is with the linguistic underpinnings and Christian meaning of the biblical text, his own explanation ultimately enlists linguistics in the service of a Christian auditory.

1 Samuel 7:6: They drew water, and powred it out before the Lord

The second passage to be examined is taken from the sermon on the Penitential Psalm 6:6–7, listed in the *LXXX Sermons* as "Preached to the King [Charles I] at White-hall, upon the occasion of the Fast, April 5, 1628" (535); as Simpson explains, "The King had ordered a public fast in consequence of the naval and military disasters which had occurred in the war which England was waging against France and Spain" (*Sermons* 8:19). Though the sermon is thereby marked as being part of a national penitence, there is evidence that it was originally preached as part of an earlier liturgical series on the Penitential Psalm 6.[37] Joan Webber discusses this sermon as mostly "organized around the word 'tears,' which becomes the controlling symbol" (*Contrary Music* 136); the following passage is taken from the section designated *Lacrymae* ("tears"). Donne writes,

> And so when at *Samuels* motions, and increpation, the people would testifie their repentance, *They drew water*, says the story, *and poured it out before the Lord, and fasted, and said, We have sinned against the Lord* [marginal note: 1 Sam. 7.6]. They poured

water, *Ut esset symbolum lacrymarum* [marginal note: Nab. Oziel.], That that might be a type, and figure, in what proportion of teares, they desire to express their repentance (*Sermons* 8:200).

The attention of Donne's auditory (perhaps originally Lincoln's Inn, and later king and court) would assuredly have been drawn to the Latin phrase, *Ut esset symbolum lacrymarum* ("So that it should be a symbol of tears"), which would have comprised for the auditory what Janel Mueller terms "a kind of oral punctuation" ("Introduction" 10). The attention of the sermon's reader, however, is just as assuredly drawn to the marginal note, which attributes this Latin phrase to "Nab. Oziel"; actually a misprint in *LXXX Sermons* (539) for the name Rab[bi Jonathan ben] Uzziel, author of the Aramaic interpretative translation *Targum Jonathan* (*Sermons* 10:366).[38] Donne's explicit citing of this Jewish exegetical source is a significant difference between the sermon as oral and printed text;[39] the published version of the sermon not only uses a change in typeface to indicate what Anderson terms the "appearance of another voice" (27–28) but also uses scholia to confirm and define that voice.

Webber has subsequently commented that "by taking his symbol from the verse of the Bible and by developing it with the assistance of commentators from various periods in church history, he [Donne] tries to give it something of the timelessness of the essential Word, which according to him informs the words of Scripture; and he makes himself not an individual voice, but what he would have liked to think of as part of a consort" (*Contrary Music* 137). The desire to uncover the voices of this "consort" should not be taken as that conclusive search for sources against which Daiches warns, but rather as a discovery of the underlying system of intertextuality that shapes the preacher's interpretation and provides it with a comprehensive exegetical context. This discovery is facilitated by Evelyn Simpson's citation of Lyre's fourteenth century commentary as the source for Donne's use of *Targum Jonathan* (*Sermons* 10:366–67).[40] Her discussion of Lyre's influence must, however, be qualified. She does indeed allow full credit to "Rabbi

Lehmann of Oxford"[41] for the citation from Lyre; in his original letter, Lehmann explains that "It therefore looks, as if Donne in saying 'ut esset symbolum lacrymarum' used the *Targum* through Lyra or a related source" (OSB MSS 90, Box 1, Folder 22). It is, however, the discovery of this letter in Evelyn Simpson's archives at the Beinecke Library that fully discloses the circuitous (and enigmatic) route of the transmission of Jewish knowledge in the twentieth century, which reflects as well on such transmission in the seventeenth century. Lehmann's letter (dated May 3, 1956) is actually addressed to Rev. C. A. Simpson, Dean of Christ Church, Oxford, who at this point was advising Evelyn Simpson on matters of Hebrew in Donne's sermons.[42] In his letter Lehmann cites Lyre's Latin commentary, as well as citing and translating into English those by *Targum Jonathan* and Kimhi (table 4)—both of which remain uncited by Evelyn Simpson—thereby marking the inaccessibility and incomprehensibility of these Jewish sources even for a twentieth century Christian Hebraist such as C. A. Simpson.

Table 7. 1 Samuel 7:6: They drew water, and powred it out before the Lord

Jewish Sources	Christian Sources
Targum Jonathan. They were gathered together at Mitspaya and poured forth their heart in repentance like water before the Lord [*ushfihu libhon bityuvta ke-maya qadam Adonai*] and fasted on that day and said: we have been guilty before the Lord (Trans. Lehman, OSB MSS 90, Box 1, Folder 22).	*Nicholas of Lyre. Postillae.* hoc fecerunt in signum humiliationsis....Jonathan filius Oziel maximae reputationis apud Hebraeos, hoc exponit de conversione cordium ad Deum, et sic per istas aquas intelliguntur lacrymae contritionis exeuntes a corde (Cited by Lehmann, OSB MSS 90, Box 1, Folder 22; *Sermons* 10:366–67).
Rashi. They drew water and poured it out: Jonathan translated [it as] "and poured forth their heart in repentance like	This they did as a sign of humiliation....Jonathan son of Uziel of great reputation among the Hebrews, explained this about the

Table 7 *(cont.)*

Jewish Sources	Christian Sources
water before the Lord." And this means that it is but a sign of humility, "Behold we are before you as these waters, which are poured out" *(Biblia Rabbinica* 2:131).	conversion of hearts to God, and so [thus] through those waters are understood the tears of contrition gushing forth from the heart.
Kimhi. They drew water and powred it out before the Lord: "And poured forth their heart in repentance like water before the Lord." One may interpret that they poured out water before the Lord as a sign of atonement for iniquities (Trans. Lehmann, OSB MSS 90, Box 1, Folder 22).	*The [Geneva] Bible.* And they gathered together to Mitzpeh and ^ddrewe water and powred it out before the Lord ("The Olde Testament" 123v). ^d The Chalde text hathe, that thei drewe water out of their heart: that is, wept abundantly for their sinnes.

Studying these various commentaries elucidates complementary exegetical issues and paths of transmission (table 7). One central issue is the invocation of the primal authority of the *Targum* by Jewish and Christian sources; both Rashi and Kimhi quote it in Aramaic, while Lyre and the Geneva Bible rather acknowledge and summarize its explanation. Also of importance is the concept of repentance and sin; Rashi's influence on Lyre is particularly evident in their shared explanation of the tears as "a sign of humility [or submission]," while Kimhi's acknowledged influence on the Geneva Bible[43] is confirmed by their shared emphasis on the reasons for repentance — the people sought "atonement for iniquities" and "wept abundantly for their sinnes." Finally, there is a progressive, figurative intensification of the act of repentance as one moves from the *Targum's* simile, which compares an emotional response ("their heart in repentance") with the act of pouring out water, to Rashi's simile comparing human beings themselves to the waters, and finally to the metaphorical intensification of feelings of guilt and repentance found in both Lyre ("tears of contrition gushing forth from the heart") and in the Geneva Bible ("thei drewe water out of their heart"). In other words, there is a move from an analysis within the simile of pre-existing shared properties (lowliness of poured water and penitent human beings) to the metaphor's integration and extension of these properties (e.g., the laborious act of drawing water and invoking penitence, the depths of well and heart out of which something is drawn, and the quenching of physical and spiritual thirst).[44]

How does this discussion of the underlying, though somewhat elusive system of intertextuality contribute to an understanding of Donne's own commentary on the biblical verse? It clearly makes him, as preacher, "part of a consort" (in Webber's terms), participating in a multitextual consideration of repentance. Significantly, Donne at once appropriates (for his auditory) as well as invokes (for his reader) the authority of the *Targum* by directly quoting it in Latin, thereby foregrounding his move from the literal reading of the Hebrew word מַיִם *mayim*, "water," to its figurative interpretation, "teares," as an expression of repentance. Moreover, Donne's Latin citation actually circumvents the *Targum's* use of simile, particularly as his explanation of the tears as "a type, and figure" is remarkable for its concurrence with the shift into metaphor found in the Genevan marginal note; in a similar manner, Donne integrates the various properties of water and human repentance (e.g., fluidity, the ability to expand and cover, and the power to cleanse). In this manner, Donne's citation of the Latin translation (itself rather more of an interpretation) of the *Targum* aligns him with the Christian exegetical texts, appropriating and ultimately redesignating Jewish authority for the purpose of both personal and national penitence.

Exodus 4:13: O my Lord, send I pray thee, by the hand, of him who thou wilt send

Donne's 1627 Christmas sermon, "Preached at Pauls" (*LXXX Sermons* 39) on Exodus 4:13, provides the third passage. The discussion of the two previous passages has demonstrated how Christian Hebraist sources both verify Donne's use of biblical terms and provide what Julia Kristeva has called a *textual system* (15). Here Donne chooses to explicitly apprise both auditory and reader of this intertextuality, using it as well to overtly expound his Christian argument. In a section designated *Mitte quem missurus* ("Send whom you will send"), he writes,

> we cannot doubt of leave to accompany the Fathers in that Exposition, that these words, *O my Lord, send I pray thee, by the hand, of him who thou wilt send,* are a petition, and not a reluctation against God. And that, not as *Lyra* takes them; *Lyra* takes them to be a petition, and not a reluctation; but a petition of *Moses,* that hee would send *Aaron;* That, if he would send any, he should send a man of better parts, and abilities, then himselfe....Nor as *Rabbi Solomon* takes it; hee takes it for a Petition, and no reluctation; but, a Petition, that God would send *Josuah;* For, (sayes that *Rabbi*) *Moses* had had a Revelation, that *Josuah,* and not he, should be the man, that should bring that People into the Land of Promise...*quid prodest ex Egypto exire, & in peccatis manere,* saies he [marginal note: Ferus];[45] what shall they bee the better, for comming out of the pressures of Egypt, if they must remaine still, under the oppression of a sinfull conscience? And that must be their case, if thou send but a Moses, and not a Christ to their succour....And so these words are a Petition, and no Reluctation, though some men have taken them so; and a Petition for the sending of Christ, and no *Aaron,* no *Josuah,* no other man; though some have taken so too. (*Sermons* 8:152–53)

Donne's first concern is to define the speech act inherent within the biblical text as a "petition" of—and not a "reluctation" (or resistance) against—God; in this argument he follows the Church Fathers, as well as the commentaries written by Rashi[46] and Lyre (table 8). His second, more imperative concern is to identify the object of Moses' petition, since the original Hebrew text reads literally and vaguely שְׁלַח-נָא בְּיַד-תִּשְׁלָח *shelaḥ-na be-yad-tishlaḥ,* "send by the hand of him whom thou wilt send." Donne had earlier quoted Justin Martyr, St. Basil and Tertullian, explaining "this to be a supplication, That God would be pleased to hasten the coming of the Messias" (*Sermons* 8:151). It is not difficult for the Christian reader—Church Fathers, Donne—to transform Rashi's reference (to Aaron or Joshua) as גּוֹאֲלָם לֶעָתִיד *go'alam le-'atid,* "their future redeemer" (table 8) into a foretelling of Christ.

Table 8. Exodus 4:13: O my Lord, send I pray thee, by the hand of him whom thou wilt send

Rashi	Lyre, *Postillae*	Lapide, *Commentarium in Exodus*
By the hand of him whom thou wilt send: [This means] by the hand of him whom you are accustomed to send, and he is Aaron. Another explanation is: by the hand of another [person] whom you wish to send, [for] it is not my end to bring them into the Land [of Israel] and to be their future redeemer, [for] you have many messengers (*Biblia Rabbinica* 2:131; *Pentateuch: Exodus* 16).	Obsecro inquit domine & c. licet Moyses de verbo Domini non dubitaret, tamen quia Aaron frater suus erat eo senior & eloquentior desiderabat eum habere socium sibi a Domino assignandum. Ideo hanc petitionem replicavit (132v). "I beseech thee, O Lord," he said, and, even though Moses did not doubt the Lord's word, nevertheless, as his brother Aaron was older than him and more eloquent, he wanted to have him as	Quare non recte Lyranus putat, his verbis Mosen orasse Deum, ut definite Aaronem fratrem suum miteret, utpote qui se esset eloquentior.... Non recte etiam Rabbi Solomon putat Mosen petiisse Josue, de quo sibi revelatum erat, quod post mortem induceret Hebraeos in Chanaan (*Sermons* 8:395). Lyre does not think correctly, [that] with those words Moses begged God to send precisely his brother Aaron, as is natural for

Table 8 (*cont.*)

Rashi	Lyre, Postillae	Lapide, Commentarium in Exodus
	his partner who would be assigned to him by the Lord. That is why he [God] replied to this request [Exod. 4:14].	a man who is more eloquent than him.... And even Rabbi Solomon does not think correctly [that] Moses asked Joshua, by whom it was revealed to him, that after his [Moses'] death he [Joshua] would lead the Hebrews into Canaan.

What, then, is the purpose of Donne's rather considerable invest-ment in laying out for his auditory at St. Paul's (and ultimately for his reader) the alternative explanations proposed by both Rashi and Lyre? The seventeenth century auditory might well have responded to Donne's sermon as did his twentieth century reader and editor; in a rather piqued evaluation, Simpson writes that "as a Christmas sermon it is a complete disappointment. It contains a great deal about Moses, and very little about Jesus Christ" (*Sermons* 8:12). Simpson's criticism notwithstanding, this passage is especially appropriate for the celebration of Christ's nativity. For here Donne involves his auditory and his reader in the very process of engaging with and refuting biblical commentaries that read the text in a purely contextual, historical sense, that is, that read the object of the petition as either Aaron or Joshua.

The overt intertextuality of this passage has attracted the atten-tion of both D. C. Allen and Evelyn Simpson, who are primar-ily concerned with the issue of *transmitted knowledge* (Allen, "Dean Donne" 220 n. 5; *Sermons* 8:393–96). Yet once again, it is the specific polemical, religious use to which Donne puts these commentaries that is most significant. Clearly echoing the 1616 commentary of the Flemish Jesuit Cornelius à Lapide, who Evelyn

Simpson argues is Donne's mediating source for Rashi (table 8), Donne first presents Lyre and Rashi—Christian Hebraist and Jewish exegete—as two alternative readers of the biblical text. In this manner, Donne aligns the Jewish and Christian authorities as jointly providing a contextual, historical explanation of the biblical verse. Moreover, when we consider his subsequent refutation of these explanations, it becomes apparent that Donne both exhibits and resolves that Christian "inbuilt ambivalence" toward Jewish authority remarked upon by Goshen-Gottstein; at once demonstrating the need to discuss the *sensus historicus* or *literalis*—"a simple explanation of the words" (Caplan 283)—even as it becomes the basis for a more figurative, Christological interpretation. This passage also provokes a discussion of Donne's conception of his auditory and his reader. Donne's references to the Church Fathers, as well as to Lyre and Rashi, presuppose a highly educated audience, knowledgeable in Latin as well as in the multilingual texts of biblical scholarship—and alternatively or concomitantly, a sophisticated audience enjoying the learned intertextuality displayed by a preacher. This conception of the seventeenth century auditory and of subsequent readers provides an appropriate answer to Simpson's twentieth century criticism of the sermon as being "intellectually able...[but] spiritually arid" (*Sermons* 8:12).

Job 16:18: O Earth cover not thou my blood

The final passage is taken from the sermon "Preached in Lent, To the King [Charles I]. April 20. 1630" (*LXXX Sermons* 127), on Job 16:17–19. Here Donne sustains a particularly complex and overt intertextuality among various biblical and exegetical texts. In a rather long passage taken from Part 2 of the sermon, he explains:[47]

> Amongst our later men, *Cajetan*, (and he, from a Rabbi of the Jews, *Aben Ezra*) takes this to be an adjuration of the Earth, as *Gregory* does, but not, as *Gregory*, does, in the person of Christ, but of *Job*

himselfe; That *Job* adjures the earth, not to cover his blood, that is, not to cover the shedding of his blood, not to conspire with the malice of his enemies so much, as to deny him buriall when he was dead....And this may also have good use, but yet it is too narrow, and too shallow, to bee the sense of this phrase, this elegancy, this vehemency of the Holy Ghost, in the mouth of *Job*....the Capuchin *Bolduc,* hath also pursued that [other] sense. That sense is, that in this adjuration, or imprecation, *O Earth cover not thou my blood;* Blood is not literally bodily blood, but spirituall blood, the blood of the soule, exhausted by many, and hainous sins, such as they insimulated Iob of. For, in this signification, is that word, *Blood,* often taken in the Scriptures....And, another [prophet says], *blood toucheth blood* [marginal note: Hosea 4.2], whom the Chalde Paraphrase expresses aright, *Aggregant peccata peccatis,* blood toucheth blood, when sin induces sin. Which place of *Hosea,* S. *Gregory* interprets too, then blood touches blood, *cum ante oculos Dei, adjunctis peccatis cruentatur anima;* Then God sees a soule in her blood, when she wounds and wounds her selfe againe, with variation of divers, or iteration of the same sins....This then will be the force of *Jobs* Admiration, or Imprecation, *O Earth cover not thou my blood*...I would mine enemies knew my worst, that they might study some other reason of Gods thus proceeding with me, then those hainous sinnes, which, from these afflictions, they will necessarily conclude against me. (*Sermons* 9:221–23)

The vivid imagery of uncovered blood in the biblical appeal from Job 16:18—אַל-תְּכַסִּי דָמִי *al- tekhasi dami,* "cover thou not my blood"—evokes associations of death and violence, which has been explained as meaning that "blood not covered by the earth was understood to have been violently shed, and was regarded as calling for revenge on the murderer" (Reichert 84). Donne seeks, however, to transmute the biblical concern with revenge into a more subtle concern with sin and penitence, particularly with what Simpson has described as "Job's passionate protestation of his innocence" (*Sermons* 9:28). To this end, the preacher is preoccupied with defining the participants and the semantics of the biblical speech act, ultimately forging a reading of the impassioned address to the earth that combines literal and figurative interpretations. First laying bare (in this rare instance) the line of Jewish-Christian exegetical transmission—from Ibn Ezra[48] to the sixteenth century Italian Dominican Cardinal Tommaso de Vio Cajetan (table 9)—Donne designates Job as the speaker who vehemently beseeches the earth not to cover his blood. Allen's disparaging remark that Ibn Ezra "comes through Cajetan and hardly counts" ("Dean Donne" 220 n. 5) reflects more on what the Oxford biblical scholar D. C. Simpson has observed as this scholar's prejudice regarding Donne than on Donne's appropriately circuitous seventeenth century use of Jewish exegetical sources. Indeed, Donne's citation of Ibn Ezra serves to affirm the primal authority of the Jewish exegete, as well as the literal, contextual reading presupposed by him and confirmed by Cajetan (table 9). Finally, one might well wonder at what seems to be Donne's largely rhetorical gesture in opposing this reading to Gregory's allegorical one of the speaker as Christ. It is only by looking more closely at Gregory's commentary *Librum B. Job* (table 9) that Donne's reason becomes apparent. For Gregory emphasizes the universal authority of the Church, whose teachings of "the mystery of his redemption in all parts of the world" belie the effort to "hide the blood of our Redeemer"—that is, literally to cover his blood or more figuratively to dispute his redemption. Donne, however, uses his reading of the biblical text rather to assert a personal repentance befitting the Lenten season, "appointed by the Church for penitence and self-examination" (*Sermons* 9:35).

This insistence on sin and innocence prompts Donne's subsequent exegetical choice as well, when he focuses on the figurative explication of the word "blood" as "the blood of the soule, exhausted by many, and heinous sins." Donne's continued insistence on revealing the route of exegetical transmission serves to underline the inherent intertextuality of Christian Hebraism. This is here of two types: a biblical intertextuality, with its connection between the word דָּם *dam*, "blood" in Job 16:18 and וְדָמִים בְּדָמִים נָגָעוּ *ve-damim be-damim naga'u*, "blood toucheth blood" in Hosea 4:2; and the scholarly intertextuality among the sermonic text, the *Targum Jonathan*—cited in Latin and termed "the Chalde Paraphrase"[49]—and the 1619 *Commentaria in Librum Job*, written by the French Franciscan Jacques Bolduc (table 10). In archival correspondence Evelyn Simpson's research assistant Mary Holtby cites the passage from Bolduc,[50] who has clearly pointed the way for Donne toward an intratextual philological reading of the two biblical passages. This reading allows the preacher to adopt the figurative interpretation of "blood" as "sin," thereby investing Job's appeal with a meaning appropriate for Lent—as Donne elides the violence and vengeance associated with the purely literal image of uncovered blood to emphasize instead the Jobian drama of suffering and sin.

Table 9. Job 16:18: O earth cover not thou my blood

Gregory, *Librum B. Job*	Ibn Ezra	Cajetan, *In Librum Job Commentarij*
Quae scilicet terra Redemptoris nostri sanguinem non abscondit...quia sancta Ecclesia redemptionis suae mysterium in cunctis jam mundi partibus praedicavit (*PL*, vol. 75, part 3, book 13, chapter 23, colimn 1029A).	*O earth cover not thou my blood*: Like wickedness, if I have seen [it] in my heart, God will not listen. Yet God listened and thus my prayer succeeded. And if I disappoint you, earth, do not cover my blood (*Biblia Rabbinica* 4:219).	Iurando autem per execrationem, apostrophat ad terram/ imprecans q non tegat ipsius sanguinem si in manibus eius iniqitas aut oro eius immunda fuit. Et per non tegi a terra sanguinem significant corpus inhumatum (53r).
Apparently this earth does not hide the blood of our Redeemer... because the holy Church already preached the mystery of his redemption in all parts of the world.		Swearing an execration, he beseeches the earth that it will not cover his blood, if in his hands there was injustice or if his words were impure. And [the fact] that the earth will not cover [the] blood means an unburied corpse.

Table 10. Job 16:18: O earth cover not thou my blood

Bolduc, *Commentaria in Librum Job*

Igitur potest hic quidem esse (ut interpretantur Caietanus & Aben Esdra) iuramenti deprecatorii forma.... *Nisi vera loquor inhumatus abjicior, neque me defunctum parens tellus sinu escipiat*.... Non enim nomine sanguinis debet hic intellegere cruor, qui in venis eius existit: sed peccatum, vel etiam gravissimum, ac detestandum facinus, ut ex quamplurimis Scripturae locus intelligitur.... Hoc etiam adnotat Gregorius. Et Chaldaeus illud Osee, *Sanguis sanguinem tetigit*, vertit, *Et aggregant peccata peccatis* (OSB MSS 90, Box 5, Folder 121).

Thus it is possible that there is here (as Cajetan and Ibn Ezra interpret) a form of imprecatory oath.... "If I do not speak the truth let me be rejected without burial," and "let mother earth not receive me in her womb when I die...." In fact by the word "blood" we should not understand the red blood that exists in his veins, but rather the sin, even very heavy, and the odious crime, that is understood from many places in the Scriptures. ... Also Gregory points out this thing. And the Chalde at Hosea [4:2] translates *Blood toucheth blood* as *And sins are added to sins.*

Yet over and above Donne's particular application of the biblical text to the Lenten season is the confirmation of Shami's perceptive observation that the "significance of Donne's method lies not simply in his refusal to reject anything potentially useful to salvation, but in his refusal to acknowledge the absolute authority of any commentator.... Donne's sermons are evidence that he can salvage saving doctrine from a variety of sources, however unlikely" (*John Donne and Conformity in Crises* 82). Bolduc's commentary clearly comprises for the preacher a nexus of sources and readings for Job 16:18—the prior commentaries of the *Targum*, Gregory, Ibn Ezra and Cajetan—as he utilizes a central strategy of many a Renaissance exegetical and sermonic text, which Eugene Kintgen describes as the "religious counterpart of intertextuality: intratextuality, the *heaping up of references* [italics added] to other parts of the Bible" (113). Donne's particular method of citation marks out, however, significant differences between the exegetical and sermonic texts. Bolduc presents his reading of "blood" as "sin…and the odious crime, that is understood from many places in the Scriptures," subsequently tersely noting Gregory as an authority as well as fully citing the *Targum* ("the Chalde"). As preacher, Donne takes on the responsibility for providing his auditory and reader with the very words of both the Christian and Jewish commentaries; in this way he takes care to directly transmit—and overtly assume—their exegetical authority. One can readily envision Donne copying out the *Targum* into his sermon notes, further expanding on Bolduc's allusion by copying out Gregory's commentary on Hosea. By means of his display of scholarship in this passage Donne thus accomplishes many things: he creates a developing intensity that progresses from the *Targum's* statement of sin and consequence—where it was written וְחוֹבִין עַל חוֹבִין מוֹסְפִין *ve-hovin 'al hovin mospin*, "And sins upon sins accumulate" (*Biblia Rabbinica* 3:343)—to Gregory's vivid and violent description of God seeing a soul *adjunctis peccatis cruentatur anima* (in Donne's explanation, a soul "in her blood, when she wounds and wounds herself again"); he preserves Latin as the nonvernacular, authoritative language for both Jewish and Christian biblical commentary, thereby having it bear the weight of exegetical and religious dialogue; he appropriates for himself as reader of the Bible the authority of Christian Hebraism by carefully eliding Bolduc's original citation of Hosea, the *Targum* and Gregory; and he establishes a reading of the biblical text that ultimately elides the vengeance (if not the violence) associated with the purely literal image of uncovered blood, so as to sever the connection between the biblical speaker's "hainous sinnes" and "these afflictions" visited upon him by God, and ultimately to emphasize instead the continued Jobian drama of suffering.

Conclusion

In the opening quotation of this chapter, cited from his essay "Reflections on (New) Philology," Siegfried Wenzel acknowledges the "love of the word" that certainly colors the response of those who argue about, translate and preach on the Hebrew Bible. Yet even more significantly, Wenzel proposes that a philologist should be "alert to the fact that a given text comes from and is shaped by a specific time and place that usually is significantly different from that of the observer" (12). In doing so, he offers an important way to reconceive and expand upon the primarily linguistic, indexical approach to Donne's Hebraism taken by D. C. Allen and Evelyn Simpson. For this proposal supports philology as aspiring to incorporate what Wenzel has previously termed "contextual information" (12)—in the present instance, the Hebrew Bible as well as Jewish exegetical commentaries, Christian polemical treatises, and English Bibles.

Such an updating of the study of Donne's Christian Hebraism must take into consideration recent advocacies for contextual studies of the English sermon. Thus Lori Anne Ferrell and Peter McCullough have demonstrated the central role in literary and historical studies of what they designate "the sermon properly considered—as theatrical, as fundamentally occasional, as literary art inextricably engaged in the public sphere" ("Revising" 2). This attention to contextual information dovetails with the complementary concept of intertextuality, raised by Marcus in her study of early modern England. This term has, as the translators of Julia Kristeva's seminal work on intertextuality explain, "nothing to do with matters of influence by one writer upon another, or the sources of a literary work; it does, on the other hand, involve the components of a *textual system*" (Kristeva 15). As such, the concept of intertextuality becomes significant for the study of sixteenth and seventeenth century England, both in its demarcation of twentieth and twenty-first century critical concerns and in the adumbration of such concerns through the shared interpretive strategies of such seemingly disparate scholars as medieval Jewish exegetes and Renaissance translators and preachers.

PART I

SERMONS ON THE PENITENTIAL PSALMS 6 AND 32

Two

The Penitential Psalm 6

Notes and Margins

Dr. Duns notes the 16th of October 1625 on the 6th psa v 5. or 6. Returne o Lord, deliver my soule…

By returneing is not meant a returne of providence for soe god is never from us, but in some particular grace punctually thus returneing may be eyther in remooveing judgmentes, in vouchsafeing mercyes, or in turning us to him self.
        —John Burley, "Manuscript Notes," Dublin, Trinity College MS
                                                              419, f. 72v[1]

Sermon and Context

Paul Stanwood's discovery of John Burley's manuscript notes on Donne's sermons, recorded in a "miscellaneous academic notebook" ("John Donne's Sermon Notes" 76), bestows a palpable presence on one member of this preacher's "learneder, and more capable auditories, and congregations" (*Sermons* 5:42–43).

The 23-year-old Burley, at this time matriculated at Oriel College, Oxford, and attached to Chelsea College, records lines from Donne's sermon preached on the Penitential Psalm 6:4–5.[2] Burley inscribed these notes in October of 1625,[3] the period during which Donne was sequestered in Chelsea, in retreat from the plague epidemic that was ravaging London (*Sermons* 6:31–35).[4] The continuing presence of these sermons is thereby confirmed for the contemporary reader by what Ceri Sullivan discusses as a sermon's "written afterlife in notes for friends, colleagues, patrons, and printers" (42). As Sullivan has shown, Burley supplies one example of what she describes as "the art of listening in the seventeenth century." Trained most probably like others of his time, Burley attentively listens and records, bringing the twenty-first century reader of Donne's sermons (in Stanwood's words) "nearer than we have ever been to Donne's actual preaching, to his first thoughts as contrasted with the eloquent contrivances of his later study" ("John Donne's Sermon Notes" 78).

The particular "afterlife" of the sermon on the Penitential Psalm 6:4–5 recorded by Burley confirms the attention that Donne pays to the biblical text, in this instance, the way in which he unfolds the meaning of the Hebrew word שׁוּבָה *shuvah*, "*Returne.*" This is one of a string of verbs in the psalmic text that are directed by the speaker to God; as he does with *shuvah*, Donne takes great care to explain each of these verbs in its original Hebrew, pausing in the midst of an impassioned discussion of penitence to base his argument on a correct reading of the biblical text (table 11).[5] Thus Donne explains (in the first of the two printed sermons on verses 6:4–5) that "*Shubah, To Returne, is Redire ad locum suum,* To returne to that place, to which a thing is naturally affected" (*Sermons* 5:368), thereby reflecting the grammatical form of the Hebrew word in which the locative letter ה *heh* is added to the root *shuv.*[6] Donne subsequently draws from this point of grammar a religious and ecclesiastical meaning when he writes that "in the Church, in the Sermon, in the Sacrament he [God] returnes to us, in the first signification of this word *Shubah,* as to that place to which he is naturally affected and disposed" (*Sermons* 5:368).

Table 11. Verbs

Biblical Passage	Sermon
6:1: O Lord, rebuke me not in Thine anger, neither chasten me in thy displeasure	This word that is here Rebuke, *Iacach* [תּוֹכִיחֵנִי *tohiheini*], is for the most part, to Reprove, to Convince by way of argument, and disputation (*Sermons* 5:332). Both these words, which we translate to *Chasten* ["*Iasar*"; תְּיַסְּרֵנִי *teyasreini*], and *Hot displeasure* ["*Camath*"; בַּחֲמָתְךָ *ba-hamatkha*], are words of a heavie, and of a vehement signification (*Sermons* 5:335).
6:2: Have mercy upon me	For this word *Chanan* [חָנֵּנִי *haneini*]...[is] Lord shed some drops of grace upon me (*Sermons* 5:340).
6:4: Returne, O Lord, deliver my soule: oh save mee	And so, *Shubah* [שׁוּבָה *shuvah*], *To Returne,* is *Redire ad locum suum,* To returne to that place, to which a thing is naturally affected (*Sermons* 5:368). This word is in the Original, *Chalatz* [חַלְּצָה *haltzah*]; which signifies *Eripere* [snatch away, pluck out] in such a sense, as our language does not fully reach in any one word. So there is some defectiveness, some slacknesse in this word of our Translation, *Delivering* (*Sermons* 5:375). *Iashang*[7] [הוֹשִׁיעֵנִי *hoshi'eini*, "save me"] is the very word, from which the name of Jesus [יֵשׁוּעַ *yeishu'ah*] is derived (*Sermons* 5:377).
6:8: the Lord hath heard the voice of my weeping	*Shamang* [שָׁמַע], is *audit,* God gives eare to our teares; sometimes it is beleeving, *Shamang,* is *Credit,* God gives faith, and credit to our teares; sometimes it is Affecting, *Shamang,* is *Miseretur,* God hath mercy upon us for our teares; sometimes it is Effecting, *Shamang,* is *Respondet,* God answers the petition of our teares; and sometimes it is Publication, *Shamang,* is *Divulgat,* God declares and manifests to others, by his blessing upon us, the pleasure he takes in our holy and repentant teares (*Sermons* 6:48).

Table 11 (*cont.*)

Biblical Passage	Sermon
6:9: the Lord will receive my prayer	for this word, which signifies *Prayer* [תְּפִלָּתִי *tefilati*] here, is derived from *Palal,* which signifies properly *Separare* (*Sermons* 6:50).[8]
6:10: let them returne and be ashamed suddenly	those words which are here rendred, *Convertentur* [return], & *Erubescent* [ashamed], and which in the Originall, are *Iashabu* [יָשֻׁבוּ *yashuvu*], and *Ieboshu* [יֵבֹשׁוּ *yeivoshu*], which have a musicall, and harmonious sound, and agnomination in them (*Sermons* 6:55).

Lastly, Donne presents an extended homiletic development of this Hebrew term. In a further passage from the first sermon on verse 6:4–5, entitled *Revertere* ("Turne"), he summarizes:

> So that word which *David* receives from the Holy Ghost in this Text, being onely *Returned,* and no more, applies it selfe to all three senses, Returne thy selfe, that is, bring backe Mercy; Returne thy Wrath, that is, Call backe thy Judgements, or Returne us to thee, that is, make thy meanes, and offers of grace, in thine Ordinance, powerfull, and effectuall upon us. (*Sermons* 5:370–71)

The multiplicity of meanings for *shuvah* is apparent in the *Hebrue Dictionaire* (see fig. 4) composed by John Udall, the sixteenth century English religious controversialist and Hebraist (Cross, "Udall"); the literal meaning of the Hebrew root שׁוּב *shuv* is "return," while its extended meanings include "conversion," "turning againe," and "answere" (154). Indeed, as Lynn Staley has noted, the "Penitential Psalms are peppered with words related to an understanding of conversion as a turning.... More than verbal play, this language takes up complex issues constituent of the penitential experience" (222–23). The rhetorically and emotionally charged quality in Donne's development of this particular term is less evident in Burley's notes than in the written sermon. For while Burley accurately records the "three senses," Donne's meticulous development of the argument in the printed sermon progresses from the "return" of mercy, to the "turn or change" of judgments and finally to the act of "conversion" or "repentance"; in conjunction with the stylistic characteristics of lexical repetition and syntactical parallelism, this intensifies the final effect of God's action upon the preacher's reader.

This comparison of Burley's notes with the sermonic text foregrounds the difference between this record of its (largely inaccessible) oral and (later) printed forms. Yet by attending to the notes in both the sermonic text and its margins, the reader can recover echoes of Donne's preaching and also perceive the complexity of his reading of the Hebrew Bible. In the present sermon, the marginal note *Revertere* as a sermon topic particularly reinforces for the reader the authority of the Vulgate term used in the body of the text (the sole record of the preacher's oral rendition). Furthermore, this "other voice" cited from the *Vulgate Bible* is part of a larger phrase—"*Revertere,* O Lord return" (*Sermons* 5:367)—which presents a double textual authority and concomitantly the very reason for Donne's explanation. For the literal meaning, "returne," of *shuva* (as translated in both the Vulgate and King James Bibles) raises an interpretive problem, which Donne expresses by explaining that "we cannot say, *O Lord Returne,* because, so, he was never gone from us...for God is absent when I doe not discerne his presence" (*Sermons* 5:367–68). Donne's response is not unique. Both Rashi and Ibn Ezra have succinctly explained that God "turns" from his anger (table 12), thereby anticipating Donne's explanation of "Returne thy Wrath," while Augustine also anticipates (and influences?) Donne in clarifying that, reciprocally, "God turns" as well as "make[s] me turn" (table 12).

This "turning" to the notes and margins of both the sermonic text and the *Biblia Rabbinica,* as well as to Augustine's *Enarrationes in Psalmos* (Expositions on the Psalms), emulates the preacher's own scholarly enterprise. For as D. C. Allen asserts, some of Donne's Hebrew certainly comes from the marginal

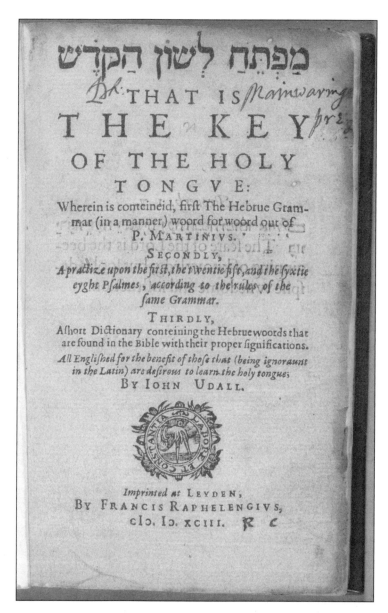

מַפְתֵּחַ לְשׁוֹן הַקֹּדֶשׁ

Dr. THAT IS *Mainwaring*

THE KEY

OF THE HOLY
TONGVE:

Wherein is conteineid, firſt The Hebrue Grammar (in a manner) woord for woord out of
P. MARTINIVS.

SECONDLY,

A practize upon the firſt, the twentie fiſt, and the ſyxtie
eyght Pſalmes, according to the rules of the
ſame Grammar.

THIRDLY,

A ſhort Dictionary conteining the Hebrue woords that
are found in the Bible with their proper ſignifications.

*All Engliſhed for the benefit of thoſe that (being ignoraunt
in the Latin) are deſirous to learn the holy tongue;*

BY IOHN UDALL.

Imprinted at LEYDEN;
BY FRANCIS RAPHELENGIVS,
cIɔ. Iɔ. XCIII.

Fig. 4. Title page of John Udall, *Mafteah Lashon Ha-Kodesh: That is
the Key of the Holy Tongue* (1593). Reproduced by permission of the
Huntington Library, San Marino, California. Manuscript call no. RB 30640.

Table 12. Penitential Psalm 6:4: Returne, O Lord

Augustine [6:5]	Rashi [6:5]	Ibn Ezra [6:5]
Convertens se, orat ut ad eam convertatur et Deus, sicut dictum est: *Convertimini ad me, et convertar ad vos, dicit dominus* (Zach. I, 3). An ex illa locutione intellegendum est, *Convertere, Domine,* id est, fac me converti, cum in ipsa sua conversione difficultatem laboremque sentiret? (*Enarrationes in Psalmos,* "In Psalmum VI, Enarratio," Vers. 5).	*O Lord, Turn:* From Your anger (*Biblia Rabbinica* 4:7; *Rashi's Commentary* 191).	*O Lord, Turn:* A turn from his fierce indignation (*Biblia Rabbinica* 4:7).
English Translation: Turning herself, she [the soul] prays that God too would turn to her, as it is said: *Turne ye unto me, and I will turne unto you, saith the Lord* (Zachariah 1:3). Or is it to be understood according to that way of speaking, *Turne, Lord,"* that is, make me turn, since the soul in this her turning feels difficulty and toil? (Coxe, *Expositions* 17).		

notes of the Geneva and King James Bibles ("Dean Donne" 213).[9] Donne states this explicitly when he writes in his Prebend sermon on Psalm 66:3: "*Mentientur tibi,* (as it is in the Originall, and as you finde it in the Margin) They shall dissemble, they shall lie" (*Sermons* 8:114). The curious reader will look to the margins of the Geneva and King James Bibles to confirm Donne's integrative explanation of the Hebrew word יְכַחֲשׁוּ *yekhahashu,* "they will lie."[10] The Geneva note explains that "the infidels for feare shal dissemble themselves to be subject" ("The Olde Testamente" 248r); the note thus creates, in Evelyn Tribble's words, "an informed, educated, and coherent community of readers" (34)—with the emphasis here on the "coherent community" as distinguished from the lying infidels. On the other hand, the King James note brings a rather less inflammatory and more literal explanation—"Or, yeild fained obedience. Heb. lie." ("The Olde Testmanet" n.p.)—which conscientiously follows the royal dictum "No Marginal Notes at all to be affixed, but only for the Explanation of the *Hebrew* or *Greek* Words" (Pollard 54).[11] Donne's citation of these specific marginal notes highlights his persistent search for the meaning of the "Originall" biblical text, as well as the variety of exegetical and interpretive voices echoing within his sermons. More generally, it also highlights Donne's lesson to his auditory and reader in—to use Donne's words—the "Art of reading" (*Essayes in Divinity* 29) the biblical text.

What, then, is the significance of the use of "notes and margins" for Donne's sermon series on the Penitential Psalm 6? The answer begins with a "return" to the list of verbs (table 11), through which Donne defines the development of the psalmic text in seventeenth century ecclesiastical terms. In the last of the six sermons, he explains:

> The Psalme hath a Deprecatory part, that God would forbeare him, and a Postulatory part, that God would heare him, and grant some things to him, and a Gratulatory part, a sacrifice of thanksgiving....*David* makes it his first worke, to stay Gods anger in a deprecatory prayer, but he stayes not upon that long, he will not prescribe his Physitian, what he shall prescribe to him, but leaves God to his own medicines, and to his own methode. But then the Postulatory prayer, what he begs of God, employes six verses: as well to shew us, that our necessities are many; as also that if God doe not answer us, at the beginning of our prayer, our duty is still to pursue that way, to continue in prayer. And then, the third part of the Psalme, which is the Gratulatory part, his giving of thanks, is, shall we say deferred, or rather reserved to the end of the Psalme. (*Sermons* 6:40–41)

Donne's recognition that these illocutionary acts—the speaker's "performance of an act *in* saying something" (Austin 99)—mark out the psalm's narrative development is not unique. Both the *International Critical Commentary,* from the early twentieth century (Briggs 1:45–49), and the *Word Biblical Commentary,* from the late twentieth century (Craigie 89–96), conceive of the psalmic text as a movement from prayer, to its intensification in a plea for delivery from misery, and finally to an expression of confidence. In other words, the psalm moves through a series of addresses to both God and the speaker's enemies: from the "Deprecatory prayer" (verse 6:1) "that asks pardon for sin and deliverance from evil" (Potter 64)—the Lord will "rebuke" and "chasten"; to the "Postulatory prayer" (verses 6:2–7) that "more actively asks for something the petitioner desires or needs" (Potter 64)—the Lord will "have mercy," will "returne" and "deliver" the soul; and finally to the "Gratulatory part" (verses 6:8–10) that designates God's response—the Lord "hath heard" weeping and will "receive prayer"—and that brings about the enemies' defeat—"let them returne and be ashamed."

Within this dialogic development verse 1 and verses 6–7 comprise pivotal units, demonstrating Harold Fisch's statement that the psalms "are not monologues, but insistently and at all times dialogue-poems, poems of the self but of the self in the mutuality of relationship with the other" (*Poetry with a Purpose* 108). While the speaker's "Deprecatory prayer" of verse 1 therefore appropriately designates the Lord as the "other" in this dialogue, verses 6–7 together complete the "Postulatory prayer" by describing the depth of the speaker's personal agony and pain. This conception of the dialogic nature of the psalm invites a consideration of the dialogic nature of the sermon, participating as it does in an intertextual system that encompasses the biblical passage, as well as the various Bibles and commentaries primarily marked out in the sermonic notes and margins. It will be demonstrated therefore that in Donne's two sermons on verses 6:1 and 6:6–7 this art of reading the biblical text ultimately empowers Donne's investigation into the dialogic relationship between God and man portrayed in the psalm, particularly as he gains access to its nature through the "Originall" language in which it was articulated.

Sermon on the Penitential Psalm 6:1: O Lord, rebuke me not in thine anger, neither chasten me in thy hot displeasure

In his sermon on verse 6:1 Donne develops the linguistic and mystical attributes of God from the Tetragrammaton — the "Name of four letters," YHWH, or *Jehovah*. Reading this passage in tandem with a strikingly similar one from the *Essayes in Divinity* marks out Donne's scholarly use of a highly intertwined exegetical tradition:

> *Essayes in Divinity*
> Of which Name [marginal note: Tetragra.] one says [marginal note: Reuclin.de verbo Mirifico l.1.c.6], that as there is a secret property by which we are changed into God, (referring, I think to that, *We are made partakers of the godly nature* [marginal note: 2 Pet. 1.4]) so God hath a certain name, to which he hath annexed himself to be present.....
>
> How this name should be sounded, is now upon the anvile, and everybody is beating and hammering upon it. That it is not *Jehova*, this governs me, that the *Septuagint* never called it so; Nor Christ; nor the Apostles, where they vouch the Old Testament; nor *Origen*, nor *Hierome*, curious in language. And though negatives have ever their infirmities, and must not be built on, this may, that our Fathers heard not the first sound of this word *Jehova*. For (for any thing appearing,) *Galatinus*, in their Age, was the first that offered it. For, that *Hierome* should name it in the exposition of the eighth *Psalm*, it is peremptorily averred by *Drusius* [marginal note: De Nomine Tetrag.] and admitted by our learnedst Doctor [marginal note: Rainolds. De. Idol. 2,3,18] that in the old Editions it was not *Jehova*. But more then any other reason, this doth accomplish & perfect the opinion against that word, that whereas that language hath no natural vowels inserted, but points subjected of the value and sound of our vowels, added by the *Masorits*, the Hebrew Cricks, after *Esdras*; and therefore they observe a necessity of such a naturall and infallible concurrence of consonants, that when

such and such consonants meet, such and such vowels must be imagined, and sounded, by which they have an Art of reading it without points; by those rules, those vowels cannot serve those Consonants, nor the name *Jehovah* be built of those four letters, and the vowels of *Adonay* [marginal note: Genebr. de leg. Orient. sine punctis]. (28–29)

Sermon on the Penitential Psalm 6:1
This is that name, which out of a superstitious reverence the Jews always forbore to sound, or utter, but ever pronounced some other name, either *Adonai*, or *Elohim*, in the place thereof, wheresoever they found *Jehovah*. But now their Rabbins will not so much as write that name, but still expresse it in foure other letters. So that they dare not, not onely not sound, not say it, but not see it.

How this name which we call *Jehovah*, is truly to be sounded, because in that language it is exprest in four Consonants onely, without Vowels, is a preplext question; we may well be content to be ignorant therein, since our Saviour Christ himselfe, in all those places which he cited out of the Old Testament, never sounded it; he never said, *Jehovah*. Nor the Apostles after him, nor *Origen*, nor *Jerome*; all persons very intelligent in the propriety of language; they never sounded this name *Jehovah*. For though in S. *Jeromes* Exposition upon the 8. Psalme, we finde that word *Jehovah*, in some Editions which we have now, yet it is a cleare case, that in the old Copies it is not so; in *Jeroms* mouth it was not so; from *Jeroms* hand it came not so. Neither doth it appeare to me, that ever the name of *Jehovah* was so pronounced, till so late, as in our Fathers time; for I think *Petrus Galatinus* was the first that ever called it so. But howsoever this name be to be sounded, that which falls in our consideration at this time, is, That *David* in his distresses fled presently to God, and to God by name, that is, in consideration and commemoration of his particular blessings; and to a God that had that name, the name of *Jehovah*, the name of Essence, and Being, which name carryed a confession, that all our wel-being, and the very first being it selfe, was, and was to be derived from him. (*Sermons* 5:324–25)

The sermonic passage is evidently one of those that evoked Dennis Quinn's twentieth century unenthusiastic assessment of the sermon's "intellectual academic tone" ("Donne's Christian Eloquence" 295–96), as Donne traces out at length the exegetical history of the name *Jehovah*. The multitude of cited sources in the *Essayes* clearly reveals Donne's (overly) avid use of exegetical and Kabbalistic sources, which necessitates the use of editorial notes for the modern reader that are provided by Evelyn Simpson (*Essays in Divinity* 117) and Anthony Raspa (*Essayes in Divinity* 138–39). Donne's detailed discussion of the exegetical aspects of the name *Jehovah*—at once informative and obliquely parodying scholarly authority[12]—cites texts from the sixteenth and seventeenth centuries by the Christian Hebraists Peter Galatin[us], Jan van der Driesche (Drusius), John Rainolds and Gilbert Genebrard,[13] as well as the church fathers Origen and Jerome, the Jewish Masorites (who composed the Masorah, critical notes on the biblical text), and the prophet-scribe Ezra (Esdras).

Yet rather than accepting Quinn's modern evaluation of the seventeenth century discussion, we may more fruitfully inquire as to its function within the sermonic context for a contemporary auditory and reader. Donne's auditory might well have been aware (at least in part) of the exegetical history, repeated as it is throughout Donne's sermons to such an extent that George Potter admits to Evelyn Simpson (in a letter dated September 29, 1952) that he had been tempted "to relate certain sermons, because they stress, say the names of God, or the meaning of Hebrew words" (OSB MSS 90, Box 2, Folder 47). In the present sermon, Donne is first and foremost concerned with educating his Christian congregation on the meaning and etymology of God's sacred name; in so doing, he enfolds within the sermonic text his scholarly research that was carried out before 1605 and which appeared previously in his earlier (pre-1615) *Essayes in Divinity* (*Sermons* 5:26–30).[14] The citation of this series of what Donne's nineteenth century biographer Edmund Gosse has termed "scholastic exercises" (2:63) is not at all accidental. For Evelyn Simpson's emphasis on the similarity between this sermonic passage and that from *Essayes in Divinity* provides an opportunity to move past source criticism to a consideration of the ways in which the "exercises" are utilized in the final, sermonic text.[15] Citing the two passages at length clearly illustrates the parallels between them, indicating how *Essayes in Divinity* serves as a preliminary draft for the final, printed sermonic text, as well as providing the scholarly addenda to the no less erudite but more admonitive and hortatory demands of the later, public genre. Most notably, the rhetoric and polemics of the sermonic text are served by various changes: leaving in the reference to the Church Fathers, while excising the confusing discussion of the various Christian Hebraists (except for Galatin); combining the details of Jewish exegesis into the general term "Rabbins"; and moving the discussion of *Jehovah* (Hebrew: YHWH) as "Essence, and Being" (from wordplay on the Hebrew root הוה / היה *hyh/hwh/hvh*, "to be, to exist") to the conclusion.[16]

Donne's evaluation of his general hortatory circumstances is quite clear; he deems it necessary to delimit the extensive scholarly account of the name *Jehovah* provided by Christian Hebraists in order to privilege early church authority and ultimately to align it against Jewish authority. This is distinctly revealed in the sermon, particularly in Donne's marking out of the "superstitious reverence" of the Jews while necessarily building upon the use of Jewish and Christian Hebraic sources delineated in the *Essayes in Divinity*. In the move from these "scholastic exercises" or in Donne's own words "Sermons...[and] solitary Meditations" (*Essayes in Divinity* 47–48), the preacher establishes his authority as a mediator of Christian Hebraism while determining the scope of such knowledge for his auditory. Reading this early text in conjunction with the printed sermonic version thus vividly demonstrates Donne's method of composition, in which he summarizes the laborious search for sources in his earlier scholarly work while heightening its polemic value in the sermonic text.

It might very well be disconcerting to the modern reader that immediately upon concluding this scholarly discussion in the sermon, Donne seems to diminish its weight by stating that "howsoever this name be sounded"; yet subsequently he confirms its importance by stating that David fled to "God by name...and to a God that had that name, the name of *Jehovah*." Moreover, the preacher's prior forging of an audience that is to some degree aware of the exegetical tradition behind the name *Jehovah* prepares them for the final discussion of its literal meaning as "Essence, and Being"—and ultimately for the development of its theological and mystical significance. In discussing this aspect, the marginal note in the *Essayes in Divinity* points directly to Johannes Reuchlin's fifteenth century Kabbalistic work, *De Verbo Mirifico* (On the wonder-working word).[17] In the second of its three books[18] Reuchlin places the following passages in the mouth of the Jew Baruch (quite likely modeled after Reuchlin's Jewish teacher, the court physician Jakob ben Jehiel Loans; Oberman 73–75):

> [Baruchias inquit] semper quasi amplissima virtus nutritiva conatur (quantum per imbecillitatem humanam licet) non amoris solum calore, verum etiam proprietate occulta, in se ipsum digerendo transformare, ut et homo migret in deum et deus habitet in homine (160).
>
> [Baruch says] the most nutritious virtue at all times prepares itself (as far as human weakness allows) not only with love's warmth, but also with an occult property, to transform by dividing himself, so that man would migrate to God, and that God would dwell within man.

> [Baruchias inquit] Dixitque deus ad Moysen: 'Ehieh, qui ero. Et dixit: Sic dices filiis Israel: Ehieh misit me ad vos' [Exodus 3:14]. Hoc nomen Plato in sua illa tam longa penes Assyrios peregrinatione didicerat: quod ad Graecos tandem duabus litteris 'on' transtulit. Nam in Timaeo sic ait: 'Est igitur secundum meam opinionem primo distinguendum, quid sit >on<, id est ens, quod semper est, ortum vero non habet, et quid quod ortum habet, est autem nunquam' (208).
>
> [Baruch says] God saide unto Moses: 'I AM THAT I AM. And he said: Thus shalt thou say unto the children of Israel: *Ehyeh* sent me to you' [Exod. 3:14]. This name Plato had learned during his very long peregrination among the Assyrians: which in the end he translated for the Greeks with these two letters 'on' [ὄv, being]. For in the *Timaeus* he says this: "Therefore in my opinion it is necessary first to distinguish, what >on< is, it is the being, that exists forever, but has no origin, and that which has an origin, never exists."

The Jew Baruch quite naturally dominates book 2 of *De Verbo Mirifico* (Blau, *Christian Interpretation of the Cabala* 41–48), in which Reuchlin's investigation into the "power of words...leads to a number of excursions into Kabbalistic and grammatical areas which are clearly meant to clarify the historical, theological, or theosophical substructure, by means of and through which the names attain power" (Maxwell-Stuart 207). Donne's citing in the first passage of the "occult or secret property" specified by Reuchlin effectively encompasses Kabbalistic thought—a term "for the esoteric teachings of Judaism and for Jewish mysticism" (Scholem, Garb, and Idel 587)—within a Christian text and context,[19] most particularly by establishing a connection between Reuchlin's Kabbalistic interpretation of the Tetragrammaton and the second Epistle of Peter (*"partakers of the godly nature"*). Whether the illocutionary power of YHWH only affirms God's existence through the "simple" verb form *Qal* ("He is here, He is present"), or whether it also evokes a distinct performative power as the "causative" verb form *Hiph'il*[20] ("He causes to be, He brings into existence"),[21] Donne utilizes this name to emphasize how God mystically transforms the divine and the human into each other. Furthermore, this would most likely activate for Donne God's performative power evident in the Gospel of St. John, where it is declared that "In the beginning was the Worde, and the Worde was with God, and that Worde was God. . . . All things were made by it; & without it was made nothing that was made" (1:1–3); as Angela Esterhammer remarks about this passage, "God's spoken word assures the presence of God as origin" (291).

For the reader of the sermon, this passage from *Essayes* therefore prompts an awareness of the mystical significance attributed to the name *Jehovah*—as "Essence, and Being"—in Donne's final assertion that "all our wel-being, and the very first being it selfe, was, and was to be derived from him." Yet Donne's reference to *De Verbo Mirifico* also highlights the inherently dialogic and polemical nature of Christian Hebraism. For Reuchlin's work is composed as a three-way discussion among a Greek philosopher Sidon, the Christian Capnion (this name being a Greek translation of the German "Reuchlin," meaning "smoke") and the Jew Baruch. The polemic weight of Reuchlin's second passage thus rests on the transmission of knowledge within a Christian Hebraist text. The mimetic level of the discourse, which presents Baruch as speaker, emphasizes the heterogeneous origins of the Jew's statement about God's nature: his words at once evoke Platonic authority and support the Jewish belief that places the roots of Greek philosophy in Judaism and in the cultures of other Eastern (e.g., Assyrian) nations (Altman 854). The narrative level, on the other hand, emphasizes the uncertain origins of such knowledge; is it the Jewish physician who is being quoted as reading Plato, or is it the Christian author Reuchlin who is responsible for such knowledge?

Reuchlin's text distinctly reveals the intellectual hybridism in the Christian Hebraist text, as well as the circuitous routes by which Jewish (and classical) knowledge was transmitted. As an advocate of Jewish knowledge and books in the controversy over their use by Christians,[22] Reuchlin is presumably on one level hedging his bets, while on another level he is foregrounding the inevitably dialogic aspect of Christian Hebraism that moves past Quinn's combative concept of the Bible as being for Christian scholars simply "an arsenal of proof-texts" ("Donne's Christian Eloquence" 281). Michael Hall has astutely commented that in *Essayes in Divinity* Donne "places himself with respect to certain points of Christian doctrine which every apprentice preacher must confront and come to terms with—the nature of God, the creation of the world, the authority of the Scriptures, the tension between reason and faith" (424). Underlying Donne's discussion in his sermon on the Penitential Psalm 6:1 of the name and nature of *Jehovah* is a wider interplay of exegetical and interpretive voices, which becomes apparent only through close attention to the notes and margins of the *Essayes* as a sermonic draft. As preacher, Donne has deemed it necessary to educate his auditory and reader in the art of reading the biblical text, providing a prolonged philological discussion of the term *Jehovah* that adapts the one in the *Essayes,* producing in the end a sermon that reverberates deeply with Christian polemics and faith.

Sermon on the Penitential Psalm 6:6–7: *I am weary with my groning, all the night make I my bed to swim: I water my couch with teares. Mine eie is consumed because of griefe; it waxeth olde because of mine enemies*

Donne's lesson on the art of reading is continued in his sermon on verses 6:6–7, which in the psalmic text completes the "Postulatory prayer" by describing the depth of the speaker's agony and pain. In Part 1 of the sermon, Donne attends to the Hebrew "Originall" to preach about *"Quid factum,* What David did" (*Sermons* 8:197). Turning to the first action, "I am weary with my groning" (6:6), he explains:

> And when he heares...these sighs of thy soule, then he puts thy name also into that List, which he gave to his messenger, (in which Commission this very word of our Text, *Anach,* is used) *Sinabis signum super frontibus virorum suspirantium & gementium* [marginal note: Ezek. 9.4], Upon all their fore-heads, that sigh and groane, imprint my mark; Which is ordinarily conceived by the Ancients to have been the letter *Tau;* of which though *Calvin* assigne a usefull, and a convenient reason, that they were marked with this letter *Tau,* which is the last letter of the Hebrew Alphabet, in signe, that though they were in estimation of the world, the most abject, and the outcasts thereof, yet God set his mark upon them, with a purpose to raise them; yet S. *Hierome* [marginal note: Hieron.] and the Ancients for the most part assigne that for the reason, why they were marked with that letter, because that letter had the forme of the Crosse...so God imprinted upon them, that sighed, and mourned, that *Tau,* that letter, which had the forme of the Crosse, that it might be an evidence, that all their crosses shall be swallowed in his Crosse, their sighs in his sighs, and their agonies in his. (*Sermons* 8:197–98)

Through a connection that moves past the agonized speech act within the psalm, Donne transforms its speaker into one of those persons marked by God in Ezekiel's prophetic vision (table 13). On the basis of the shared Hebrew root אנח, *anaḥ*, "groan," Donne creates an intertexual link between the psalmic phrase "I am weary with my groaning" *yagati be-'anḥati,* and the phrase in Ezekiel 9:4 that reads *ve-hitvita tav 'al mitzḥot hane'enaḥim ve-han'enaqim,* "put a mark on the foreheads of the men who moan and groan" (*Tanakh* 903). Donne's marginal note confirms the biblical source for his reader, while his citation of both the Hebrew term *Anach* and the Latin phrase underlines the bilingual aspect of reading the Bible, confirming the authority of such bilingualism well into the period of Reformation English Bibles. Ultimately, this move within the sermonic passage to the verse from Ezekiel brings with it an interpretive focus on the tension between the iconic character of the Hebrew term *tav* and its meaning, which is concerned with suffering and redemption. This tension is evoked by the inherent ambiguity of the term *tav,* since it denotes both the last letter of the Hebrew alphabet ת (Jerome and Kimhi; table 13) as well as the word "mark" or "sign" (King James note; table 13). Donne places the two explanations of this term—Calvin and Jerome, Protestant and Catholic, semantic and iconic—in opposition. Calvin's Protestant concern with the issue of "God's *Election* from all eternity of certain persons to salvation and eternal life" (Lewalski 16) is prominent, when he writes about how "the world has treated the sons of God as if they were castaways" (table 13). Such a reading of the term *tav* both echoes Kimhi's prior explanation about distinguishing the righteous from the evil (table 13), and is itself echoed, not surprisingly, in the later Genevan note, which (as an "annotation upon all the hard places," "To the Reader" iiii[v]) explains that they are "God's children, whom he marketh for salvation" (table 13).[23]

Donne concludes by focusing on the iconic and theological transformation of the Hebrew letter *tav* into the Cross, which has its basis—cited specifically from Jerome—in the original form of the letter ת as a cross turned on its side (**X** = †; Chomsky 87). As he previously retained the Hebrew and Latin words of the

Table 13. Ezekiel 9:4: Set a Marke

Jerome, *Commentariorum in Hiezechielem*	Kimhi	Calvin, *Ezekiel*	Reformation Bibles[24]
extrema "tau" littera crucis habet similitudinem, quae christianorum frontibus pingitur (106–07). the last letter *tau* is similar to the cross, which the Christians put on their forehead.	*Mark a Mark.* Our Rabbis of blessed memory explained that *tav* is the letter which is called *tav* [ת]. The Holy One, blessed be He, said to [the angel] Gabriel: "Write on the foreheads of the righteous a *tav* of ink and on the foreheads of the evil a *tav* of blood" (*Biblia Rabbinica* 3:23).	If puzzles please you, it would be a better reason why the faithful were marked with the last letter, because they were the last among men, and as it were the offscouring of the world. Since therefore from the beginning, the world has treated the sons of God as if they were castaways, therefore I have said that they may be signed with the last letter (Lecture Twenty-Fourth, n.p.).	*The [Geneva] Bible.* And the Lord said unto him, Go through the middes of the citie, *even* through the middes of Jerusalém, and set ‖ a marke upon the foreheads of them that ᶠ mourne, and crye for all the abominacions that be done in the middes thereof ("The Olde Testament" 336v). ‖ Or, *marke* with Thau ᶠ He sheweth what is the maner of Gods children, whom he marketh to salvation. *The Holy [King James] Bible.* And the LORD sayd unto him, Goe through the middest of Jerusalem, and set † a marke upon the foreheads of the men that sigh, and that cry for all the abominations, that bee done in the middest thereof ("The Old Testament," n.p.). † *Heb. marke a marke*

biblical text in his preaching on the English Bible, so too Donne retains and reworks the Catholic affirmation of the image within the Protestant pulpit. Ann Hurley has argued that for Donne, images such as the Cross were uniquely "'visible things' that provide access to the living God and to the living mind" (142); in his poem "The Cross," for example, Donne concludes by writing "Then doth the crosse of Christ worke faithfully / Within our hearts, when we love harmlesly / The Crosses pictures much, and with more care / That Crosses children, which our crosses are" (*Poems* 344). The resonating syntax of the sermonic passage, created in its concluding parallel clauses ("all their crosses shall be swallowed in his Crosse, their sighs in his sighs, and their agonies in his"), holds up to Donne's auditory and reader those very "Crosses pictures." The preacher also skillfully integrates the semantic and iconic aspects of *tav* as both "mark" and "cross," maintaining the vividness of Kimhi's iconic *tav* of ink and *tav* of blood[25] as well the import of the marginality and suffering of Calvin's "sons of God" being treated "as if they were castaways" (table 13). In this manner Donne fashions the central symbol of Christian suffering and salvation out of the very materiality of the Hebrew language.

This lesson in the art of reading verse 6:6 from the Penitential Psalm is enhanced by the placement of Jerome, Calvin, and Donne within the Kristevan *textual system* that links both to the medieval Kimhi and to the Reformation Bibles of sixteenth and seventeenth century England. The Christian response to the biblical text is of course not determinate; Jerome's Christianization of the biblical term *tav* stands in contrast to the Calvinist and Genevan reworking of Kimhi's interpretation, while Donne's integrative solution to the issue of the image forefronts the exegetical dialogue among Jewish and Christian sources. His discussion of verse 6:7 further enriches this dialogue by providing scholarly notes on a particular dilemma in biblical interpretation. In the following passage, entitled *Turbatus*,[26] Donne's searching for—and weighing of—different interpretations of the biblical verse, *'asheshah mi-ka'as 'eyni,* "mine eie is consumed because of griefe" is evident:

> For the second word, which in our Translations, is, in one *dimmed* [*Geneva Bible*], in the other *consumed* [King James], and in the Vulgat *troubled,* a great Master in the Originall [marginal note: Reuchlin] renders it well, elegantly, and naturally out of the Originall, *Verminavit* [it is covered with worms], *Tineavit* [it is covered with moths], which is such a deformitie, as wormes make in wood, or in books.... And against this Vermination, (as the Originall denotes) against this gnawing of the worme, that may bore through, and sink the strongest vessel that sailes in the seas of this world, there is no other varnish, no other liniment, no other medicament, no other pitch nor rosin against this worme, but the bloud of Christ Jesus.... And therefore whensoever this worme, this apprehension of Gods future indignation, reserved for the Judgement, bites upon thee, be sure to present to it the bloud of thy Saviour; Never consider the judgement of God for sin alone, but in the company of the mercies of Christ. It is but the hissing of the Serpent, and the whispering of Satan, when he surprises thee in a melancholy midnight of dejection of spirit, and layes thy sins before thee then. (*Sermons* 8:204–07)

What is immediately manifest is Donne's explicit citing of multiple biblical translations in order to bring to the forefront his concern with the problem of the opaque Hebrew verb עָשְׁשָׁה *'asheshah,* which in its verbal form literally means "decayed," while its adjectival form עֲשֵׁשָׁה *'asheishah* means "dimmed." In his commentary, Rashi not only supplies these literal meanings (table 14), but also a comparison (though he is mistaken about the philological connection with the Hebrew term for "lantern") between weak eyesight, and the glass surrounding and dimming the lantern's light. Yet a reader of the biblical text might well ask, How does the emotion of anger actually *cause* the eye's physical decay or—by extension—dimming? In answer, one can point to the interpretive tradition, supported by Mayer Gruber's explanation that the biblical expression *'asheshah 'ayin* means "my eye dries up from sadness," which refers to "to the drying up of the eye in consequence of its running out of tears from profuse crying"

(*Aspects of Nonverbal Communication* 386–90).[27] This tradition is evident in Calvin's commentary on *The Psalmes of David*, as well as in *The Whole Book of Psalmes* composed by Sternhold and Hopkins, which was a highly popular metrical translation that was "the most widely known volume of verse in English" (Hamlin 38) during the sixteenth and seventeenth centuries (table 14). In both of these instances, there is an emphasis on the penitent speaker's intense emotional state and consequent corporeal blindness ("his eye wexed dim," "my sight is dim and waxeth old")—perhaps also a metaphor of spiritual blindness—that only God can heal.

Table 14. Penitential Psalm 6:7: 'Asheshah as "Dimmed"

Rashi [6:8]	Calvin, *The Psalmes of David* [6:8]	Sternhold and Hopkins, *Psalmes*
'Asheshah. (It becomes glassy) is a cognate of [the noun] 'ashashit [*lanterne* in O.F.]. [The psalmist speaks of] an eye, whose perception of light is weak so that it seems to him [the person whose eye is here described] that he is looking through [foggy] glass, which is [placed] before his eye. And Menahem [ben Saruq] explained it as meaning "decay," as in 'atsamay 'asheishu ["my bones decayed"; Psalm 31:11] (*Biblia Rabbinica* 4:7; *Rashi's Commentary* 191–92).	As towching the woordes, he sayth that his eye wexed dim, because the greef of the mynd dooth bothe easly perce unto the eyes, and from thence moste chiefly utter it self (part 1, folio 18).	My sight is dim and waxeth old, with anguish of mine heart: For feare of those that are my foes, and would my soule subvert (9).

Yet attention should be paid to an alternative interpretive tradition, an outstanding example of which is Philip Sidney's translation of the Penitential Psalm 6. A great admirer of this translation, Donne dedicates a "Divine Poem" to it ("Upon the translation of the Psalmes by Sir Philip Sydney, and the Countesse of Pembroke his Sister"), writing: "Two, by their bloods, and by thy [God's] spirit one; / A Brother and a Sister, made by thee / The Organ, where thou are the Harmony.... / They shew us Ilanders our joy, our King, / They tell us why, and teach us how to sing" (*Poems* 366). In Sidney's imaginative reworking of the Hebrew Bible, he develops the imagery of insects in three out of eight stanzas:

[1]
Lord, lett not mee, a worm, by thee be shent
    While thou art in the heate of thy displeasure:
    Ne let thy rage, of my due punishment
            Become the measure.

[6]
Woe, like a Moth, my faces beautie eates,
    And age, pul'd on with paines, all freshness fretteth;
    The while a swarm of foes with vexing feates
            My life besetteth.

[8]
The Lord my suite did heare, and gently heare;
    They shall be sham'd and vext, that breed my cryeng:
    And turn their backs, and straight on backs appeare
            Their shamfull flying.
            The Psalms of Sir Philip Sidney (12–13)

It is the idiosyncratic explanation put forth by Ibn Ezra, and subsequently copied into Kimhi (table 15), that is the most probable source for this interpretive tradition. Turning to Isaiah 50:9, these Jewish exegetes explain that the word *'asheshah* is related to the Hebrew word עָשׁ *'ash*, "worm or moth," a meaning supported by Rashi in his explication of the term as "clothes worm." This alternative (though philologically incorrect) tradition finds its way into the Genevan note ("mine eye is eaten as it were with wormes"; table 15), suggested by the broader signification in English of "moth" as both the larva and the adult insect;[28] Rivkah Zim has pointed out "the realistic and horrifying image of the eaten face which would have had a special affective power for an Elizabethan reader" (*English Metrical Psalms* 161–62). Thus the penitent speaker envisions the physical and spiritual ravages brought on by sin: in stanza 1, the image of the speaker as a worm, a prostrate and groveling creature, enforces his despair, while in stanzas 6 and 8 the supplicant transfers to the enemies—those "who in my ill rejoice" (stanza 7)—his own affective and psychological content of being attacked by an at once exasperating and overwhelming force (so that "they shall be sham'd and vext").

Table 15. Penitential Psalm 6:7: 'Asheshah as "Worm"

Isaiah 50:9	Jewish Exegetes	The [Geneva] Bible and Holy Scriptures
The Holy [King James] Bible. Behold, the Lord God wil helpe me, who *is* he *that* shall condemne mee? Loe, they all shall waxe olde as a garment: the moth shall eate them up ("The Old Testament" n.p.). *Rashi: 'Ash* ['mothe']. The clothes worm *(Biblia Rabbinica* 2:79).	*Ibn Ezra: 'Asheshah.* A cognate of [the noun *'ash* meaning 'moth' in] 'the moth will consume them' [Isa. 50:9] *(Biblia Rabbinica* 4:7). *Kimhi: 'Asheshah.* A cognate of [the noun *'ash* meaning 'moth' in] "the moth will consume them" [Isa. 50:9], as if he had said "decayed" *(Complete Commentary* 21).	^{ll} Mine eye is dimmed for despite, & sunke in because of all mine enemies ("The Olde Testament" 236v). ^{ll} Or, mine eye is eaten as it were with wormes.

This meaning certainly appeals to Donne's poetic and polemic imagination. Moreover, his preaching on the biblical term makes direct reference to Reuchlin and indeed develops his explication of the Hebrew word *'ash,* found in both his Hebrew grammar and dictionary, *De Rudimentis Hebraicis* (*On the Fundamentals of Hebrew*) and the accompanying annotated translation *In Septem Psalmos Poenitentiales* (*On the Seven Penitential Psalms*). Reuchlin writes:

> *De Rudimentis Hebraicis*
> עָשֵׁשׁ. Tinea. Vermis. Per apocopen ultime litera. Isaia .L. Tinea comedet eos (412).
> *Ashash.* Moth larva. Worm. As in the closing words of Isaiah 50 [50:9]: "A moth larva consumes them."

> *Septem Psalmos Poenitentiales* [6:8]
> Vermanivit ex iracundia species me inveteravit in omnibus tribulantibus me.
> My face became wormy because of anger; it grew old because of all my troubles.

Reuchlin's echoing of Kimhi is not all surprising, since *De Rudimentis Hebraicis,* "the real pioneering work of its kind by a Christian scholar," was based mainly on the work of this Jewish exegete (Silverman and Scholem 247). In this instance, Donne does not consult Reuchlin the Christian Kabbalist, but rather Reuchlin the philologist, who utilizes "a philological method which traces the meaning of every word in the original Hebrew" thereby establishing "philology as an autonomous discipline entitled to discuss the meaning of words in the Bible...[and] to discover the truth hidden in God's word" (Schwarz 78–79). Expanding on Reuchlin's image of the worm and its physical ravaging, the Protestant preacher establishes a continuously transforming series of comparisons and metaphoric assertions ("a deformitie [in the eye] as wormes make in wood"; "worme, this apprehension"; "worme bites upon thee"; "it is the hissing of the serpent"; "it is the whispering of Satan") to remind his audience of their sins and their dependence upon Christ for salvation.

Donne's intensifying characterization of sin as "licentiousnesse," "intemperance" and "the drawing in of others" is accompanied by an intensifying characterization of language's illocutionary power. Paradoxically, it seems, Donne transmutes the worm's bite first into the "hissing of the Serpent" and then into the "whispering of Satan," adding in the course of his interpretation a linguistic element; for the first verb is bereft of speech, while the second is a metaphoric and fantastic representation of a Christian's psychological surrender to melancholy and dejection. Moreover, Donne's prefiguring of Milton's post-Fall Satan as speaking only (in book 10) in "hiss for hiss return'd with forked tongue to forked tongue" (249) creates a density of meaning that underlines the psalmic speaker's sin as tainted with the implications of the temptation and fall. This is appropriate for a psalm that is in the Christian tradition the first of the seven Penitential Psalms, traditionally associated with David's sin of sexual transgression with Bathsheba.[29] This penitential force is thus at the heart of the theological consequence of Donne's exegetical choice, resetting as it does the prior Christian tradition of psalm translation, as well as revealing to his auditory and reader the scholarly sources and authorities—the very process of evaluation—by which a Christian reader construes the meaning and message of the Hebrew biblical text.

Conclusion

While Burley's manuscript notes highlight "the art of listening" to sermons, which was so important in the seventeenth century, Donne's own sermonic and textual notes—and his attention to other notes and commentaries—highlight "the art of reading" that very biblical text on which he preached. This art is disclosed through attention paid by the modern reader of Donne's sermons on the Penitential Psalm 6 to his *Essayes in Divinity*, as well as to the various exegetical and interpretive readings which both exist independently of these sermons and influenced them. Attending to the notes and margins of Donne's sermons, and of the varied biblical texts and commentaries, thus emphasizes an interplay of voices which creates (in an adaptation of Bakhtinian terms, "Discourse" 272) a tension between the centrifugal and centripetal forces of reading that first flings Donne's auditory and reader out to the notes and margins of the *Biblia Rabbinica* and the Reformation Bibles, as well as of the Christian commentaries, and then ultimately and necessarily pulls them back to the central biblical text. For in Donne's own words (from a 1630 Whitsunday sermon preached on John 14:20), "though he interline it with other studies, and knowledges, yet the Text it selfe, in the booke it selfe, the testimonies of the conscience, will shine through and appeare" (*Sermons* 9:237).

THREE

The Penitential Psalm 32

The Sacred Philology of Sin

*Sacred philology was not an end in itself, not even for the most
bookish and pedantic of Renaissance humanists, much less for
Reformation theologians.... Whatever new insights into Hebrew
grammar or Greek lexicography may have come from the scholars of
the fifteenth and sixteenth centuries, their biblical scholarship had
as its goal to derive meaning from the text—indeed the meaning of
the text, which each of them believed could be found, and had been
found by him—and to communicate that meaning both to other
scholars and theologians and to the church.*
—Jaroslav Pelikan, *Reformation of the Bible*

Sermon and Context

Donne's series of eight sermons on the Penitential Psalm 32
evoked a rather piqued response from Evelyn Simpson, who writes
that the "great block of sermons on the Penitential Psalms [32] is
a bit of a drag."[1] Perhaps Simpson's response reflects her unease

with Donne's apparent insistence in these sermons on subordinating the theological and moral aspects of sin to its philological one. Yet Simpson's unequivocal statement can be tempered by turning to the opening citation from Pelikan, highlighting as it does the scholarly and theological implications of positioning sacred philology—that "humanist tradition of biblical philology" (Kristeller 79)—within what Debora Shuger has aptly termed a "culturally specific discursive system" (*The Renaissance Bible* 26–27).[2] This is indeed the crux of the Henrician debate over the Hebrew word *yevam*, in which its two alternative translations of "brother-in-law" or "kinsman" respectively endorse either the Levitical concern with incest and familial purity or the Deuteronomic concern with dynasty and familial continuity. It is also very much in evidence, for example, when Donne subsumes the Hebrew word *eizov*, "hyssop" (from the Penitential Psalm 51:7) and *tav*, alphabetical letter or "mark" (from Ezekiel 9:4), within a Christian system of ritual and belief—theologically transforming the hyssop from a Jewish instrument of purification into one of Christian redemption, as well as iconically and theologically transforming the Hebrew letter [ת] *tav* into the Cross [†].

Yet a reader of Donne's sermons might well inquire about the exegetical strategies by which such a transformation of meaning is accomplished. In answer, it is worth citing John Chamberlin's discussion of the sermon on verses 32:1–2 as "a representative instance of Donne's preaching" (137);[3] Chamberlin writes,

> These procedures—dividing and associating, particularizing and diffusing [the biblical word]—can go on at the same time because the sectioning of the verbal statement from Scripture *is* the division of a whole entity of meaning conceived by the mind. Thus the sermon can come together in a discourse both as a structure of ideas and as a grammatical commentary on the words of the text. (153–54)

In other words, the biblical intratextuality (associating and diffusing) utilized so consistently by Donne is balanced by his equally consistent use of philology with its lexical, grammatical and etymological issues ("dividing and particularizing"). What is more, Chamberlin perceptively notices the way in which Donne conceives of the biblical word as a highly significant unit of meaning that structures the sermonic text itself. Such exegetical strategies are not, of course, unique to Donne's preaching. Indeed, comparative discussion of Donne and his contemporary Lancelot Andrewes (1555–1626)[4] can clarify the ways in which attending to sacred philology directs the sermonic text. Andrewes, considered to be a *Stella praedicantium* or "star preacher," was also a noted Hebrew scholar and one of the translators of the King James Bible.[5] His sermon on Psalm 106:29–30, printed in *XCVI Sermons* as "A Sermon Preached at Cheswick in the Time of Pestilence" (August 21, 1603),[6] is particularly interesting. For in this instance Andrewes organizes the sermon's narrative and thought entirely around a discussion of the two alternative meanings of the Hebrew word יְפַלֵּל *yefalel*—either "prayed" or "executed judgement." The sermon's prefatory citation of the biblical text is taken from the Bishops' Bible (a revision of Coverdale's Great Bible that was considered a "dignified and 'safe' version for public reading"; Gilmore 32), augmented by parenthetical, alternative meanings from the scholarly but more radical Geneva Bible;[7] this reads: "*Thus they provoked Him to anger with their owne inventions, and the plague was great (or, brake in) among them. Then stood up* Phinees, *and prayed (or, executed judgement) and so the Plague was ceased (or, stayed)*" (*XCVI Sermons* 159).[8] Andrewes then explains (*XCVI Sermons* 160 and 167):

> The *Cure* is likewise set downe; and it is twofold, out of *two* significations of one word, the word (*Palal*) in the Verse. *Phinees prayed* (some read it:) *Phinees executed judgement* (some other;) and the word beares both.
>
> ········
>
> There are two persons. Both of them were in *Phinees*. For, as he was a *Priest*, so he was a *Prince of his Tribe*. So then, both these must joyne together, as well as the *devotion* of the *Priest in praier*,

> which is his *Office:* as the *zeale* of the *Magistrate* in executing
> *judgement,* which is His. For, *Phinees the Priest,* must not onely
> *stand up,* and *pray:* but *Moses (the Magistrate* also*) must stand in
> the gap to turne away the wrath of God, that he destroy not the
> people....*But what if *Moses* gives no charge; what if *Phinees* doe
> no execution, as oft it falleth out? How then? In that case, every
> private man is to bee *Phinees to himselfe;* is not onely to *pray* to
> God, but to be *wreaked* [marginal note: 2 Corinthians 7:11], do
> *judgement, chasten his owne body* [marginal note: 1 Corinthians
> 9:27]; and so *judge himselfe, that he may not be judged of the Lord*
> [marginal note: 1 Corinthians 11:31].

The psalmic text refers to the events recorded in Numbers 25:7–8,
in which the Israelites' idol worship brings down upon them the
divine punishment of a plague. It is the violent act of "Phinehes
the sonne of Eleazar, the sonne of Aaron the priest" that saves
them, for "he rose up out of the myddes of the companie, and
tooke a javelin in his hande, And went after the man of Israel
into the tent, and thrust both of them through, both the man
of Israel, and also the [Madianitishe] woman, even thorowe the
belly of her: And the plague ceased from the children of Israel"
(*The Holie [Bishops'] Bible.* First Part. lxxxv[v]). In Psalm 106,
however, the description of Phinehes's act—*yefalel*—is more
ambiguous; for it comprises in the psalmic text the "intensive"
verb form (*Pi'el*) of the root *pll* and therefore means to "pray,"[9]
but can in its causative verb form (*Hiph'il*) as *hiphlil* mean to
"judge or punish" (Even-Shoshan 5:1491).[10] Ibn Ezra, for example,
expounds on the psalmic term *yefalel* by explaining that Phinehes "executed judgement like a criminal offence [*'avon pelili*]"
(*Biblia Rabbinica* 4:98).

   This is a highly effective and fascinating biblical text for a plague
sermon, encompassing the season of sickness and death within
the biblical issues of moral and religious responsibility, the effi-
cacy of prayer, and the administration of justice.[11] Significantly,
Andrewes's preaching on the Hebrew word *yefalel* serves these very
issues; thus he extends its dual meaning to discuss the responsibilities of the religious and judicial leaders—invoked in Phinehes

as both "Priest" and "Prince"—and consequently raises several interesting, potentially subversive though oblique questions: Is Andrewes suggesting a comparison between the biblical and the English political (monarchical) and religious leaderships? Is he calling attention on this occasion to the anticipated role of King James I, at whose recent coronation (July 25, 1603) he had assisted (McCullough, "Andrewes, Lancelot")? And finally, Is he (somewhat surreptitiously) advocating the individual appropriation of political and judicial responsibility and power?[12] What is more, the three citations from Corinthians serve to construct a reading that integrates the Hebrew Bible with the Christian Scriptures, emphasizing the natural progression from the Pentateuchal story of plague and judgment, to the psalmic retelling and reinterpretation, and finally to the Pauline exhortations regarding penitence and self-judgment.[13] Andrewes's sermon thus demonstrates how skillfully he makes use of sacred philology, particularly "the culturally specific discursive system" of divine justice, within which the plague is understood to be divine retribution visited upon a sinful populace who must consequently examine its moral and religious responsibilities.

In this manner Andrewes points the way to a better understanding of how Donne uses sacred philology in his sermons on the Penitential Psalm 32. Jeanne Shami has conceived of this series as following "a pattern similar to that already observed in the *Anniversaries,* showing the drama of a sinner's gradual awakening from lethargy, his sense of God's heavy hand upon him, his growing sense of his responsibility and potential, and his decision to celebrate the newly established commerce between himself and God with joy and confidence" ("Anatomy and Progress" 230).[14] Within this penitential development, the first sermon (on verses 32:1–2) focuses intensively on Hebrew words in order to delineate the various types of sin, as well as the ways in which God's mercy is proffered to the sinner. These two aspects are developed in subsequent sermons, as Donne successively draws out the theological and polemic meanings of the "Originall" biblical text. Ultimately, the point is not to contrast Andrewes's learned scholarship with what Evelyn Simpson terms Donne's (simply) "considerable interest" (*Sermons* 10:308), but rather to examine Janel Mueller's statement that "unlike Andrewes Donne does not go to great pains in consulting the Hebrew and Greek texts and the numerous translations available in his day to establish an authoritative and authentic reading of a verse. (Donne's philological research has, in fact, the opposite objective: to open many possibilities of nuance and meaning, not to settle upon one)" ("Introduction" 10). In the course of this examination, Janel Mueller's pointed distinction between Andrewes and Donne will be somewhat qualified, and turned into a discussion about issues of sermonic genre and exegetical agenda.

Sermon on the Penitential Psalm 32:1–2: Blessed is he whose transgression is forgiven, whose sinne is covered. / Blessed is the man unto whom the LORD imputeth not iniquitie: and in whose spirit there is no guile

In his third sermon on the Penitential Psalm 32 Donne notes that there "are few things in the Scriptures, which the Holy Ghost hath exprest in so many names, as Sin; *Sin, Wickednesse, Iniquity, Transgressions, Offences,* Many, many more; And all this, that thereby we might reflect upon our selves often, and see if our particular actions fell not under some of those names" (*Sermons* 9:305–06). The specific meanings of each of the three   Hebrew terms cited in verses 32:1–2 (פֶּשַׁע *pesha,* "transgression"; חַטָא *ḥeit,* "sin"; and עָוֹן *'avon,* "iniquitie") are acknowledged by Kimhi, when he writes concerning the evaluation of a righteous man:

> *Whose transgression is forgiven.* This is a reference to three degrees in which righteous men can be. It begins with the lowest degree, and this is "whose transgression is forgiven": he sinned, committed an iniquity and committed a crime, but then fully repented and was forgiven. *Whose sin is covered over:* He has done many good deeds and only committed a small sin. So this [sin] is covered over,

and is not seen amongst his good deeds....*Imputeth not iniquitie:* He has many merits and good deeds and only a small sin. (*The Complete Commentary on the Psalms* 75)

Such a graduated reading of the parallel structure of these biblical verses is apparent in Donne's first sermon of this series, in which he makes his own, singular use of these differences.[15] He variously explains:

The Originall word is *Pashang* [*pesha*],[16] and that signifies sin in all extensions. The highest, the deepest, the weightiest sin; It is a malicious, and a forcible opposition to God (*Sermons* 9:257).

Sin in this place is not so heavy a word, as *Transgression* was in the former; for that was sin in all extensions, sinne in all formes, all sin of all men, of all times, of all places, the sin of all the world upon the shoulders of the Saviour of the world. In this place, (the word is *Catah*, and by the derivation thereof from *Nata*, which is to Decline, to step aside, or to be withdrawne, and *Kut*, which is *filum*, a thread, or a line) that which we all sin here, signifies *Transilire lineam*, To depart, or by any tentation to be withdrawne from the direct duties, and the exact straightnesse which is required of us in the world, for the attaining of the next. (*Sermons* 9:259–60)

To which purpose, we consider also, that this word, which we translate here *Iniquity*, *Gnavah* ['*avon*], is oftentimes in the Scripture used for punishment, as well as for sinne: and so indifferently for both, as that if we will compare Translation with Translation, and Exposition with Exposition, it will hard for us to say, whether *Cain* said [marginal note: Genesis 4:13], *Mine iniquity is greater then can be pardoned,* or *My punishment is greater then I can beare;* and our last Translation, which seems to have been most carefull of the Originall, takes it rather so, *My punishment,* in the Text, and lays the other, *My sinne,* aside in the Margin. So then, this Imputing, being an Imputing which arises from our selves, and so may be accompanied with error, and mistaking, that we Impute that to our selves, which God doth not impute. (*Sermons* 2:62)

Donne's use of sacred philology is apparent not only in his graduated reading from the most serious to the least serious terms for misdeed (similar to the reading put forward by Kimhi), but also in his iconic development of what he considers to be the

etymology of the word *ḥatah* (constructed from נָטָה "natah" and
חוט *ḥut*) as "withdrawne from the direct duties, and the exact
straightness."[17] This iconization of Hebrew philology is also apparent in Donne's discussion of the term *'avon* in his sermons on
the Penitential Psalm 38 (table 16); in this instance he distinctly
echoes Benedict Pererius's sixteenth century commentary[18] in a
shared emphasis on the concurrent literal and figurative meanings
of the word עָוָה *'avah*—"crooked" and "pervert"—as the root of
'avon, "iniquitie." Indeed, Donne's focus on the etymological and
iconic aspects of the Hebrew word is supported by a variety of
Hebrew dictionaries; James Strong's nineteenth century biblical
dictionary explanation in particular emphasizes the iconic aspect
of the letter [ע] *ayin* as a "turn" (table 16). This convergence of
the literal meaning of *'avon/'avah* as "crooked" or "bent" with
the image of the crooked, inclined body—and the subsequent,
figurative transformation both philologically and psychologically
into "perversion" and "iniquity"—provides Donne as preacher
with a powerful image of sin. In his homiletic extension of these
etymological and iconic aspects of the Hebrew word Donne thus
renders language, in Judith Anderson's important distinction, as
"something quite other than an incidental or a transparent system of notations....in short, substantial *res*, things opaque and
self-sustaining" (191–92).

Donne's emphasis in the present sermon on the dual meaning
of *'avon* as both "inquity" and "punishment" echoes the semantic ambiguity of this Hebrew term, as noted by Even-Shoshan's
Hebrew dictionary (table 16). This ambiguity is put to good use by
Donne in his letter (dated October 26, 1624) "To the Honourable
L. the Lady Kingsmel upon the death of her Husband."[19] Seeking
to console her, Donne writes,

> To say that our afflictions are greater than we can bear, is so near to
> despairing, as that the same words express both; for when we con-
> sider *Caines* words in that originall tongue in which God spake, we
> cannot tell whether the words be, My punishment is greater than
> can be born; or My sin is greater than can be forgiven. But Madame,

Table 16. 'Avon as "Crooked"

Benedict Pererius, *Commentariorum et Disputationum in Genesim*	Dictionaries	Donne, Sermons on Psalm 38:4
Pro Latina voce Iniquitas, Hebraicè est עבן *Havon* proprie significans curvitatem. Incedit autem quis curvus, vel ob sensum ed dolorem sceleris a se commissi" (Page Proofs, OSB MSS 90, Box 5, Folder 116).	Udall, *Hebrue Dictionaire.* עָוָה *he hath done wickedlie.* Niph. *he was bowed.* Piel, *he perverted.* עָוֹן, עָוֹן *Iniquitie.* עֲוֹנוֹת *Iniquities.* עָוָה *Froward* (105–06).	Psalm 38:4: For mine iniquities ['*avonotai*] are gone over my head, as a heavy burden
Instead of the Latin word *Iniquitas* [injustice], the Hebrew [word] is *Havon,* that means exactly crookedly. Someone bent crooked moves forward or because of the sense and the pain of the crime [that was] committed by himself.	Strong. *Dictionary* 5753. *'Avah.* A primitive root; to crook, literally or figuratively (as follows):—do amiss, bow down, make crooked, commit iniquity, pervert, (do) perverse(-ly), trouble, turn, do wickedly, do wrong. 5771. *'Avon.* From 'avah; perversity, i.e. (moral) evil:—fault, iniquity, mischief, punishment (of iniquity), sin.	...they are as heavy, as a heavy *Burden;* And the nature, and inconvenience of a Burden is, first to *Crooken,* and bend us downward from our naturall posture, which is erect, for this incurvation implies a declination in the inordinate love of the Creature, *Incurvat....* It crookens us, it deprives us of our *rectitude* (*Sermons* 2:97).
	Even-Shoshan. *Dictionary* (4:1352). *'Avah* [Close to '*avt;* Arabic, make crooked]	*Inclinat;* That a Burden *sinkes* a man, *declines* him, *crookens* him, makes him *stoop.* So does sin (*Sermons* 2:132).

Table 16 (*cont.*)

Benedict Pererius, *Commentariorum et Disputationum in Genesim*	Dictionaries	Donne, Sermons on Psalm 38:4
	Pa'al [*Qal;* simple form]. Sinned, transgressed. *Niph'al* [Reflexive]:[20] Be bent, twisted. *Pi'el* [intensive form]: Bend, make crooked, pervert. *'Avon* [From *'avah*]. 1. Sin, crime. 2. Punishment for sin. 3. [In modern Israeli legislation] A crime that is less severe than *pesha* [transgression] and more severe than *ḥeit* ["sin"].	

you who willingly sacrificed your self to God, in your obedience to him, in your own sickness, cannot be doubted to dispute with him, about any part of you, which he shall be pleased to require at your hands. (*Letters to Severall Persons of Honour* 9)

This is the fifth and final letter addressed by Donne to Lady Bridget [White] Kingsmill (d. 1672), "a patroness of literary men over a long period of years" (Bennett 134).[21] Its significance in echoing crucial issues from Donne's writing has already been noted; the discussion of physical decay in the opening passage[22] particularly reflects his two poems "The Dissolution" (Levine 304) and the "First Anniversarie: An Anatomy of the World" (Hirsch 75). As Lady Kingsmill's "Chaplaine" (*Letters to Severall Persons of Honour* 10), Donne frames his consolation to her within the more

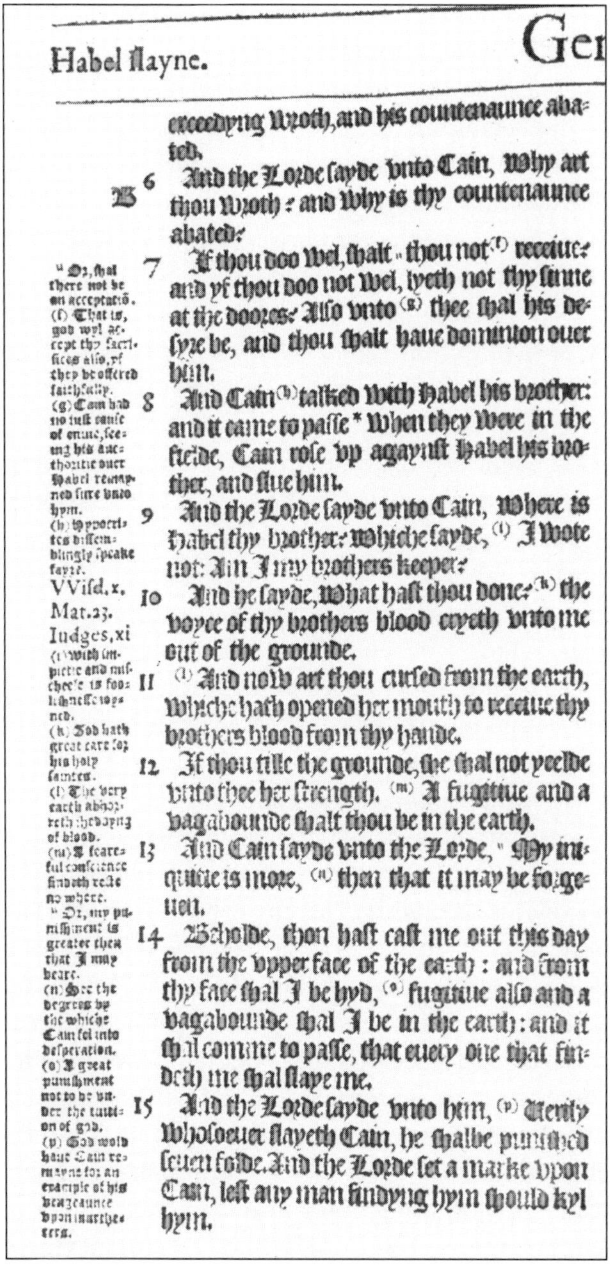

exceedyng wroth, and his countenaunce aba∣
ted.

6 And the Lorde sayde vnto Cain, why art
thou wroth? and why is thy countenaunce
abated?

7 If thou doo wel, shalt " thou not (f) receiue?
and yf thou doo not wel, lyeth not thy sinne
at the doores? Also vnto (g) thee shal his de∣
syre be, and thou shalt haue dominion ouer
him.

8 And Cain (h) talked with Habel his brother:
and it came to passe * when they were in the
fielde, Cain rose vp agaynst Habel his bro∣
ther, and slue him.

9 And the Lorde sayde vnto Cain, where is
Habel thy brother? Whiche sayde, (i) I wote
not: Am I my brothers keeper?

10 And he sayde, what hast thou done? (k) the
voyce of thy brothers blood cryeth vnto me
out of the grounde.

11 (l) And now art thou cursed from the earth,
whiche hath opened her mouth to receiue thy
brothers blood from thy hande.

12 If thou tille the grounde, she shal not yeelde
vnto thee her strength. (m) A fugitiue and a
vagabounde shalt thou be in the earth.

13 And Cain sayde vnto the Lorde, " My ini∣
quitie is more, (n) then that it may be forge∣
uen.

14 Beholde, thou hast cast me out this day
from the vpper face of the earth : and from
thy face shal I be hyd, (o) fugitiue also and a
vagabounde shal I be in the earth : and it
shal comme to passe, that euery one that fin∣
deth me shal slaye me.

15 And the Lorde sayde vnto him, (p) Verily
whosoeuer slayeth Cain, he shalbe punished
seuen folde. And the Lorde set a marke vpon
Cain, lest any man findyng hym should kyl
hym.

" Or, shal
there not be
an acceptatiō.
(f) That is,
god wyl ac∣
cept thy sacri∣
fices also, yf
they be offered
faithfully.
(g) Cain had
no iust cause
of enuie, see∣
ing his autho∣
ritie ouer
Habel remay∣
ned sure vnto
hym.
(h) Hypocri∣
tes dissem∣
blingly speake
fayre.
Wisd. x.
Mat.23.
Iudges.xi
(i) With im∣
pietie and mis∣
chiefe is foo∣
lishnesse ioy∣
ned.
(k) God hath
great care for
his holy
saintes.
(l) The very
earth abhor∣
reth the dOyng
of blood.
(m) A fearo∣
ful conscience
findeth rest in
no where.
" Or, my pu∣
nishment is
greater then
that I may
beare.
(n) See the
degrees by
the whiche
Cain fel into
desperation.
(o) I great
punishment
not to be vn∣
der the tuiti∣
on of god.
(p) God wold
haue Cain re∣
maine for an
example of his
vengeaunce
vpon murthe∣
rers.

Fig. 5. *The Holie [Bishops'] Bible* (1572), leaf iii[v]. Reproduced courtesy
of the Rare Book and Manuscript Library of the University of Illinois at
Urbana-Champaign.

general concept of divine providence, and requires her not to "be doubted to dispute with him [God], about any part of you, which he shall be pleased to require at your hand."

It is at the beginning of the cited passage that Donne reveals his art of reading the Hebrew Bible. Unmarked though they are within this epistolary text, "*Caines* words" can be readily identified as cited from two different translations of Genesis 4:13 (tables 17 and 18): "My punishment ['*avon*] *is* greater, then I can beare" from the Geneva Bible; and "My iniquitie ['*avon*] is more, then it may be forgiven" from *The Holie [Bishops'] Bible* (see fig. 5). Cain's arrogant accusation against God's punishment "as a cruel judge" is noted in the Genevan scholia, while his sin of "desperation" at God's sentencing him to be "a fugitive, and a vagabond in the earth" (Gen. 4:14) is noted in the scholia of the Bishops' Bible; both are evident in Donne's acknowledgment of Lady Kingsmill's "afflictions" and the sin of "despairing." Indeed, Cain was seen in medieval and Renaissance tradition as the ultimate image of pride and despair, which were linked in him through his "refusal to acknowledge insufficiency of self and ask for God's help" (Snyder 32). By thus anonymously quoting Cain in this letter, Donne revitalizes the emotional aspects of the biblical story and bestows as well (for the reader cognizant of the source) a biblical resonance on the seventeenth century experience of grief.

Both of these alternate readings are suggested by Ibn Ezra (table 19), who explains that while "all the other commentators" have relied on the literal translation of the Hebrew term '*avon* as "iniquity" (as, for example, Rashi; table 17), in the wider context of Cain's subsequent citing of his divine punishment (Gen. 4:14) it should preferably be understood as "punishment" for sin. Donne chooses here to retain both meanings, and astutely indicates his comprehension of Kingsmill's emotional state by warning that an overwhelming "dispute" over divine "afflictions" or punishment (her husband's death) transmutes into the sin of despair. Clearly, then, the scholarly recording of alternate readings (evident in the Reformation Bibles) is acknowledged by Donne in this epistle not

Table 17. Genesis 4:13: *'Avon* as "Iniquity"

Rashi	The Holie [Bishops'] Bible	Luther, *Lectures on Genesis*
With surprise, "You bear the worlds above and below, and it is impossible to bear my sin?" (*Biblia Rabbinica* 1:22; *Pentateuch*, Genesis 18–19).	And Cain sayde unto the Lord, My ‖ iniquitie is more, (n) then it may be forgiven. ‖ Or, my punishment is greater then I may beare. (n) Bee the degrees by the whiche Cain fel into desperation ("The First Part" iii[v]).	These two words, מִנְּשֹׂא and עָוֹן, are linguistic cruxes. Jerome translates them: My inquity is greater than I deserve forgiveness." Santes Pagninus, a learned philologist and apparently also an industrious one, translates thus: "My punishment is greater than I can bear." But in this way we would make a martyr out of Cain and a sinner out of Abel. However, I stated above that where the word נָשָׂא is applied to sin, it means to lift sin up or take it away, just as we use a common figure and speak of "remission of sins," and of "remitting sin." Thus we read in Ps. 32:1: אַשְׁרֵי נְשׂוּי-פֶּשַׁע, which literally means "becoming blessed, having been relieved of guilt or sin." This we express by "Blessed is he whose sin has been forgiven," or "whose sin has been taken away"....But עֲוֹנִי here denotes "inquity," or "sin," the same as in many other passages of Scripture, as the verb "to lift up," which has been added, also indicates. Thus we see that philologists who are nothing but philologists and have no knowledge of theological matters have their perplexing difficulties with such passages and torture not only Scripture but also themselves and their hearers. First the meaning should be established in such a manner that it is everywhere in agreement, and then philology should be brought into play. But the rabbis do the opposite. For this reason I regret that our teachers and holy fathers have, for the most part, followed their lead (1:297–98).

Table 18. Genesis 4:13: 'Avon as "Punishment"

Ibn Ezra	The [Geneva] Bible and Holy Scriptures	The Holy [King James] Bible
My punishment ['avoni] is greater than I can bear. All the commentators explained this to mean that [Cain] confessed his sin [as they translate 'avon literally as iniquity]. They explained that *neso* [bear] means forgiveness, as [in Exodus 34:7] *noseh 'avon* [forgiving iniquity]. In my opinion, in Hebrew [the word] "reward" is called *'eqev* [עֵקֶב] [because it follows as a result of something], and the harsh punishment that comes as a result of iniquity [is called] "sin" [*ḥatat*]. Similarly [in Genesis 15:16] "the Amorite's punishment ['avon] is not yet complete," [in 1 Samuel 28:10] "no punishment ['avon]] will happen to you," [in Lamentations 4:6] "the punishment ['avon] of my people is severer [than the punishment of Sodom]." The meaning [of our verse] is that "this punishment ['avon] is greater than I can bear [mi-neso]." The succeeding verse demonstrates the correctness of this interpretation [Gen. 4:14: "Behold, thou hast driven me out this day from the face of the earth, and from thy face shall I be hid, and I shall be a fugitive, and a vagabond in the earth"] (*Biblia Rabbinica* 1:22; *Ibn Ezra's Commentary on the Pentateuch*, Gen. 84–85).	Then Káin said to the Lord, [m][II] My punishment is greater, then I can beare. [m] He burdeneth God as a cruel judge ("The Olde Testament" 2v). [II] Or, my sinne is greater then can be pardoned.	And Cain said unto the LORD, [II] My punishment *is* greater, then I can beare. [II] Or, my iniquitie is greater, then that it may be forgiven ("The Old Testament" n.p.).

simply as an exegetical perspective on the biblical text, but rather as an opportunity to draw out a parallel between two particular, personal tragedies.

Donne in this letter explores the alternate meanings of the Hebrew term *'avon* much as Andrewes does regarding the Hebrew term *palal* in his sermon on Psalm 106. Yet interestingly enough, their exegetical strategies part company when they preach on this passage from Genesis. The importance of understanding their differences in strategy is articulated by Luther, in his commentary on the two "linguistic cruxes" of Genesis 4:13: עָוֹן *'avon* as "sin" or "punishment"; and מִנְּשׂוֹא *mi-neso* as "than be born" or "than be forgiven" (table 17). He subsequently condemns those philologists "who are nothing but philologists and have no knowledge of theological matters"—thus in his opinion following the "Rabbis"—arguing instead for the precedence of "meaning" over "philology" in reading the Hebrew Bible. Janel Mueller's distinction between the different uses of sacred philology by Andrewes and Donne may therefore be more fruitfully conceived of as serving particular issues of genre (a lecture series; a Lenten series on sin and penitence) or exegetical agendas (accusation against divine judgment or desperation over one's sin).

Andrewes's sermon on Genesis 4:13 was preached at St. Giles on September 2, 1599; he explains "the double reading" of this verse:

> The one in the Text, *My punishment is greater than I can bear.* The other in the Margent, *My sin is greater than can be pardoned:* So in the Text the word is translated the punishment of sinne, in the Margent the sinne itself, which is the primarie signification of the word. And they that turn it punishment for sinne, doe thereby expresse *Cain's* murmuring against God: They that turn it for sinne doe shew *Cain's* desparation. I rather follow that in the Margent, (*viz.*) that the sense is thus; *My sinne is greater than can be pardoned.* First, because punishment of sinne. Secondly, because the Hebrews expound it so. Thirdly, for that all the old Fathers read it so. Fourthly, for that there is no mention of the third person. Lastly, because the full sense is comprehended in the next

verse. So that we are to take it thus, That *Cain* being examined, and hearing the sentence pronounced by God upon him, breakes forth into this complaint, *My sinne is greater than can be forgiven.* (*Apospasmatia Sacra* 435)

At the heart of Andrewes's discussion is his attempt to make a specific decision about the meaning of the word *'avon,* and to this end he turns once again to the text and margins of the Geneva Bible. He thus carefully explains the alternate meanings and their interpretive consequences for the word *'avon,* which emphasize (as "punishment") Cain's pride in "murmuring against God" or (as "sin") his "desparation." Andrewes's reliance on contextual meaning to establish one overriding definition of the biblical text echoes Ibn Ezra, though he arrives at a different solution: the Jewish exegete understands the verse as a further expression of Cain's understanding of the full gravity of his situation (*'avon* as "punishment"), while the Christian preacher emphasizes the pronouncement of Cain's punishment in Genesis 4:14 as the *consequence* of sin, which itself further breeds the sin of despair. In setting out his exegetical authorities against the reading in the text (and in line with the Genevan "Margent"), Andrewes provides a lesson in the art of reading the Bible that culminates in a clear-cut interpretive solution emphasizing Cain's despair as "the case of all his progenie" (*Apospasmatia Sacra* 435).

Andrewes's ultimate intention in this lecture is indeed to establish the "authoritative and authentic reading of a verse" as asserted by Janel Mueller. This is particularly accomplished by his emphatic and rather pedantic heaping up of reasons in support of his interpretive decision to read *'avon* as "sin," thereby corroborating Cain's status as a biblical exemplar of despair for his late sixteenth century Christian auditory. The passage in Donne's sermon on the Penitential Psalm 32:1–2 in which he preaches on Genesis 4:13 certainly reiterates the scholarly process of reading demonstrated by Andrewes, but sharpens it by carefully maintaining those "possibilities of nuance and meaning" so evident in the Kingsmill letter. Thus in the third passage cited from this sermon, Donne echoes Andrewes's use of biblical sources, acknowledging the two alternative meanings of *'avon*. Yet he does not, as Andrewes does in his lecture on Genesis, bypass that process of scholarship in sacred philology that had culminated in the English Reformation Bibles. Rather, Donne takes care to point out the necessity of comparing "Translation[s]" and "Exposition[s]," and refrains from endorsing only one exegetical conclusion. In this, he essentially follows the lead of Andrewes's exposition on the dual meaning of the Hebrew term *yefalal* in the sermon on Psalm 106; putting this homiletic practice to good use, Donne creates a complex intertwining of the two alternate meanings of the Hebrew term.

The "Chaplaine's" concern with personal tragedy—be it Lady Kingsmill's or Cain's—therefore shapes his use of sacred philology in warning against the transmutation of her "dispute" over divine punishment into despair. The preacher's concern, on the other hand, is shaped by the "literary and devotional tradition" focused on the Penitential Psalms (Stanwood, "Donne's Earliest Sermons" 366), as well as his sermons' connection with the Lenten season (preached as they were between January and June 1626, and between January and March 1627). In his sermon, Donne consequently reconciles the dual meaning of *'avon* ("iniquity" and "punishment") by suggesting that a false imputation of "sinne to my self," may arise out of God's "punishments and corrections inflicted upon us"; in other words, he warns the members of his auditory that divine punishment may lead them to believe there is sin where there is none. Concerned as he is with both the personal and the collective, ecclesiastical experiences of sin, Donne develops this admonition to encompass the other psalmic statements of divine forgiveness ("transgression is forgiven," "sinne covered," "imputeth not iniquitie"). In both the epistolary and sermonic genres, therefore, Donne explores the relationship between divine judgment and sin, drawing out a lesson from the biblical text that speaks to the emotional states of both personal loss and collective penitence.[23]

Reading the texts of Andrewes and Donne in juxtaposition therefore invites consideration of the issues of sermonic genre and exegetical agenda. The choice of homiletic practice—whether to establish one authoritative reading or whether to open up alternative possibilities of meaning—should be understood as significantly related to a specific text's designation as either a plague sermon preached (on Psalm 106) in the difficult circumstance of death and grief, or as part of a lecture series on Genesis preached at Andrewes's parish church of St. Giles, or as part of Donne's series at St. Paul's concerned with confession and penitence. One can then better understand the attention to Hebrew terms in the sermon (most probably) preached at the Westminster Abbey's estate in Chiswick,[24] the more didactic tone of Andrewes's lecture series, and the detailed use of Hebrew in Donne's series preached to the auditory of St. Paul's Cathedral (which certainly included the other senior Prebendaries). One can also better understand the effect of the lecture series on Andrewes's decisive establishing of Cain's despair as "the case of all his progenie," as well as the impact of the plague and penitential seasons on both preachers' interest in sin and judgment—whether it is Andrewes preaching on moral and religious responsibility or Donne preaching on the emotional effect of punishment and sin. In this manner, both preachers exploit the variances of sacred philology, adapting the biblical text to a particular venue, auditory and the appropriate "culturally specific discursive system."

Sermon on the Penitential Psalm 32:1–2: Blessed is he whose transgression is forgiven, whose sinne is covered

Sermon on the Penitential Psalm 32:6: Surely in the floods of great waters, they shall not come nigh unto him

Sermon on the Penitential Psalm 32:7: Thou art my hiding place, thou shalt preserve me from trouble

Throughout his sermon series on the Penitential Psalm 32 Donne is meticulous in following the biblical text and in fitting the types of mercy to those of misdeeds: for *pesha* ["transgressions"], it is "*Nasa*...the word does not onely signifie *Auferre*, but *ferre*; not onely to take away by sin, by way of pardon, but to take the sin upon himselfe (*Sermons* 9:259); for *catah* ["sins"] it is a "*Covering*...a part of Gods mercy, in spreading, and applying the merits and satisfaction of Christ upon all them (*Sermons* 9:260); for *gnavah* ["iniquities"] it is a "not Imputing of Iniquity, is that *Serenitas Conscientiae*, That brightnesse, that clearnesse, that peace, and tranquility, that calme and serenity, that acquiescence, and security of the Conscience" (*Sermons* 9:263). It is, however, in his repeated development of the psalm's evocation of mercy as a type of conceptual metaphor—a "container metaphor," with its attributes of physical boundaries, in-out orientation, and territoriality (Lakoff and Johnson 29–30)—that Donne provides his audience with a concretely visual and tactile experience, which effectively moves past the abstraction of theological discourse.[25] In his sermon on verses 32:1–2, he explains:

> So the word (the word is *Casah*, which we translate *Covering*) is used, *a wise man concealeth knowledge* [marginal note: Proverbs 12:23]; that is, Does not pretend to know so much as indeed he does: So our mercifull God, when he sees us under this mantle, this covering, Christ spread upon his Church, conceales his knowledge of our sins, and suffers them not to reflect upon our consciences....this *Covering* is *Tegere attingendo*, To cover sin, by coming to it, by applying himselfe to our sinfull consciences, in the means instituted by him in his Church...they have in that language another word, *Sacac*, which signifies *Tegere obumbrando*, To cover by overshadowing, by refreshing....But *Tegere attingendo*, is when thus I lay my hand upon mine eye, and cover it close, by that touching....not onely *obumbrando*, as hee hath spread himselfe as a Cloud refreshing the whole World, in the value of the satisfaction, but *Attingendo*, by comming to me, by spreading himself upon me, as the Prophet did upon the dead Child, Mouth to mouth, hand to hand. (*Sermons* 9:260–61)

The two Hebrew terms at the center of this passage are: כָּסָה *casah*, "to cover by touch" *(tegere attingendo)*; and סָכַךְ *sakhakh*,

"to cover by shade" (*tegere obumbrando*). Donne begins by trop-
ing God's mercy as "this mantle, this covering," thereby providing the spiritual act with an impression of physical boundaries
and territoriality. He subsequently draws out a semantic distinction between the words *casah* and *sakhakh* (table 19)[26] in order
to develop a progressively intensifying awareness of the sense
of touch, through which this act of "covering" with a mantle
is transmuted into a physically intimate, restorative act that
bespeaks resurrection in Christ. This reading is substantiated
from an earlier sermon (the second preached on Matt. 4:18–20),
in which he directly compares Elisha the Prophet's "raysing the
Shunamits dead child" (table 19) to his own "conformity with
Christ": "so when my crosses have carried mee up to my Saviours
Crosse, I put my hands into his hands, and hang upon his nailes,
I put mine eyes upon his....I put my mouth upon his mouth"
(*Sermons* 2:300).[27] In both sermons Donne's effect is to turn an
abstract theological discourse into a concrete experience, particularly by depicting mercy (and salvation) as part of a physically and
emotionally symbiotic relationship with Christ in which there is
an overriding (even violation) of the self's physical boundaries.

Donne's physical experience of divinity is also evident in his
sermon preached on verse 32:4 ("thy hand was heavy upon me"),
about which he writes that "the hand of divine Justice shall grow
heavy upon him, in a sense of an unprofitable retirednesse, in
a disconsolate melancholy, and at last, in a stupidity, tending
to desperation" (*Sermons* 9:292–93).[28] Certainly the metaphoric
transformation of divine judgment into a physical experience
once again emphasizes the violation of the self, just as it iconically depicts an emotional state in terms of a physical burden.
These various aspects are placed at the forefront of Donne's subsequent sermon on verse 32:7, in which he focuses successively
on the components of the Hebrew psalmic text:

> First then, this is an acknowledgement of the Church, contem-
> plating her selfe in her low estate; for the word *Sether* implies,
> *Tu absconsio,* Though I were in the darke, it was thou that didst

Table 19. Penitential Psalm 32:1: Whose sinne is covered

2 Kings 4:32–36	Hebrew Bible	Dictionaries
32: And when Elisha was come into the house, behold, the child was dead, *and* laid upon his bed.	Proverbs 12:23 A prudent man concealeth [כֹּסֶה *koseh*] knowledge.	Alabaster. *Lexicon* כָּסָה כסה, Chaldaicè כְּסָא *texit, operuit, abscondit, occultavit* [weaves, covers, conceals, hides].
33: He went in therefore, and shut the doore upon them twaine, and prayed unto the LORD.	Donne. *Lamentations of Jeremy* 3:44 Cover'st [סַכֹּתָה *sakotah*] thy selfe with clouds (*Poems* 381).	Arab: כסוה cesua *operimentum, tegumentum, vestis* [blanket, covering, cloth] (232).
34: And he went up, and lay upon the child, and put his mouth upon his mouth, and his eyes upon his eyes and his hands upon his hand, and he stretched himselfe upon the child, and the flesh of the child waxed warme (*The Holy [King James] Bible.* "The Old Testament" n.p.).		סָכַךְ סכך, Chaldaicè: סְכַךְ & סַךְ *operuit, texit, protexit, contexit, velavit* [covers, weaves, protects, veils] (323). Strong, *Dictionary* 3680. *Casah.* A primitive root; properly, to plump, i.e., fill up hollows; by implication to cover (for clothing or secrecy):—clad self, close, clothe, conceal, cover (self); (flee to) hide, overwhelm. 5526. *Sakhakh.* A primitive root; properly, to entwine as a screen; by implication, to fence in, cover over, (figuratively) protect:—cover, defense, defend, hedge in, join together, set, shut up.

over-shadow me, Though I were in danger, it was thou that didst hide me from them....*Tu absconsio,* may the Primitive Church, and the Reformed Church say, *Thou hast beene our hiding place*...The Lord is able to hide them, able to cover them. (*Sermons* 9:336, 339)

. . . .

So far this word [Trouble] of our Translators assists our devotion, *Thou shalt preserve me from Trouble,* Thou shalt make me unsensible of it, or thou shalt make me victorious in it. But the Originall word *Tzur* hath a more peculiar sense; It signifies a straite, a narrownesse, a difficulty, a distresse; *I am distressed for thee, my brother Jonathan* [marginal note: 2 Samuel 1:26], says *David,* in this word, when he lamented his irremediable, his irrecoverable death....So that the word expresses *Angustiam,* narrownesse, pressure, precipitation, inextricablenesse, in a word, (that will best fit us) Perplexity; and, *The Lord shall preserve me from perplexity.* (*Sermons* 9:341–42)

Donne in these passages focuses on two Hebrew words: סֵתֶר *seiter,* "covering" or "secret/hiding place"; and צוּר *tsur* (more correctly the biblical word צַר *tsar*) "straight, narrow, difficulty and distress" (Even-Shoshan 5:1578, 1616). The sense of an "in-out orientation" regarding the "container metaphor" appears in Donne's emphasis on the image of *seiter* as a dark and constricted space, echoing the various translations of this Hebrew word as "covering," or "hiding" place, proposed in their respective dictionaries by both Udall and Strong, and readily apparent in the translation by the King James Bible (table 20). Indeed, this physical orientation is specifically realized in this sermonic passage as an aspect of refuge, with the physical, spatial sense intensified as an apprehension of danger from the enemies of the Church in its different historical periods.

Secondly, Donne turns his attention to the word *tsar,* emphasizing its meanings as "straite, a narrownesse, a difficulty, a distresse." In this he correctly follows the literal, lexical meaning recorded by Udall, as well its extension into the figurative meaning explained in Strong's dictionary and noted in the King James Bible (table 20). This dual meaning allows the preacher linguistic

Table 20. Penitential Psalm 32:7: Thou art my hiding place, thou shalt preserve me from trouble

Seiter	*Tzur*
Udall, *Hebrue Dictionaire* סָתַר *He hid.* סֵתֶר *A covering, a hiding* or *secret* (103).	Udall, *Hebrue Dictionaire* צָרַר *he vexed* or *straitened...* מֵצַר, צָרָה *Distresse* (132).
The Holy [King James] Bible Thou *art* my hiding place ("The Old Testament" n.p.).	*The Holy [King James] Bible* Thou shalt preserve mee from trouble ("The Old Testament" n.p.).
Strong, *Dictionary* 5643. A cover (in a good or a bad, a literal or a figurative sense): hiding place, privily, protection, or secret(-ly, place).	Strong, *Dictionary* 6862. Narrow; (as a noun) a tight place (usually figuratively, i.e., trouble).

license; thus he underlines the intertextual connection with the story of David's lament over the dead Jonathan—in which the phrase *tsar-li*, "I am distressed" appears—as well as extending this figurative meaning to include political and theological polemics. The previous encompassing of Church history within the metaphor of *seiter* appears again in Donne's remarks upon *tsar* as a preservation of the Church "from perplexities of all kinds": "perplexing of Princes...matter of Religion towards Heretiques...differences of opinions amongst our selves" (*Sermons* 9:342–43). In this way, Donne develops the intertwined imagistic and psychological meanings of a Hebrew word within the psalmic text, and ultimately draws out the constrained sense of space into an iconic representation of an emotional and a polemical state.

It is in his sermon on verse 32:6 that Donne radicalizes these various aspects of the "container metaphor"; in two sections respectively entitled *"Aquae"* and *"Diluviam,"* he explains the phrase "floods of great waters":

> The Holy Ghost who is a direct worker upon the soule and conscience of man, but a Metaphoricall, and Figurative expresser

of himselfe, to the reason, and understanding of man, abounds in no Metaphor more, then in calling Tribulations, *Waters*.... S. *Augustine* understands these *waters*, to be *Variae Doctrinae*, those diverse opinions, that disquiet and trouble the Church.... Christ and his Apostles had carried two Waters about his Church: The water of Baptisme.... And then Christ gave another Water, by which, they came to another Ablution, to Absolution from actuall sins, the water of contrite teares, and repentance.... But yet for all these Waters, other Waters soaked in, and corrupted them earely; for, for Baptisme, the Disciples of *Simon Magus* annulled Christs Baptisme, and baptized in *Simons* name.... And then, for the other Water, Repentance, the Heretiques drained up that shrewdly, when they took all benefit of repentance for sins committed after Baptisme.

....

Therefore does *David*, in this text, call these many waters, *Diluvium*, *A flood of great waters;* many and violent. For this word *Shatach, Inundans*, signifies Vehemence, Eagernesse, and is elegantly applied to the fiercenesse of a horse in Battel, *Equus inundans in Bellum*, A horse that overflowes the Battell, that rushes into the Battell [marginal note: Jeremiah 8:6]. Therefore speaks the Prophet of *waters full of blood* [marginal note: Isaiah 15:9];[29] What Seas of blood did the old Persecutions, what Seas have later times poured out, when in the Romane Church, their owne Authors will boast of sixty thousand slaine in a day, of them that attempted a Reformation in the times of the *Waldenses!* (*Sermons* 9:328–30)

In an intermediate passage Donne has taken care to correctly note the dual, literal meaning of the Hebrew word רַבִּים *rabim* as both "many" and "great," explaining of the phrase *mayim rabim* that "*Aquae multae, Many waters;* so the vulgat reads this, that wee Translate here [King James Bible], *Great waters*" (*Sermons* 9:329). His sustained emphasis on a more figurative meaning is prompted, however, by the absence of a literal (that is, agricultural, seasonal) context for the psalmic image, which is evident in the Geneva Bible, whose marginal note explains this image as "the waters, and great dangers"; and in Andrewes's psalm paraphrase, which explains it as "*floods*, and swelling of the *great* waters of afflictions" (table 21). Donne chooses, moreover, to situate his exposition of the phrase within the specific discursive system of Christian religious polemics. His invective in the first passage against the baptismal practices of the second century Simonian sect (followers of the Samarian magician Simon Magus) and the more contemporary "Heretiques" (such as the sixteenth and seventeenth century Anabaptists) who denied the validity of infant baptism (*Sermons* 9:329) continues in the second one, against the Catholic attack on the late-medieval, proto-Reformation sect of the Waldenses.[30] Donne transforms the theological discourse over baptism into an image of a besieged sanctuary, wherein the baptismal waters are hyperbolically changed into the psalmic floodwater, and then into the vivid concluding metaphor "seas of blood." Indeed, this convergence of the flood image with the Waldenses appears once again in Donne's second sermon on John 14:26 ("Preached at S. Pauls upon Whitsunday. 1628"). There he writes "that they put themselves in the gap, and made themselves a Bank, against this torrent, this inundation, this impetuousnesse, this multiplicity of Fryars, and Monks, that surrounded the world in those times" (*Sermons* 8:264). The image of waters takes on the metaphorical meaning of "heresies" in this sermon, expressing not only the flood's violent, devastating, vehement force but also the palpable, protective counterforce of Christianity's reformation groups.

At the beginning of the second passage Donne establishes the literal meaning of the Hebrew word *sheitef* [*Shatach*] שֶׁטֶף, "flood or torrent," thereby conveying the intensity of Augustine's exposition on "waters" as *Variae Doctrinae*. A similar polemic reading is maintained by Rashi, who explains the psalmic verse to mean "that he will not fall into the hand of the Gentiles, who are like a flood" (table 21). The flood's violent energy becomes the unrestrained physical violence of Rashi's "Gentiles" (הָאֻמּוֹת, *ha-umot*; literally "the nations"), taking on a contemporary relevance with regard to the attacks wreaked upon Jewish communities during the First Crusade (1096–99). Through his commentary Rashi thereby enfolds within the psalmic text several important issues:

Table 21. Penitential Psalm 32:6: The floods of great waters

Rashi	The [Geneva] Bible and Holy Scriptures	Andrewes, *Holy Devotions*
Only at the rushing of mighty waters [so that] they will not overtake him. So that he will not fall into the hand of the Gentiles [הָאֻמּוֹת, *ha-umot;* literally "the nations"], who are like a flood. Similarly we have found that when David prayed for this [that he will not fall into the hands of the Gentiles], he said "Let me fall" into the hands of the LORD, for his compassion is great, and let me not fall into the hands of men [2 Sam. 14:14] (*Rashi's Commentary* 298).	Surely in the flood of great waters ("The Olde Testament" 241r).ᵍ ᵍ To wit, the waters and great dangers.	7 For *this* remission of sin, as it was necessary for me to pray for it, so *shall every one,* of what condition soever, *that is godly,* (for the just also fall) *pray unto thee,* O Lord, *in a time when thou mayest be found,* in a fit season. But *in the* greatest danger of *floods,* and swelling of the *great* waters of afflictions, God will so preserve the just man, that *they shall not* have power to *come nigh unto him,* to oppose or overwhelm him (323).

the concept of the religious other; the precarious existence of a community in the face of impending danger; and ultimately the sustaining of religious identity in the face of physical violence. Indeed, the fears of this medieval exegete recall Luther's later remarks, who expounded upon the waters as "these scourges, these evils, above all, the spiritual ones, which have come with great wrath upon the Jewish people" (table 22).

Table 22. Penitential Psalm 32:6: The floods of great waters

Augustine (31:6)	Cassiodorus	Luther, *Psalms*
Quid est diluvium aquarum multarum? Multiplicitas variarum doctrinarum. Intendite, fratres. Multae aquae sunt variae doctrinae. Doctrina Dei una est, non sunt multae aquae, sed una aqua, sive sacramenti baptismi, sive doctrinae salutaris (*Enarrationes in Psalmos*. "In Psalmum XXXI. Enarratio." II:18). What is the floods of many waters? (There is) a multiplicity of various doctrines. Understand, brothers. Many waters are various doctrines. God's doctrine is one, it is not many waters, but one water, of the baptismal sacrament, or (the water) of the salvation's doctrine.	*Diluvium* enim *aquarum multarum* est error hominum pessimorum, qui variis pravitatibus fluctuantes, multiplices sibi doctrinas constituunt, quas a vero Magistro nullatenus acceperunt. Quae sententia maxime haereticos arguit, qui *in diluvio* perversitatis suae tempestuosas et naufragas excitant quaestiones. Et hi *ad eum non approximabunt*, quoniam a vera religione discedunt. Quae figura dicitur metaphora, id est translatio, cum mutatur nomen aut verbum ex eo loco ubi proprium est, in eum in quo aut proprium deest, aut translatum proprio melius est (*In Psalterium Expositio*. "Expositio in Psalmum XXXI. Expositio Psalmi" 9).	And thus these many waters are these scourges, these evils, above all, the spiritual ones, which have come with great wrath upon the Jewish people to the present day.... [Another meaning] According to Augustine and Cassiodorus, that flood of waters is the multitude of errors and heresies because of which men are prevented from drawing near to God (10:149–50).

Table 22. (*cont.*)

Augustine (31:6)	Cassiodorus	Luther, *Psalms*
	Indeed, *flood of many waters* is an error of the worst men who, fluctuating among various depravities, establish for themselves many doctrines that would not be in any way accepted by the real Master. This sentence reveals very precisely [the] heretics, who, *in the flood* of their perversity, raise tempestuous and shipwrecking questions. And those *shall not reach him*, for they move away from the real religion. This image is called metaphor, i.e. transfer, since we move a name or a verb from the place where it properly is, to [the place] where it is not properly, or, after having being transferred, it is better than proper.	

Rashi's fears are adopted and sharpened by the Christian expositors, who ultimately extend the primary biblical concern with a general form of misfortune into a polemical involvement with particular forms of heretical "otherness." This is clearly seen in Luther's commentary (table 22), which proceeds from anti-Jewish rhetoric to citation of the two patristic authors Augustine and Cassiodorus,[31] in whose works the groups of Christian heretics comprise the functional equivalent of Rashi's Gentiles. While Augustine constrains their "multiplicity of doctrines" into the "one water" of the "baptismal sacrament," Cassiodorus's acknowledged reworking of this commentary (Lejay and Otten) intensifies the flood into a vivid imagery of the "tempest and shipwreck" that are evoked as consequences of the psalmic flood (table 22). Donne, in his turn, develops the psalmic image of waters into the polarized images of a life-sustaining force ("water of Baptisme") and of destruction ("waters soaked in and corrupted")—images respectively of Christian repentance and grace, and of heretical doctrines. In this manner Rashi's interpretation of the psalmic phrase as a confrontation between religious groups is sustained, as is the attempt to obliterate another's physical and spiritual integrity.

Yet it is Donne's emphasis on the flood's visceral, dynamic qualities of "Vehemence, Eagerness" that shows how this term *sheitef*, "floods," readily acquires a metaphoric meaning—as when Jeremiah's horse is said to have the quality of being שׁוֹטֵף *shoteif*, "overflowing" or "rushing" into battle. As such, Donne's emphasis on this shared quality reciprocally and interactively redefines both the waters and the horse in terms of a potentially destructive energy that is at once a natural force and a bestial intensity. Though this intertextual reference does strongly suggest Donne's use of a concordance, ultimately he puts this lexical work to good use by not only affirming the fundamental integrity of the Scriptures, but also by demonstrating a basic aesthetic appreciation of its figurative language—that "Metaphoricall, and Figurative expresser of himselfe." Donne's attention to the

Hebrew term *sheitef* allows him, therefore, to impart a tangible and overwhelming sense of danger to the heretical "other." The dual meaning of the Hebrew word allows Donne "to open many possibilities of nuance and meaning, not to settle upon one" (in Janel Mueller's words), as he juxtaposes the translations of the King James and the Vulgate Bibles. Inviting his auditory and reader to consider the different meanings, he ultimately concludes that these "many waters" are therefore "great waters," thereby emphasizing the overpowering violence of the many heresies that threaten the English church. In this instance Donne marshals the various meanings of the biblical text in order to mark out its relevance and lesson within the specific doctrinal debates and religious polemics of the English church.

Conclusion

Both Andrewes and Donne comprise outstanding examples of what Horton Davies has discussed as "English Metaphysical Preaching," displaying (among other characteristics) a "great fondness for puns and paronomasia in English and ancient languages...[as well as] frequent citations from Greek and Latin originals, and occasional use of Hebrew etymology" (106–07). This fascination with language has been shown to comprise, however, not merely an intermittent occurrence, nor simply a fascination with words. For just as Andrewes is certainly more than "the strict, philologically oriented, exegete" (Gane 31), Donne's use of Hebrew exceeds the somewhat limited conclusion that his "definitions are exact according to the lexicons of his day, and he obviously knows how to find the place in the text" (Allen, "Dean Donne" 215). Both preachers share a remarkable attention to the "Originall" Hebrew Bible, integrating the authority and variable meanings of its words and phrases into the very fabric of the sermonic text. Reading these two preachers together within the context of sacred philology further confirms the appropriateness of a move from discussion of linguistic knowledge (*how much* Hebrew is known) to that of *ways and means*—in other words, issues of transmitted knowledge, discursive systems, sermonic genres, and exegetical agendas. Emphasizing these different aspects of English Reformation preaching widens the boundaries of previous, lexical discussions of Donne's knowledge of Hebrew, affording an opportunity for a study of such knowledge within the larger context of the sermonic text.

PART II

SERMONS ON THE PENITENTIAL PSALM 38
AND THE PREBEND PSALMS

FOUR

The Literal Sense

Moralized Grammar

Grammar has the duplicity, and sometimes the advantage, of keeping some of its best secrets to itself. Not by the perilous byways of syntax only: the inflections of single verbs can, and should, give pause for thought.
— Brian Cummings, *The Literary Culture of the Reformation*

Sermon and Context

In his religious treatise *The Obedience of a Christen Man* (1528) (see fig. 6), William Tyndale devotes a section to "The Four Senses of the Scripture." In a passage considered to be "a most seminal and original contribution to English hermeneutics" (Janel Mueller, "Introduction" 19), Tyndale sets out his exegetical agenda:

> Thou shalt understonde therefore that the scripture hath but one sence, which is the literall sence. And that literall sence is the rote

and grounde of all and the ancre that never fayleth where onto yf thou cleve thou canst never erre or goo out of the waye. And if thou leve the literall sence, thou canst not but goo out of the waye. Never the later the scripture useth proverbes / similitudes / redels or allegories as all other speaches doo / but that which the proverbe / similitude / redell or allegory signifieth is ever the literall sence which thou must seke out diligently (cxxix[v]–cxxx[r]).

Complementing his work as the first English translator of the Bible to rely on the original Hebrew text,[1] Tyndale constructs an interpretive dichotomy that enforces both religious and hermeneutic parameters. Thus he strives to reclaim the "literall sence" from the Pope (who, he has previously claimed, "hath taken it cleane awaye and hath made it his possession"; cxxix[v]), and then subsequently to redeem it by effectively subsuming under it all the nonliteral senses. Yet the reader of Tyndale's passage is left somewhat confused as to the nature of the "literall sence" that concomitantly is signified by "proverbs, similitudes, riddles and allegories." How does one clarify the opacity—or the "possible strangeness" (Richardson 93)—of this seeming equivalence between the literal and the figurative? How does one understand, by extension, Donne's statement in his 1624 Easter sermon (on Apocalypse 20:6) "that in many places of Scripture, a figurative sense is the literall sense" (*Sermons* 6:62)? Finally, how does one propose an exegetical method for realizing Stephen Greenblatt's rhetorically oriented explanation that "it appears that by the 'literal sense' here Tyndale means a clear, moral lesson or principle of faith that is openly stated elsewhere in the Bible. . . . Allegory, along with the related forms of similitude, example, and figure, are not used to express a dark mystery but rather to heighten the effect upon the reader" (100–02)?

   In answer, it is instructive to look at another exegetical manifesto, namely that written by Abraham Ibn Ezra. For whether cited from the Hebrew original[2] or from Latin translations generated by European scholars,[3] Ibn Ezra's commentaries on the Hebrew Bible comprised a significant resource for sixteenth and early

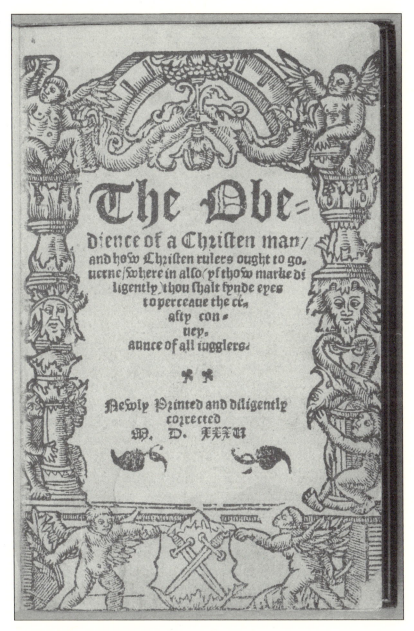

Fig. 6. Title page of William Tyndale, *The Obedience of a Christian Man* (1535). Reproduced by permission of the Huntington Library, San Marino, California. Manuscript call no. RB 42270.

seventeenth century English biblical translators and commentators (see fig. 7).[4] In the explanation of his exegetical method in the "Introduction" to his *Commentaries on the Torah [Pentateuch]*,[5] he writes,

> This is Abraham the poet's *Seifer Ha-Yashar*,
> Bound by cords of grammar.
> The eyes of reason will find it fit,
> Happy are those who adhere to it.
>
> ....
>
> The fifth method, My commentary on it is founded, Correct is this method, Before God, That of him alone I am in awe, I will not show favoritism in [interpreting] the Torah, I will search the grammar of every word with all my might, Afterwards I will explain it as I see right. (*Commentaries on the Pentateuch* 1–10)

In the prefatory rhymed prayer[6] Ibn Ezra terms his book *Seifer Ha-Yashar*, "The Book of the Straight [Path]," so named because the Hebrew term *yashar*, "straight" is a synonym for *peshat*, or the literal meaning of the text.[7] By utilizing metaphors that conjointly underline the need for restraint and clear thinking, he vividly sets out his method of biblical commentary as based on grammar and reason. In the subsequent cited passage he marks out two major methodological points: *ve-lo esa panim be-torah*, "I will not show favoritism" in relying on accepted authorities; and *ahapeis heiteiv diqduq kol milah*, "I will search the grammar of every word." Together these points reinforce the polemic tone of Ibn Ezra's treatise, following as they do his discussion of various other exegetical "paths,"[8] an aspect certainly shared by Tyndale. To see this one need only to return to the discussion of the Hebrew word *yevam*, in which each author is embroiled in exegetical debates that ultimately convert philology into theology (chapter 1); thus the concern over the meaning of the Hebrew ("husband's brother"? "kinsman"?) becomes the touchstone for a debate over issues of familial purity versus dynasty.

Furthermore, Ibn Ezra's emphasis on a rational, grammatical reading provides a highly usable strategy, particularly of value for

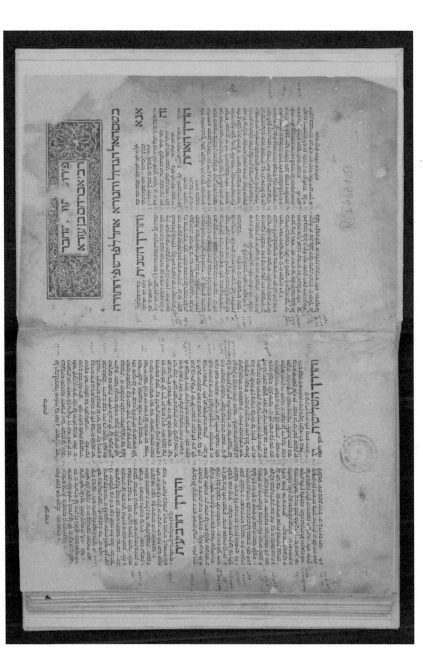

Fig. 7. Abraham Ibn Ezra, *Commentary on the Torah [Pentateuch]* (1488), p. 2. Reproduced by permission of The National Library of Israel.

Reformation exegesis in its attempt to recover the literal sense of the biblical text. This aspect is echoed in Donne's own statement (in a sermon on John 1:8), which maps out the often overlapping but still distinct meanings that this "literal sense" can bear when he calls for "an Historicall, such a Grammaticall, such a Logicall beliefe of our Bible, as to preferre it before any other, that could be pretended to be the Word of God" (*Sermons* 3:359). Lastly, the acknowledgment by both Ibn Ezra and Tyndale of the coexistence of the various exegetical methods offers the opportunity to reconceive of their discussion in terms of Roland Barthes's concept of *scriptible* or "writerly" text, whose goal "is to make the reader...a producer of the text...the writerly text is *ourselves writing*" and in which "the networks are many and interact, without any of them being able to surpass the rest" (4–5).[9] The Bible is thus reconceived as a text that evokes an interpretive process whose indispensable literal reading subsequently transforms into a figurative meaning of religious and theological consequence, specifically through the knowledge and use of Hebrew grammar.

This concern with these different aspects of exegetical strategy is at the very heart of Donne's two sermon series on the Penitential Psalm 38 and on the Prebend Psalms. Rivkah Zim has drawn attention to how Donne's "art of interpretation" structures these sermons "through a three-fold system of applications of the biblical text" ("The Reformation" 98) while for her part, Judith Anderson underlines Donne's alignment of "the presence of eternal preconceptions in God with verbal practice, whether human or divine" (190). Juxtaposing passages from Donne's sermons on the Penitential Psalm 38:2 and on the Prebend Psalm 63:7[10] makes clear his use of these exegetical strategies:

> *Penitential Psalm 38:2 (For thine arrowes sticke fast in me)*
> literally, primarily, this text concerns *David*....The Psalm hath a *retrospect* too, it looks back to *Adam,* and to every particular man in his loines, and so, *Davids* case is our case, and all these arrowes stick in all of us. But the Psalm and the text hath also a *prospect,*

and hath a *propheticall* relation from *David* to our Saviour Christ
Jesus. And of him, and of the multiplicity of these arrows upon him
in the exinanition, and evacuation of himself, in this world for us,
have many of the *Ancients* interpreted these words literally, and as
in their first and primary signification; Turne we therefore to *him*,
before we goe, and he shall return home with us. (*Sermons* 2:69)

*Prebend Psalm 63:7 (Because thou hast bene my helpe; therefore
in the shadow of thy wings will I rejoyce)*
That language in which God spake to man, the Hebrew, hath
no present tense; They forme not their verbs as our Westerne
Languages do, in the present, *I heare,* or *I see,* or *I reade,* But they
begin at that which is past, *I have seene* and *hearde,* and *read.* God
carries us in his Language, in his speaking, upon that which is past,
upon that which he hath done already; I cannot have better security for present, nor future, then Gods former mercies exhibited to
me....From this one word, That God hath been my *Helpe,* I make
account that we both these notions; first That God hath not left
me to my selfe, He hath come to my succour, He hath been my
Helpe, but he hath left some thing for me to doe with him, and by
his helpe." (*Sermons* 7:62–63)

Though not completely overlapping, these threefold patterns of
exposition (literal-moral-anagogical; past-present-future) demonstrate Donne's intense concern with time,[11] particularly in his
(literal) "historicall" reading of the Hebrew Bible that becomes
a (figurative) "propheticall" prefiguring of the Christian Scriptures. In the first passage, Donne clearly is seeking to encompass
the concepts of punishment and penitence within the threefold
method of biblical exegesis that demarcates various "senses":
literal, historical (David of the present, contextual biblical situation); tropological, moral (Adam of the biblical past); and ana-
gogical, mystical (Christ as the biblical future).[12] In a similar
manner, Donne reflects in the second passage on concepts of past
or prevenient grace ("hath been my Helpe") and future or subsequent grace ("hath left some thing for me to doe") particularly
as they provide the "security" accorded thereby to David in that
situation (as Donne had emphasized earlier) of "distresse put him
upon for the present" (*Sermons* 7:52).[13]

The discussion of Hebrew tense therefore becomes of particular significance for Donne's discussion of grace, most distinctly as he relates to the two expressed tenses in the psalmic verse: "thou hast bene [הָיִיתָ *hayita*]" and "I will rejoyce [אֲרַנֵּן *aranein*]." Reflecting contemporary accounts such as Ralph Baynes's 1550 *Prima Rudimenta in Linguam Hebraem* and John Udall's 1593 "Hebrue Grammar" (see table 23), Donne sets out the distinctiveness of biblical Hebrew grammar, in which tense is defined as being either completed (past) or continuous (future).[14] He then moves forward to its radical reconception (in Eugene Hill's words) as a "moralized account...of the verbal structure of Hebrew by which he links morphological fact (absence of a present tense) with intended psychological effect (the arousal of expectation and faith)" (190). Whether Donne's attention to Hebrew is acknowledged as what Hill terms a "moralized grammar," or as what Janel Mueller and Heather Asals respectively term the "grammar of the soul" ("Introduction" 50) and "the grammar of redemption" ("John Donne"), the consequence is a transformation of the grammatical circumstances of the biblical text into both a rhetorical structure and a theological statement about the relationship between God and humankind.

Such a use of Hebrew grammar for homiletic purposes is developed at length throughout the sermon on the Penitential Psalm 38:2, which depicts God's intensely physical, violent relationship with humankind, particularly by using Hebrew noun forms to move between the literal and the figurative. What is more, Donne's concern with grace and predestination in the second Prebend sermon is further developed throughout the subsequent, third Prebend sermon,[15] which carefully explicates both Hebrew noun and verb forms, as well as Hebrew etymology, to set out the ways of "godly men." Read in tandem, these sermons demonstrate that whether he was preaching at the very different venues of Lincoln's Inn or St. Paul's Cathedral, Donne foregrounds his sustained concern with involving his auditory (and reader) in the exegetical project set out by the twelfth century Jewish commen-

Table 23. Verb Tense

Baynes, *Prima Rudimenta*	Udall, "Hebrue Grammar"
Post praeteritum apponimus participium praesens, quod בְּנוֹנִי vocatur cum inter praeteritum & futurum, medium locum obtineat. Nam verbum praesentis temporis non habent Hebraei. Flectuntur participia more nominum: & idcirco numeris & generibus non personis variantur (15).	A tense is the difference of a verb according to the time past, called the praeter tense, or the time to come, called the future tense. *There is one praeter tense, or tyme past in the Hebrue tongue, as* פָּקַד [paqad] hee visited, he hath visited, *but there bee two* future tenses, *or verbs noting the tyme to come.*
After the past we put the present participle, which is called *benonee* ["intermediate"] because between the past and the future, one obtains the middle [point]. In fact, the Jews do not have the present tense. Participles are declined in the same way as nouns: for this reason there is no change of number and gender of the person.	The first future [imperative], as פְּקוֹד [peqod] visit thou; *the second future tense, as* יִפְקוֹד [yifqod] hee shall visit (First Book 43).

tator Ibn Ezra and exemplified by the sixteenth century English translator Tyndale.

Sermon on the Penitential Psalm 38:2: For thine arrowes sticke fast in me; and thy hand presseth me sore

Debora Shuger's statement that "divine power fascinates Donne largely in its destructive and catastrophic aspect" ("Absolutist Theology" 171)[16] is especially relevant to his Lenten preaching on Psalm 38:2, which continues to describe the biblical experience of divine punishment established in verse 38:1: "O Lord, rebuke me not in thy wrath; neither chasten me in thy hot displeasure." Donne concentrates on the infliction of divine violence upon the psalmic speaker, writing at one point: "*Thy hand presses me sore;* so the Vulgat read it, *Confirmasti super me manum tuam, Thy hand is settled upon mee;* and the Chalde paraphrase carries it farther then, to *Mansit super me vulnus manus tuae; Thy hand hath wounded mee, and that hand keeps the wound open*" (*Sermons* 2:66). In this passage he conscientiously returns to the Jewish source, the *Targum* (the "Chaldee paraphrase")—which reads "The [מְחַת *mehat*] blow/wound of your hand rested upon me" (*Biblia Rabbinica* 4:35)—to accurately expand upon the raw physicality of this act. Yet it is through the treatment of the image of arrows ("For thine arrowes sticke fast in me"), which is read in modern biblical criticism as a "metaphorical description of the divine origin of malady" (Craigie 303), that Donne fully develops the grammatical possibilities of the Hebrew language.[17]

Whether it is a development of the biblical iconization of disease as Resheph the Archer, the Canaanite god of pestilence (Craigie 303), or whether it is an echo of Ibn Ezra's "diseases and pain," "the Doway Bible's "afflictions," or the "sicknenes" of Kimhi and the Geneva Bible (see table 24), this image supports the concept that "one of the foundation pillars of Old Testament piety, [was] that all suffering is punishment for sin" (Leslie 373). Donne readily accepts this figurative reading of the arrows, writing that this is "a Metaphore, in which Gods indignation is often expressed in the Scripture" (*Sermons* 2:55). Yet he subsequently takes great care to ground this reading in Hebrew grammar, carefully and steadily developing his homiletic lesson regarding that "*propheticall* relation" from David to Christ, particularly in that grace given by the "exinanition, and evacuation of himself, in this world for us" (*Sermons* 2:69).

In a passage, entitled "*Plures*," Donne first establishes his concern with these grammatical possibilities of Hebrew. He explains:

> Wee finde many mentions in the Scriptures of filling of *quivers*, and emptying of *quivers*, and *arrows*, and *arrows*, still in the *plurall*, *many arrows*. But in all the Bible, I think, we finde not this

Table 24. Psalm 38:2: Thine arrowes sticke fast

Vulgate Bible (37:3)	Jewish Exegetes	Reformation Bibles
Quoniam sagittae tuae infixae sunt mihi, et confirmasti super me manum tuam (*Biblia Sacra* 580).	*Ibn Ezra. Niḥatu.* The [verb] form *niphal* as in *ninḥatu*, a cognate of *va-tinḥat alai yadekha* [your hand has descended upon me] and it means diseases and pain like arrows (*Biblia Rabbinica* 4:35).	*The [Geneva] Bible.* For thine ^carrowes have light upon me, and thine hand lyeth upon me ("The Olde Testament" 242v).
Because ^d thy arrows are fast sticked in me: and thou hast fastened thy hand upon me (*The Holie Bible*, Doway 2:77).		^c Thy sickenes, wherewith thou hast visited me
^d Afflictions of mind and bodie, sent by thy just judgement.	*Kimhi. For your arrows.* Sicknesses, which are the arrows. *Niḥatu bee.* From the [verb] form *niph'al* (*Complete Commentary* 93).	*The Holy [King James] Bible.* For thine arrows sticke fast in me; and thy hand presseth me sore. ("The Old Testament" n.p.)

word (as it signifies tentation, or tribulation) in the *singular, one arrow*, any where, but once, where *David* cals it, *The arrow that flies by day* [marginal note: Psalm 91:5]; And is seen, that is, known by every man; for, for that, the Fathers, and Ancients runne upon that Exposition, that that one arrow common to all, that day-arrow visible to all, is the *natural death;* (so the Chalde paraphrase calls it there expressly, *Sagitta mortis*, the arrow of death) which every man knows to belong to every man: (for, as clearly as he sees the Sunne set, he sees his death before his eyes.) Therefore it is such an arrow, as the Prophet does not say, *Thou shalt not feel*, but, *Thou shalt not feare the arrow that flies by day*. The arrow, the *singular* arrow that flies by day, is that arrow that fals upon every man, *death*. But every where in the Scriptures, but this one place, they are plurall, many, so many, as that we know not when, nor what they are. Nor ever does any man receive one arrow alone, any one tentation, but that he receives another tentation, to hide that, though with another, and another sin. And the use of arrows in the war, was not so much to *kill*, as to *rout*, and *disorder* a battail; and upon that routing, followed *execution*. Every tentation, every tribulation is not *deadly*. But their multiplicity disorders us, discomposes us, unsettles us, and so hazards us. . . . For as it is said of the spirit of wisdome [maginal note: Wisdome 7:22] that it is *unicus multiplex, manifoldly one, plurally singular:* so the spirit of tentation in every soul is *unicus multiplex, singulary plurall, rooted* in some *one* beloved sin, but derived into infinite branches of tentation (*Sermons* 2:61–62).

Through a multilinguistic encounter with the biblical text—English, Aramaic, Latin—Donne creates a palimpsest that successively exposes, erases and finally authorizes selected Christian and Jewish sources. The result is a highly figurative development of the image of arrows[18] that comprises what Dennis Quinn has termed "an image of the mechanics of temptation," wherein "the exhaustiveness of Donne's parallels suggests not comparability but identity in the two terms of the metaphor" ("Donne's Christian Eloquence" 288–89). This sounds remarkably similar to Donne's poetic use of the ingenuity and wit of the conceit that, as Helen Gardner writes, impels the reader "to concede likeness while being strongly conscious of unlikeness" ("Introduction" 19). Much as in his poem "The Bait," for example (in which he explores the relationship between "courtship" and "fishing"), in this sermon the various metaphors ("arrow/s" as "death," "tentation," "sin," "tribulation") "progressively modify, underline, elaborate, realize, and dispel various potentialities for meaning" (Goodblatt and Glicksohn 216).

It is in his exploration of these "potentialities for meaning" that Donne marks out various distinctive hermeneutic gaps in the psalmic text, evoked both by an emphasis on intertextual meaning and by the significance of the word "arrow" in both its singular and plural forms. His (auditory and) reader might well be surprised at first by the protracted discussion of the plural term חִצֶּיךָ, *hitsekha*, "your arrows" in connection with its singular form *hets* in Psalm 91:5, which reads in its entirety "Thou shal not bee afraid for the terrour by night: *nor* for the arrow *that* flieth by day." Donne is intent, however, on making use of this philological discussion to clarify the psychological and moral consequences of grammatical form, concluding in this passage with a warning against the multiple consequences proceeding from a single act of sin.

The reader of this sermon can complement Donne's explanation by looking conjointly at the commentaries on Psalm 91:5 by the *Targum* and Ibn Ezra (see table 25), to see how they introduce the figurative meanings for the words פַּחַד *paḥad*, "terrour" and חֵץ *ḥets*, "arrow." While the *Targum*'s interpretative translation simply connects both words to frightening icons of evil, supernatural figures—"demons" and the "Angel of Death"—Ibn Ezra substantiates this figurative reading through an examination of biblical parallelism. To do so he considers verse 91:5 in juxtaposition with verse 91:6, which together read: "Thou shalt not bee afraid for the terrour by night: *nor* for the arrow *that* flieth by day: / *Nor* for the pestilence *that* walketh in darknes: *nor* for the destruction, *that* wasteth at noone-day." This recurrent use of short, syntactic units creates a feeling of correspondence between the two parts (Kugel 1–2), and thus allows Ibn Ezra to conceive of the list as a reiteration that establishes an equivalent meaning, thereby not only explaining the *Targum*'s personifications of disease but also maintaining a causal effect between human fear and the etiological explanation of such disease.

Ibn Ezra's consideration of the biblical text in terms of psychology certainly has echoes in Donne's argument concerning these subtleties of grammatical form. The Christian preacher first turns to Psalm 91 and its *Targum* in order to substantiate a metaphorical meaning for the term "arrow" as "natural death." Having established this meaning, Donne refines it by making psychological (and moral) distinctions between death and sin; in other words, he develops a distinction between the image of death as an arrow, single and common to all humankind, and the image of sin as a "multiplicity" of arrows caused and intensified by an unrelenting series of temptations and tribulations. Reflecting

Table 25. Psalm 91:5: The arrow that flies by day

Targum	Ibn Ezra
Be not afraid of the fear of demons [*mazikqei*] who walk at night, of the arrow of the Angel of Death [*girera demalakh motah*] which flies by day (*Biblia Rabbinica* 4:86).	*Not, from the terror by night.* From the events of the night and not from the events of the day that fly like arrows, as shall be explained [in the following verse].
	Psalm 91:6 *From the plague [that stalks in the darkness, or the scourge that ravages at noon].* Because most of the plague is at night, if the reason is the cold, and if [the reason is] from the heat, it will be during the day at noon (*Biblia Rabbinica* 4:86).

Ibn Ezra's concern with literal meaning (regarding the etiological explanation of disease), Donne establishes here the details of an actual situation (the strategic use of arrows in warfare) in order to present a detailed description of a psychological response to sin and temptation. Finally, this passage concludes with a citation from the apocryphal *Book of Wisdom*, in which Donne turns the phrase *unicus multiplex* "single, manifold" around—as *"singulary plurall"*—in order to warn against the multiple "tentations" to sin (murder, involvement of others in sin, spiritual blindness) that are the consequences of David's singular sin (of adultery). Donne's subsequent noting of Hebrew grammar (in a section entitled *"Fixae"*) is concerned with projecting its aspect of gender onto a psychological situation, as he preaches on the distinction between grammatical masculine and feminine:

> But we complain with Jeremy, *the Sons of his quiver are entred into our reins* [marginal note: Lamentations 3:13]. The Roman Translation reads that *filias, The daughters of his quiver;* If it were

but so, *daughters*, we might limit these arrows in the signification of *tentations*, by the many occasions of tentation, arising from
that sex. But the Originall hath it *filios*, the sons of his quiver, and
therefore we consider these arrows in a stronger signification, *tribulations*, as well as *tentations; They stick in us.* (*Sermons* 2:62)

In this passage, Donne asserts that the Hebrew "Original" signifies not only sexual temptation, but also, rather, the more comprehensive "tribulation," thereby continuing the intensification, the
multiplication, of sin out of David's adulterous act. Donne's reference to the philological dispute over the literal meaning of this
phrase—as either "daughters" or "sons" (see table 26)—brings to
the fore various exegetical strategies: the projection of meaning
synchronically from one part of the biblical text onto another; the
careful investigation of alternative translations; and the investing
of the Hebrew phrase with semantic consequences. The hermeneutic gap in the biblical text is produced by the use of the figurative phrase בְּנֵי אַשְׁפָּתוֹ *benei ashpato* (*Biblia Rabbinica* 4:294),
which literally means "sons/children [*benei*] of his quiver"; interestingly enough, Ibn Ezra's explanation that the term *benei* is
indicated because "the quiver is like a pregnant belly" complements the narrative of sexuality and illicit pregnancy in 2 Samuel
11–12, which not only is believed to have generated the Penitential Psalms, but also highlights Donne's own focus on grammatical gender and its moral consequences. In this manner, Donne
shares Ibn Ezra's concern with providing a rational explication of
the relationship—in the latter's words, עֵינֵי הַדַּעַת *'einei ha-da'at*,
"the eyes of reason"—between a particular linguistic form or
phrase and its meaning; thus the preacher takes care to explain
that while arrows as "daughters of his quiver" mean "tentations"
arising from sexual enticement, arrows as "sons of his quiver"
mean "tribulations" as a general term for the ordeals inflicted by
one's enemies. In this manner Donne provides the rhetorical and
homiletic justification for his focus on grammatical gender.

Table 26. Lamentations 3:13: The arrowes of his quiver

Vulgate Bible	Jewish Exegetes	Reformation Bibles
Misit in renibus meis filias faretrae suae (*Vulgate Bible* n. pag.). He hath shot in my reines the daughters of his quiver (*The Holie Bible. Doway* 2:656).	*Rashi* *Benei ashpato.* Arrows that are placed in a quiver (*Biblia Rabbinica* 4:294). *Ibn Ezra* The quiver is like a pregnant belly (*Biblia Rabbinica* 4:294).	*The [Geneva] Bible.* He caused ‖ the arrowes of his quiver to entre into my reines ("The Olde Testament" 332r). ‖ *Ebr. sonnes* *The Holy [King James] Bible.* Hee hath caused the † arrowes of his quiver to enter into my reins ("The Old Testament" n. pag.). † *Heb. sons*

It is in two final passages that Donne, again befittingly for the Lenten season, turns his attention to repentance. Writing of the term נִחֲתוּ *niḥatu,* "sticke fast," he explains in two passages:

> *Tua ut Peccatum*
> Yea, let this arrow be considered as a *tentation,* yet *his* hand is upon it; at least God *sees* the shooting of it, and yet *lets* it flie.... And so he shoots arrow after arrow, permits sin after sin, that at last some sin, that draws affliction with it, might bring us to understanding; for that word, in which the Prophet here expresses this sticking, and this fast sticking of these arrows, which is *Nachath,* is here, (as the Grammarians in that language call it) in *Niphal, figere factae,* they were made to stick; Gods hand is upon them, the *work* is his, the *arrows* are his, and the *sticking* of them is his, whatsoever, and whosoever they may be. (*Sermons* 2:67)

> ....

> *Tua ut Medicamenta*
> though this be a shooting of arrows, *Non fugabit eum vir Sagittarius* [marginal note: Job 41:28], *The arrow,* (as we read it) *The Archer,*

as the Romane Edition reades it), cannot make that child of God afraid, afraid with a distrustful fear, or make him loth to come hither again to hear more, how close soever Gods arrow, and Gods archer, that is, his word in his servants mouth, come to that Conscience now, nor make him mis-interpret that which he does hear, or call that *passion* in the Preacher, in which the Preacher is but *sagittarius Dei*, the deliverer of Gods arrows; for Gods arrows are *sagittae Compunctionis*, arrows that draw bloud from the eyes; Tears of repentance from *Mary Magdalen*, and from *Peter*. (*Sermons* 2:68)

Ibn Ezra's systematic emphasis on Hebrew grammar clarifies Donne's concern with נִחֲתוּ *niḥatu*, "sticke fast" as the passive verb form *niph'al* (Table 24), meaning "stuck" or "pierced" (Even-Shoshan 4:1189).[19] This grammatical distinction possesses great significance for Donne's image of God's "destructive and catastrophic aspect"; indeed, as preacher, Donne is echoing the concerns of his Holy Sonnet "Batter my Heart," in which the poetic speaker appeals to God to "bend / Your force, to break, blow, burn, & make me new" (*Poems 1635* 340). The truly shocking nature of this poem is recast in the sermon in terms of an issue of grammatical, verbal form, as Donne skillfully utilizes the authority of "the Grammarians in that language" to provide a rational basis for such a depiction of the divine. Choosing to follow the translation of the King James Bible, "sticke" (see table 24), Donne thereby draws out the semantic consequences of the Hebrew verb form to place the full intention of action and violence firmly in God's hands. In doing so, he underlines the psalmic text as straining against the boundaries of imagination and theology by apostrophically forging the image of the divine in terms of a physically violent, yet also intimate relationship.

The results of God's action are presented graphically in the second passage, as "bloud from the eyes, Tears of repentance." This gruesome image evokes that metaphoric "blinding of the intellect" (Lewalski 15), which in 2 Samuel 12 (the traditional context for the Penitential Psalms) is revealed in David's lack of recognition that the "Parable of the Ewe-Lamb" is directed at his own acts of adultery and murder. His subsequent repentance,

Table 27. Job 41:28: The arrow cannot make him flee

Vulgate Bible [41:19]	Jewish Exegetes [41:20]	Reformation Bibles
Non fugabit eum vir sagittarius (Vulgate Bible n.p.).	Rashi *Lo yavriḥenu ven-qashet.* He will not flee from the owner of the bow *Miqra'ot Gedolot* (5:216).	*The [Geneva] Bible.* [41:19] The archer can not make him flee ("The Olde Testament" 234v).
The bowman shal not put him to flight (*The Holie Bible, Doway* 1:1108).	Ibn Ezra *Ben-qeshet.* It is the arrow (*Biblia Rabbinica* 4:259).	*The Holy [King James] Bible.* The arrow cannot make him flee ("The Old Testament" n.p.).

precipitated by the prophet Nathan's accusation "Thou art the man" (2 Sam. 12:7), is the biblical background against which Donne integrates the two alternative meanings of the figurative Hebrew phrase בֶּן קֶשֶׁת *ben-qeshet*,[20] "son of the arrow" as either "arrow" or "archer" (see table 27). By revealing these two meanings for his Lenten auditory—the object (the arrow shot, God's word,) and the subject (the archer, God's preacher) of the biblical action (the shooting of the arrow)—Donne fulfills his exegetical objective of opening up for his auditory (to repeat Janel Mueller's important statement) the "many possibilities of nuance and meaning, not to settle upon one" ("Introduction" 10), thereby effectively authorizing the preacher's role in the call to penitence.

Sermon on the Prebend Psalm 64:10: The righteous shalbe glad in the LORD, and shall trust in him; and al the upright in heart shall glory

In the third Prebend sermon, "Preached at S.Pauls, November 5. 1626. *In Vesperis*" (*LXXX Sermons* 673), Donne (as Evelyn Simpson writes) "strives to cheer and comfort his congregation.

Once again he attacks the Calvinists for their belief that God predestines certain men to damnation" (*Sermons* 7:17). It is in the following two passages that this homiletic purpose intersects at length with Donne's exegetical search for the literal sense of the "Originall" Hebrew:

> *Laus*
> This Retribution is expressed in the Originall, in the word *Halal;*
> And *Halal,* to those Translators that made up our Booke of
> Common Prayer, presented the signification of *Gladnesse,* for it
> is there, *They shall be glad;* So it did to the Translators that came
> after, for there it is *They shall rejoyce;* And to our last Translators
> it seemed to signifie *Glory, They shall Glory,* say they. But the first
> Translation of all into our Language (which was long before any
> of these three) cals it *Praise,* and puts it in the Passive, *All men of
> rightfull heart shall be praised.* He followed *S. Hierom,* who reads
> it so, and interprets it so, in the Passive, *Laudabunter, They shall
> be praised.* And so truly *Iithhalelu,* in the Original, beares it, nay
> requires it; which is not of a praise that they shall give to God, but
> of a praise, that they shall receive for having served God with an
> upright heart; not that they shall praise God in doing so, but that
> godly men shall praise them for having done so. All this will grow
> naturally out of the roote; for, the roote of this word, is *Lucere,
> Splendere,* To shine out in the eyes of men, and to create in them a
> holy and reverentiall admiration. (*Sermons* 7:248–49)
>
> ....
>
> *Laus danda aliis*
> And for our selves, it is truly the most proper, and most literall
> signification of this word, in our Text, *Iithhalelu,* That they shall
> praise themselves, that is, They shall have the testimony of a recti-
> fied conscience, that they have deserved the praise of good men, in
> having done laudible service to God. (*Sermons* 7:251)

Donne is intent in these passages on showing the ability of the "righteous" to determine their own fate, so that (in his earlier words) "persons obsequious to his [God's] grace, when it comes, and persons industrious and ambitious of more and more grace, and husbanding his grace well all the way, such persons God proposes to himselfe" (*Sermons* 7:240). He does so by discussing the literal, grammatical sense of the Hebrew root הלל *hll* in its verb form יִתְהַלְלוּ *yithalelu*, generating a series of alternative translations that require his auditory (and reader) to share in his own philological curiosity. Yet his insistence on citing the verb's various translations also comprises an example of Reformation scholarship, that "heaping up of references" (Kintgen 13), as well as the scholarly concern of each translation as it vies with its predecessors in creating what may at first seem minimally different, yet ultimately for Donne, semantically significant editions. Thus he first discards the Reformation translation "shall glory" (see table 28) as inappropriately emphasizing the actions of the "righteous" in praising God. Subsequently, he conceives of the alternative translation of the Vulgate and Wycliffe Bibles (see table 29)[21] — the passive form "shall be praised" — as representing admiration for the humility of the "righteous" in their "having served God with an upright heart;"[22] this meaning is emphasized by Donne's semantic connection of variants of the Hebrew term *halal: Lucere*, "shine," and praise (see table 30). Finally, Donne echoes Rashi's more radical interpretation of *yithalelu* as a reflexive verb that is "the most proper, and most literall signification"; in other words, he argues that the righteous "shall praise themselves" (table 29), empowering them to realize the situation of grace previously set out in distinctly legal terms, in which "God accepts and condemnes Man *Secundum allegata & Probata*, according to the Evidence that arises from us" (*Sermons* 7:241).

Donne's use of a literal, grammatical "sense" in order to advance this "interrelational understanding" (Jeffrey Johnson 127) of predestination is also apparent in a subsequent section, entitled *Futurum*. In two of its passages he is concerned with preventing a misinterpretation of his statements as supporting "Pelagianisme" ("disposed by nature, without use of grace"; *Sermons* 7:240) or "Semi-pelagianisme" ("disposed by preventing grace, without use of subsequent grace"; *Sermons* 7:240) that he himself had previously rejected. Thus he preaches:

Table 28. Psalm 64:10: Yithalelu as Active

Book of Common Prayer	The [Geneva] Bible and Holy Scriptures	The Holy [King James] Bible
The righteous shal rejoyce in the Lord, and put his trust in him: and all they that are true of heart, shalbe glad (n. pag.).	*But* the righteous shal be glad in the Lord, & trust in him: and all that are upright of heart, shal rejoyce ("The Olde Testament" 248r).	The righteous shalbe glad in the LORD, and shall trust in him: and all the upright in heart shall glory ("The Old Testament" n.p.).

Table 29. Psalm 64:10: Yithalelu as Reflexive or Passive

Vulgate Bible [63:11]	Rashi [64:11]	Wycliffe Bible [63:11]
Laetabitur justus in Domine, et sperabit in eo; et laudabuntur omnes recti corde (*Biblia Sacra* 599). The just shal rejoice in our Lord, and shal hope in him, and al the right of hart shal be praised (*The Holie Bible. Doway* 2:117).	*Let all the upright in heart praise themselves.* Let them praise their uprightness, and let them laud themselves for they are certain that the Holy One Blessed be He is at their assistance (*Biblia Rabbinica* 4:56; *Rashi's Commentary* 434).	The just man schal be glad in the Lord, and schal hope in hym; and alle men of riytful herte schulen be preisid (n.p.).

Table 30. Etymology: hll

Udall, "Hebrue Dictionaire"	Strong, *Dictionary*	Even-Shoshan, *Dictionary*
הול he was mad. הוֹלְלוּת Madnes (34).	1984. *Halal.* A primitive root; to be clear (orig. of sound, but usually of color); to shine; hence, to	a. Akkadian: *alâlu, elêlu;* Arabic: *halal* ["praise," "glorify"] (2:391).

Table 30. (*cont.*)

Udall, "Hebrue Dictionaire"	Strong, *Dictionary*	Even-Shoshan, *Dictionary*
הָלַל he praysed. הָלוּל, תְּהִלָּה, מְהַלָל Prayse. הֵילֵל The day starre (35).[23]	make a show, to boast; and thus to be (clamorously) foolish; to rave; causatively, to celebrate; also to stultify: (make) boast (self), celebrate, commend, (deal, make), fool(-ish, -ly), glory, give (light), be (make, feign self) mad (against), give in marriage, (sing, be worthy of) praise, rate, renowned, shine.	b. Akkadian *ellu* "clear," "bright"; Arabic: *hala* "shine" (2:391). c. Only Hebrew? "to be wild/ unruly"; to be mad/ confounded" (2:391).

In the Hebrew there is no Present tense; In that language wherein God spake, it could not be said, *The upright in heart, Are praised;* Many times they are not. But God speaks in the future; first, that he may still keepe his Children in an expectation and dependance upon him, (you shall be, though you be not yet) And then, to establish them in an infallibility, because he hath said it, (I know you are not yet, but comfort your selves, I have said it, and it shall be.) As the Hebrew hath no Superlatives, because God would keepe his Children within compasse, and in moderate desires, to content themselves with his measures, though they be not great, and though they be not heaped; so, considering what pressures, and contempts, and terrors, the upright in heart are subject to, it is a blessed reliefe, That they have a future proposed unto them, That they shall be praised, That they shall be redeemed out of contempt. (*Sermons* 7:252)

. . . .

Nay, not onely the Expectation, (that is, that that is expected) shall be comfortable, because it shall be infallible, but that very present state that he is in, shall be comfortable, according to the first of our three Translations, *They that are true of heart, shall be glad thereof;* Glad of that; glad that they are true of heart, though their future retribution were never so far removed; Nay, though there were no future retribution in the case, yet they shall finde comfort enough in their present Integrity. Nay, not onely their present state of Integrity, but their present state of misery, shall be comfortable to them; for this very word of our Text, *Halal,* that is here translated *Joy,* and *Glory,* and *Praise,* in divers places of Scripture [marginal note: Psalm 75:4; Isaiah 44:25; Job 12:17], (as Hebrew words have often such transplantation) signifies *Ingloriousnesse,* and *contempt,* and *dejection of spirit;* So that Ingloriousnesse, and contempt, and dejection of spirit, may be a part of the retribution; God may make Ingloriousnesse, and Contempt, and Dejection of spirit, a greater blessing and benefit, then Joy, and Glory, and Praise would have been. (*Sermons* 7:253)

In the first passage Donne complements the second Prebend sermon by seizing upon the essence of biblical Hebrew grammar, with its lack of the present tense, to designate the essence of grace as a timeless "cooperation" (*Sermons* 7:63) between the divine and human. He thereby encompasses both past and future, prevenient and subsequent grace by focusing intensively on the future tense of the word *yithalelu* ("shall be praised"), to reflect God's resolution to preserve human "expectation and dependance" as well as divine "infallibility." Indeed, the manner in which this second characteristic is couched—"I have said it, and it shall be"—is evocative of God's name as *Jehovah,* of which Donne himself explains (in his 1627 Christmas sermon) "that literally in the Originall, this name is conceived in the future; it is there, *Qui ero, I that shall be*" (*Sermons* 8:144). This conception of grace is further underlined in Donne's subsequent statement that "Hebrew hath no superlatives,"[24] as he utilizes this ostensible linguistic flaw to substantiate God's restraining of "his Children" in "moderate desires, to content themselves with his measures." While Donne does not in this instance provide his auditory with an adequate example, his somewhat perfunctory statement can be expanded through the study of an earlier (1617) sermon, preached on Proverbs 22:11 (see table 31). In this sermon Donne echoing Kimhi's commentary, is intent on explaining how the Hebrew phrase *Tardeimat Jehovah*, "the heavy slepe of the Lord" (Geneva Bible) functions as a superlative (intensifying the quality of the sleep) and thereby effectively demonstrating God's support of David's good deed (refusing exhortations to harm Saul).[25] While Donne's auditory at St. Paul's must necessarily have taken this point about Hebrew superlatives on its preacher's authority, the reader of this sermon can find in its homiletic precedent continued evidence of Donne's agile (and definitely learned) use of Hebrew grammar for specific theological purposes.

Table 31. Tardeitmat Yehovah

Kimhi, 1 Samuel 26:12	The [Geneva] Bible and Holy Scriptures, 1 Samuel 26:12	Sermon on Proverbs 22:11
A deep sleep from the Lord. The construct state is [to be understood] in one of two ways: either its meaning is *a great sleep* because the thing which [one] wishes to increase, [one] juxtaposes to the Holy One, Blessed be He...or its meaning is to state that the sleep had been caused by God in order that they will not be aware of David and Avishai as they take the flask and spear (*Biblia Rabbinica* 2:184).	For ‖ the Lord had sent a dead slepe upon them ("The Olde Testament" 133v). ‖ Ebr. the heavy slepe of the Lord was fallen upon them.	As it is frequent and ordinary in the Scriptures, when the Holy Ghost would express a *superlative,* the highest degree of any thing, to express it, by adding the name of God to it (as when *Saul* and his company were in such a dead sleep, as that *David* could take his Spear, and pot of water from under his head, It is called *Tardemath Jehovah, sopor Domini, The sleep of the Lord* [marginal note: 1 Samuel 26:12], The greatest sleep that could possess a man....) (*Sermons* 1:210).

The second passage is cited above at considerable length, providing as it does a theological and grammatical complement to the preceding one. It continues to reinforce the cooperation between God and humankind, arguing once again for the existence of that state of "infallible Expectation" and of "future retribution." Yet it is significant that it does so by recovering the psalmic translation from the *Book of Common Prayer* ("shalbe glad") previously discarded by Donne, while he argues here for a gladness and comfort "in present Integrity." This recovery of erased meaning evokes the Barthesian concept of the *scriptible* or "writerly" text, creating as it does a network of coexistent, alternative translations. What is more, it enables the reconception of the (at once assiduous and curious) reader as that Barthesian "producer of the text," emulating the preacher Donne in retranslating and hence re-"writing" the Bible.

Donne places this dynamic rereading and rewriting of the Bible at the service of his preaching on penitence and grace in his subsequent application of Hebrew etymology. He returns again to the etymology of the word *halal*, "glory, praise," establishing the multiple meanings of the biblical text through his discussion of the (apparently) polysemic nature of this individual biblical word.[26] The meaning of the word as *"Lucere, Splendere"* is extended here by explaining that *"Halal, that is here translated Joy, and Glory, and Praise, in divers places of Scripture . . . signifies Ingloriousnesse, and contempt, and dejection of spirit."* Donne conscientiously cites three different biblical passages[27] to support his polysemic interpretation, correctly reflecting the scholarship recorded in John Udall's sixteenth century "Hebrew Dictionaire" (and confirmed in Strong's nineteenth century *Dictionary*). It is advantageous to see how this interest in etymology works in another, densely developed passage from Donne's sermon on the Penitential Psalm 32:7. Entitling this passage "Perplexity," Donne preaches on the translation of the psalmic phrase (briefly discussed in chapter 3) "Thou shalt preserve mee from trouble [מֵצַר]":

But the Originall word *Tzur* [*tsur* צוּר] hath a more peculiar sense; It signifies a straite, a narrownesse, a difficulty, a distresse; *I am distressed [*צַר *tsar] for thee, my brother Jonathan* [marginal note: 2 Samuel 1:26], says *David*, in this word when he lamented his irremediable, his irrecoverable death. *So is it also, Pangs [*צִרִים *tsirim] have taken hold of me, as the pangs of a woman that travaileth* [marginal note: Isaiah 21:3]. And so the word growes to signifie, *Aciem gladii, Thou hast turned the edge [*צוּר *tsur] of the sword* [marginal note: Psalm 89:44], and to signifie the top and precipice of a rock; *He clave the rocks [*צֻרִים *tsurim] in the wildernesse* [marginal note: Psalm 78:15]. So that the word expresses *Angustiam*, narrownesse, pressure, precipitation, inextricablenesse, in a word, (that will best fit us) Perplexity; and, *The Lord shall preserve me from perplexity;* And this may the Church, and this may every good soule comfort it selfe in, *Thou shalt preserve me from perplexity.* (*Sermons* 9:341–42)

Donne's delight in the very substance of Hebrew words, particularly their phonological and etymological extensions, takes on a highly intertextual character as he makes his way among various books of the Hebrew Bible. This heaping up of biblical verses seems very much, as D. C. Allen rightly "suspects," the work of a concordance ("Dean Donne" 215). John Udall's *Hebrue Dictionaire*, for example, explains the Hebrew word *tzur* as meaning: "Straitninge, straitens, Opressions, tribulation, a rocke, distresse, perplexion" (128).[28] Neither Udall nor Donne is entirely correct in concluding that all of these homonymic words were created from one polysemic root; while *tzur* does mean both (literally) "straight, narrow" and (figuratively) difficulty and distress," the words *tzirim*, "pangs," *tzur*, "rock" and *tzur-harbo*, "blade of his sword" are not related (Even-Shoshan 5:1578–1616).[29] Yet this wordplay and his own *fingerfertigkeit*, "finger dexterity" (to use Allen's term; OSB MSS 90, Box 1, Folder 1) together afford Donne an additional opportunity to integrate scriptural quotations that set out the varied experiences and images so central to the penitential season and spirit, translating as he does the psalmic speaker's emotional distress into the physical discomforts of "narrowness," the pains of childbirth and the tactile sharpness of a rock and sword. Donne is primarily interested in expanding the meaning of this word through a series of semantic and metaphoric permutations, particularly appropriate to a Lenten sermon, in order to enfold within it various states of physical and emotional perplexity, and ultimately to bring into full relief the consolation available through divine intervention.

Donne's focus, therefore, on the etymology of these two words *tsur* and *halel* provides additional, intriguing evidence regarding his exegetical agenda, which seeks to maintain the potentialities of meaning available in a single term or phrase. Just as intriguing is the way in which this focus uncovers the shared desire of varied philological and homiletic sources for preserving the polysemic nature of Hebrew words. While the earlier dictionaries confirm the seventeenth century preacher in his search for the polysemic meaning of biblical text and words, they comprise something of a pitfall for a more modern reader of both the Bible and of Donne's sermons.[30] For accepting the view of the root *hll* as rather homonymous allows that reader to cast a critical eye on the sustained attempt to create a polysemic text as well as an intricate linguistic and semantic intertextuality among the several books of the Bible. It consequently allows the reader to acknowledge Donne's use of the Hebrew language not simply as a reflection of contemporary lexical and philological sources, but also as a part of this extended exegetical project with its own intertwined grammatical and theological agendas.

Conclusion

Cumming's insightful remark cited at the opening of the chapter highlights the centrality of grammar (Latin, Hebrew, Greek) to the Reformation project (translation, commentary, preaching and theology). This can be seen as an appropriate answer to the reservations expressed by Evelyn Simpson, when she notes in an early essay that Donne's sermons are "based on a too literal interpretation of the Scriptures, [and] their constant appeals to the Fathers becomes wearisome" (Spearing, "Donne's Sermons" 41). Simpson's response is reminiscent of Samuel Johnson's well-known eighteenth century statement about Metaphysical wit, asserting that "their learning instructs and their subtilty surprises; but the reader commonly thinks his improvement dearly bought" (14). Johnson and Simpson raise similar reservations about Donne's demands upon his reader, whether as poet or preacher, most particularly regarding his fascination with learning that might seem to belabor a particular linguistic or exegetical point. Yet just as poetic taste changes, so does homiletic sensibility. Most significantly, the respective dismissals of Donne's "too literal interpretation," his "learning" and "subtilty" illustrate a change in this sensibility that raises various questions about the acumen and expectations of Donne's seventeenth century auditory and readers, especially regarding their knowledge of scholarly sources, diligent note taking, and attention to critical notations. These diverse responses emphasize the shared concerns of sixteenth and seventeenth century biblical readers and Reformers, which should necessarily be taken into account by the new readers of Donne's sermons. The recognition of this aspect of Donne's sermons therefore provides a wider historical and intellectual context in which to evaluate the preacher's emphasis on the very "literal interpretation of Scriptures," particularly through a meticulous attention to the "byways of syntax," the "inflections of single verbs" and their variable, intriguing potentialities for meaning.

FIVE

The Literal Sense

Genesis

*In the first book of the Scriptures, that of Genesis, there is danger in
departing from the letter. . . . As then to depart from the literall sense,
that sense which the very letter presents, in the book of Genesis,
is dangerous, because if we do so there, we have no history of the
Creation of the world in any other place to stick to.*
　　　　　　　　　　　—John Donne, "Sermon on Apocalypse 20:6"

Sermon and Context

In his book on *The Legend of Noah,* the literary historian D. C.
Allen makes a provocative statement about the "literal sense" of
Scripture, writing that "I shall not consider the evolution of the
three allegorical senses, because the danger for the Renaissance
resided in the literal interpretation and it is in the danger that
I am interested" (*The Legend of Noah* 66–67). Allen conceives
of the literal interpretation of biblical events—in this instance

139

the Flood and the subsequent restoration of humankind—as fostering the development of a rational explanation, which in due course both destroyed the credibility of the biblical narrative and stimulated the development of "sciences of great modern value" (66).[1] For his part, Donne is concerned about the danger of departing from the literal sense, attested to in the opening citation from the 1624 Easter sermon that he preached at St. Paul's Cathedral. Though he recognized the impact of contemporary scientific thought on traditional religious concepts,[2] as a preacher Donne is predominantly concerned in his exegetical and homiletic works with utilizing the literal interpretation of biblical events, particularly the creation narrative, to preserve their historical credibility against the dangers besetting it from both sides of the hermeneutic process, that is, from expansive, unqualified allegorical interpretation on the one hand, and from the encroaching "rational explanation" posited by Allen on the other.

Such a reading of the book of Genesis in its literal sense invites a consideration of the exegetical tradition that seeks to both understand and sustain it. Allen's 1949 study of *The Legend of Noah* is one of several seminal works of that decade—the others being David Daiches, *The King James Version of the English Bible*, Beryl Smalley, *The Study of the Bible in the Middle Ages*, and Arnold Williams, *The Common Expositor*—which together highlight a confluence of interest in Christian biblical commentaries and translations. This twofold scholarly tradition, in which twentieth century scholars reconstruct medieval and early modern areas of scholarship and knowledge, encourages the reader of Donne's sermons to pay heed to those Jewish voices that resounded throughout Christian exegesis in sixteenth and seventeenth century England. Indeed, more recent studies (Philip Almond, *Adam and Eve in Seventeenth-Century Thought*; Ilona Rashkow, *Upon the Dark Places*; Jason Rosenblatt, *Torah and Law in Paradise Lost*; and Jeffrey Shoulson, *Milton and the Rabbis*) have taken up the challenge, examining how the understanding of the literal sense of the Genesis creation narrative brings to the fore a concern with the origin and nature of the world and humankind; as Anthony Raspa has pointed out, "with its opening assertion on how the world began, and how time and space came into being, Genesis was the Revealed reply to the origin of humanity that had to be addressed" ("Introduction" xxxvii–xxxviii).

Donne's interest in the creation narrative is most distinctly evident in four sermons he preached at various times and circumstances:[3] the marriage sermon preached on woman's creation in Genesis 2:18 (February 1620);[4] the two court sermons preached on man's creation in Genesis 1:26 (April 1629); and the Whitsunday sermon preached (at St. Paul's Cathedral) on the creation of the world in Genesis 1:2 (May 24, 1629). A chronological and critical divide between the marriage sermon and the latter three recommends, however, a significant distinction. For while providing instruction about the consequence of woman's nature as "an helpe meet for" man regarding her marital responsibilities and status,[5] Donne removes from consideration his usually predominant concern with the Trinitarian nature of God, explaining that "in the creation of man, there is intimated a Consultation, a Deliberation of the whole *Trinity* [*faciamus*, 'let us make']; in the making of *women*, it is not expressed so; it is but *faciam* ['I will make']" (*Sermons* 2:337). In contrast, the three 1629 sermons elucidate Donne's "theological first principle" (Jeffrey Johnson x), his Trinitarianism, as well as its bearing on the nature of man, who was created in this image. This is very much the case in the Whitsunday sermon, in which Donne commemorates the descent of the Holy Ghost by expounding on Genesis 1:2 ("And the spirit of God moved upon the face of the waters") to set out its role in the creation of the world and the governing of the Church. His concern with the Trinitarian nature of God in creation is also underscored in an earlier, 1620 Trinity Sunday sermon on Genesis 18:25 preached at Lincoln's Inn. In this instance Donne rewrites the biblical story of the divine visitation to Abraham, during which the patriarch pleads against God's judgment of the cities of Sodom and Gomorrah ("Shall not the Judge of all the earth doe right?"). Read in tandem, these two homiletic texts clarify as well the importance of grammar to Donne's theology, "wherein a grammatical plural of the Hebrew word for God must necessarily imply a plural *form* of the Godhead, a Trinity" (Adlington, "Preaching the Holy Ghost" 205). In the following passages, Donne specifically explains the issues raised by the biblical phrase בָּרָא אֱלֹהִים *bara Elohim*, "God [gods] created" in Genesis 1:1:

> [Trinity Sunday]
> those men in the Church, who have cryed downe that way of proceeding, to goe about to prove the Trinity, out of the first words of *Genesis, Creavit Dii*, That because God in the plural is there joined to a Verb in the singular, therefore there is a Trinity in Unity; or to prove the Trinity out of this place, that because God, who is but one, appeared to Abraham in three persons [at Mamre], therefore there are three Persons in the God-head; those men, I say, who have cryed downe such manner of arguments, have reason on their side, when these arguments are imployed against the Jews, for, for the most parts, the Jews have pertinent, and sufficient answers to those arguments. But yet, betweene them, who make this place, a distinct, and a literall, and a concluding argument, to prove the Trinity, and them who cry out against it, that it hath no relation to the Trinity, our Church hath gone a middle, and a moderate way, when by appointing this Scripture for this day, when we celebrate the Trinity, it declares that to us, who have been baptized, and catechized in the name and faith of the Trinity, it is a refreshing, it is a cherishing, it is an awakening of that former knowledge which we had of the Trinity, to heare that our onely God thus manifested himselfe to Abraham in three Persons (*Sermons* 3:143).

> [Whitsunday]
> In this Text [Gen. 1:2] is the first mention of this Third Person of the Trinity; and it is the first mention of any distinct Person in the God-head; In the first verse, there is an intimation of the Trinity, in that *Bara Elohim*, That *Gods*, Gods in the plural are said to have made heaven, and earth...so *Moses* having given us an intimation of God, and the three Persons altogether in that *Bara Elohim*, before, gives us first notice of this Person, the Holy Ghost, in particular, because he applies to us the Mercies of the Father, and the

Merits of the Son, and *moves upon the face of the waters,* and actuates, and fecundates our soules, and generates that knowledge, and that comfort, which we have in the knowledge of God.... The Jews who are afraid of the Truth, lest they should meete evidences of the doctrine of the Trinity, and so of the Messias, the Son of God, if they should admit any spirituall sense, admit none, but cleave so close to the letter, as that to them the Scripture becomes *Litera occidens, A killing Letter* [2 Cor. 3:6], *and the savour of death unto death* [2 Corinthians 2:16]. They therefore, in this *Spirit of God,* are so far from admitting any Person, that is, God, as they admit no extraordinary operation, or vertue proceeding from God in this place; but they take the word here (as in may other places of Scripture it does) to signifie onely a *winde* (*Sermons* 9:92–96).

As Udall's contemporary "Hebrue Grammar" attests (table 32), the grammatical problem lies in the juxtaposition of the plural name *Elohim,* literally "gods" (the singular *Eloha* with the suffix *im*), with the third-person singular verb *bara,* "created." The solution that Ibn Ezra sets out rests on what Arnold Williams has termed "a crux, demanding a firm grip on Hebrew idiom for successful solution" (11); in this case the Jewish exegete explains that the term *Elohim* is "employed stylistically" in Hebrew as a sign of respect, much as in the case of the *pluralis majestatis* or (in Donne's terms) the "Royal Plurall" (*Sermons* 9:90). In his study of this phrase in *Essayes in Divinity* Donne reveals his sound understanding of this grammatical problem by citing two biblical passages to attest to the existence of the singular *Eloha* (confirmed by Ibn Ezra),[6] and also echoes the Jewish exegete's statement about Hebrew stylistics by calling the phrase *bara Elohim* a "meer Idiotism [Idiom]" (table 32).

It is advantageous to return here to Williams's discussion of the "Devotional, Moral, and Doctrinal" purposes of Genesis (233), as designated by sixteenth and seventeenth century commentaries. His survey of the Christian commentaries (243–45) complements Donne's own in the *Essayes in Divinity* (29–31), from which only a small passage is cited here (table 32).[7] For what is of primary significance regarding the two sermonic passages is the specific

Table 32. Genesis 1:1

Ibn Ezra	Udall, *Hebrue Grammar*	Donne, *Essayes in Divinity*
Elohim. Afer we found *Eloha* [Ps. 114:7] we knew that *Elohim* is a plural. This is employed stylistically, because every language has honorific terminology. In the non-Hebrew languages, when an inferior addresses a superior he says the plural. In Arabic [it is] respectful for a dignitary such as a king to speak in the plural. In the Holy Tongue [it is] respectful to speak of a superior in the plural (*Biblia Rabbinica* 1:13; *Ibn Ezra's Commentary. Genesis* 24).	The construction of a verb with a noun is in number, gender, and person.... The speciall out-rule; and first of number. Gen. 1, 1 בָּרָא אֱלֹהִים בְּרֵאשִׁית ["bereishit bara Elohim"] In the beginning God created, *here the verb and the noun are of divers numbers* (2:165–67).	Hereupon hath an opinion, that by this name of *God*, *Elohim*, because it is *plurally* pronounced in this place, and with a *singular* verbe, the Trinity is insinuated.... For, when *Cajetan* had said true, that this place was not so interpretable, but yet upon false grounds, That the word *Elohim* had no singular [marginal note: Eloah. Job 12 & 36], which is evidently false.... It satisfies me, for the phrase, that I am taught by collation of many places in the Scriptures, that it is a meer Idiotism [Idiom]. And for the matter, that our Saviour never applied this place to that purpose: and that I mark, the first place in which the Fathers in the *Nicen* Councel objected against *Arius* his Philosopher, was, *Faciamus hominem* [marginal note: Genesis 1:26], and this never mentioned (30).

use to which Donne puts this earlier scholarship; as Williams remarks, "John Donne, in the sermons, apparently veers to the position that *bara elohim* is an intimation of the Trinity.... The *Essayes in Divinity*, written before the sermons, makes it clear that there is no indication of the Trinity in Genesis 1:1. Thus Donne illustrates both points of view, the acceptance of the text as proof of the Trinity for popular use, and its rejection for professional use" (244). What is evident from the juxtaposition of the two sermonic passages is Donne's homiletic moderation of the erudite and unequivocal expunging of Trinitarian meaning that he had set out previously in the *Essayes in Divinity*. He argues therefore (in the earlier sermon) for "an awakening of that former knowledge which we had of the Trinity" through two biblical texts (Gen. 1:1, 18:25) which provide (in the words of the later sermon) "an intimation of the Trinity." Consequently, Donne provides a more flexible hermeneutics for his auditory as readers of the Bible, an exegetical process of "equitable reasoning" (in Katrin Ettenhuber's terms) that allows them to "deviate from the strict *letter* of Old Testament law to refresh and advance the lawyer's faith in the salvific *spirit* of the New Dispensation" (141–42).

Such an argument is sustained and supplemented by Donne's participation in the philological and theological debate focused on the phrase *bara elohim, Creavit Dii*, "gods created" (and not *creavit deus* as in Jerome's Vulgate). For as employed here by Donne, the phrase's literal sense—whether the noun is singular or plural, semantically significant or simply idiomatic—reflects directly upon God's Trinitarian nature. What is more, Ettenhuber's transposition of the legal term of equity onto the sermonic genre by (re-) conceiving of it as an exegetical process reverberates in Donne's pointed, legalistic discussion of the appropriate parameters for conducting a Jewish-Christian debate over Trinitarianism. Standing before the lawyers of Lincoln's Inn during his Trinity Sunday sermon, Donne mitigates the image of the Jews as a lightening-rod either for the "cultural anxieties" (James Shapiro 1) of sixteenth and seventeenth century English Christians or for the "English apocalyptic interpretation of history" (Zakai 214), rather setting them out as a juridical opponent who is capable of assembling "pertinent, and sufficient answers to those arguments" posed by the Christians.[8] Moreover, in preaching his Whitsunday sermon before the more public auditory of St. Paul's Cathedral, he again advocates the literal sense of the Scripture while simultaneously warning against what he conceives of as a strict legalistic Jewish adherence to it that turns the Bible into "a killing Letter" and narrows the hermeneutic boundaries against a Christian, "spirituall sense."

The exegetical parameters regarding God's creation of the world as variously literal, grammatical and "spirituall" in Donne's Whitsunday (and Trinity) sermon have been held to affirm the Trinitarian concept of God. It is particularly in his first court sermon on Genesis 1:26 that Donne extends this concept to encompass a deliberation of its consequences upon human nature in general, and upon monarchic rule in particular. Moreover, these deliberations are most effectively read within a wider system of homiletic and exegetical texts previously used by Donne in his earlier sermons preached on the ecclesiastical Penitential and Prebend occasions. Thus while the first and second Prebend sermons (on Psalms 62:9 and 63:7) establish the "concurring" Trinity as a "picture" or "patterne" for human actions, the sermon on the Penitential Psalm 38:3 carefully sets out the symbolic and psychological significance evoked by the different names for man; subsequently Donne transposes these discussions onto the particular political circumstances of the spring of 1629. Juxtaposing these various sermons thus provides an opportunity to extend the discussion of Donne's sermon series on the Penitential and Prebend Psalms, demonstrating his adaptation of the literal sense of the biblical creation narrative to occasion, audience, and historical moment.

Faciamus Hominem: Let Us Make Man

The situation in which Donne preached his two sermons on Genesis 1:26 to "the King, at the Court" in April 1629 was a charged one, both politically and theologically. It came in the aftermath of the dissolution of Parliament by King Charles on March 10, 1629, in response to the submission of a resolution "which declared favourers of Arminianism, and collectors *or payers* of Tonnage and Poundage to be capital enemies of King and kingdom" (Jeffrey Johnson 18); in other words, attacking the King "as a committed Arminian" (Smith 268) as well as his desire to secure permanent revenue from import and export taxes.[9] This situation imparts a distinctive significance to the way in which the preacher utilized exegetical debates over the biblical text. The grammatical problem in this instance resides in the juxtaposition of the name *Elohim* with both a singular and a plural verb: *Va-yomer Elohim, na'aseh adam be-tsalmeinu kidmuteinu*, "And God said [*va-yomer*; third person singular],[10] Let us [*na'aseh*; first person plural] make man in our Image, after our likeness." Within the context of the previous exegetical and theological discussion of Genesis 1:1, this verse poses new questions about the multiple aspect of God's nature: Is this an additional example of that idiomatic use of the grammatically plural term *Elohim?* Is the plural verb *na-'aseh*, "let us make," to be considered an expression "of either self-deliberation or consultation with other divine beings" (Skinner 30)? Does this verse, as Donne writes (in the second sermon on Genesis 1:26), comprise a solution to the conundrum of Genesis 1:1, so "that in this text beginnes our Catechisme. Here we have, and here first the saving knowledge of the Trinity" (*Sermons* 9:57)?

Not surprisingly, Genesis 1:26 (as Janel Mueller notes) is "perhaps the most frequently cited text in Donne" (*Donne's Prebend Sermons* 234). It will therefore be productive to look first at how the preacher utilizes this verse in two related passages in his Prebend sermons:

[First Prebend Sermon]
God had a picture of himselfe from all eternity; from all eternity, the Sonne of God was the *Image of the invisible God* [marginal note: Colossians 1:15]; But then God would have one picture, which should bee the picture of Father, Sonne, and Holy Ghost too, and so made man to the Image of the whole Trinity. As the Apostle argues, *Cui dixit, To whom did God ever say, This day have I begotten thee* [Hebrews 1:5], but to Christ? so we say, for the dignity of man, *Cui dixit*, of what Creature did God ever say, *Faciamus*, Let us, us make it, All, all the Persons together, and to imploy, and exercise, not only Power, but Counsaile, in the making of that Creature? (*Sermons* 6:296).

[Second Prebend Sermon]
And therefore let him [God] be our patterne for that, to worke after patternes; To propose to our selves Rules and Examples for all actions; and the more, the more immediately, the more directly our actions concerne the service of God. If I ask God, by what Idea he made me, God produces his *Faciamus hominem ad Imaginem nostram* [marginal note: Genesis 1:26], That there was a concurrence of the whole Trinity, to make me in *Adam*, according to that Image which they were, and according to that Idea, which they had pre-determined.... God does nothing, man does nothing well, without these Idea's, these retrospects, this recourse to pre-conceptions, pre-deliberations (*Sermons* 7:61).

Preaching on these psalms in fulfillment of his ecclesiastical duty as Prebendary of St. Paul's, Donne briefly turns his attention to the meaning of Genesis 1:26 not only in terms of Trinitarianism but primarily in terms of its consequences for human nature and behavior. The Trinity is clearly an essential element of his conception of God, as Donne sets out the lesson for his auditory by stressing the necessity of their emulating the divine taking of "Counsaile" put forth by *na'aseh*, "let us make." One sermonic passage complements and extends the other as the import of the plural verb in these passages and on these occasions lies in the endorsement of the "concurrence" of the Trinity in the creation of man, as well as in the transmutation of the iconic "picture" and "Image" into the more abstract "Idea's" and "pre-conceptions, pre-deliberations" according to which such creation

Table 33. Genesis 1:26: Christian Sources

Lancelot Andrewes, *Sermon on Genesis*	Nicholas Gibbens, *Questions and Disputations*
First, there is a partition wall, there is a difference, between this work of man and all the former. There stile now is changed, *fiat* & *fit* into *faciamus:* God before was Commander, now he is a Counsellor....here in *faciamus* is deliberation, for that now he makes him, for whom all the former Creatures were made....The Arrians and Jews doe say, that in the creating of man God consulted with Angels, and had the help of Elements; which opinion is without all discretion....Men are not the patern of the Angels, but the image of God. Some Jews say here God speaketh like a Prince in the plural number, denying the Trinity; but *Philo Judeus,* the best of the Jews, disclaimeth that opinion. We say therein is expressed the Trinity....In creating man is great deliberation, it is joynt work of the Trinity (*Apospasmatia Sacra* 93–94).	But to whom said God, *let us make man?* Not to the Angels, as the[q] Jewes affirme, for he used none of their helpe in mans creation, neither did he create man after the image of Angels but of *Elohim,* of God himselfe (30). [q] Rabb. Solom. & alii Rabbini, Angelos Deum adiuvisse admittunt: imo alii, Deum, terrae, elementis, etaim animantibus fuisse allocutum, potius statuunt; quam trinitatem deitatis, & divinitatem Iesu Christi agnoscant, tam profunde traduntur in sensum reprobum. Rabbi Solomon & other Rabbis admit that the Angels helped God: though others prefer to affirm that God was talking (together) with the earth, the elements, even the animals, rather than to recognize the trinity of God and the divinity of Jesus Christ, (thus) offering a translation so deeply wrong (30).

is accomplished. This suits Donne's concern in these sermons with the consolation he offers his auditory, to be balanced against the judgment and misery of man evoked by the continuous use of the image of weights and measures.[11]

Yet Donne offers little perspective on the exegetical crux of "Let us make man," relying on his auditory's presumed familiarity with this biblical phrase. This familiarity is corroborated by the continuous presence and explication of the phrase in contemporary homiletic and exegetical texts, such as Lancelot Andrewes's 1591 sermon and Nicholas Gibben's 1602 commentary (table 33). Both preacher and commentator demonstrate their awareness of the exegetical tradition and controversy raised by the hermeneutic gap in the biblical text; their citing of this tradition delineates the issues raised by their attention to the literal, grammatical sense of the text, and also defines their different responses. As preacher, Andrewes clearly sets out how the grammatical change of the Genesis creation narrative from *"fiat & fit* into *faciamus"* — in other words, from phrases of Genesis 1:3 (*yehi or | fiat lux,* "let there be light"; *va-yehi or | facta est lux,* "and light became") to the phrase of Genesis 1:26 (*na'aseh adam | faciamus hominem,* "let us make man") — effects a theological re-conception of God from "Commander" to "Counsellor." Subsequently, he underlines (and intensifies) the prolonged interchange among Jews and Christians,[12] countering the collective heresy of the "Arrians [fourth century Christians who denied the divinity of Jesus Christ] and Jews" with the (apparent) repudiation by the first century Greek-Jewish philosopher Philo Judeaus.[13] For his part, Gibbens[14] directs his reader's attention both to the hermeneutic gap of the biblical text (asking rhetorically "to whom said God, *let us make man?"*) and to the "deeply wrong" answers offered by "Rabbi Solomon & other Rabbis."[15] These polemic citations of the Jewish exegetical tradition draw attention not only to Rashi's own attack on the *minim* (literally "sectarians" or "heretics," but understood as a term for Christians), but more significantly to his echoing of the Midrashic compilation *Genesis Rabbah*[16] in the depiction of God as a monarch consulting his "judicial counsel" (his angels) in order to teach "proper conduct and the virtue of humility, namely, that the greater should consult and take permission from the lesser" (table 34).

These various exegetical and hermeneutic potentialities echo in Donne's first sermon on Genesis 1:26, throughout which his Christian Hebraism is particularly evident. In an extended pas-

Table 34. Genesis 1:26: Jewish Sources

Babylonian Talmud	Genesis Rabbah	Rashi
It is related of King Ptolemy [Ptolemy II Philadelphus, King of Egypt; 285–246 BCE] that he brought together seventy-two elders and placed them in seventy-two [separate] rooms, without telling them why he had brought them together, and he went in to each one of them and said to him, "Translate for me the Torah of Moses your master." God placed advice in the heart of each and every one [of them] and they all were of one mind and they wrote for him...*I shall make man in my image and likeness* (Tractate of *Megillah*, p. 9, side 1; Soncino 49). *Rashi. I shall make man:* Because here the sects heretically said "They are Two Powers," as it is written *"na'aseh adam."*	*And God said, Let us make man.* With whom did he take counsel? Rabbi Joshua in the name of Rabbi Levi said, "With the works of heaven and earth he took counsel. The matter may be compared to the case of a king who had two advisers, and he would do nothing without their express approval." Rabbi Samuel bar Nahman said, "It was with the things that he had created each prior day that he took counsel. The matter may be compared to the case of a king, who had a privy counselor, and he would do nothing without his express approval (*Parashah* 8:3, *Otsrot Yisra'el* n.p.; *Genesis Rabbah* 76).	*Let us make man.* We learn from here about the humility of the Holy One, blessed be He, since man is in the image of the angels and they might envy him, therefore He took counsel with them....Although they [the angels] did not assist Him in forming him [the man] and although there is opportunity [because of the plural form] for the sectarians [heretics] to rebel [argue in favor of their own views], yet the passage does not refrain from teaching proper conduct and the virtue of humility, namely, that the greater should consult, and take permission from the lesser; for had it been written, "I shall make man," we could not, then, have learned that He spoke to His judicial council but to Himself (*Biblia Rabbinica* 1:16; *Pentateuch, Genesis* 6–7).

sage from Part 1 of the sermon, entitled *"Oriens"* ("East"), Donne discusses where "this world beganne; the Creation was in the east" (*Sermons* 9:50). He writes therefore of the nature of God as creator:

> And therefore the Jewish Rabbins say that the Septuagint, the first translators of the Bible, did disguise some places of the Scriptures, in their translation, lest *Ptolomee* [Ptolemy II Philadelphus; 285–246 BCE],[17] for whom they translated it, should be scandalized with those places, and that this text was one of those places, which, (say they) though it be otherwise in the Copies of the Septuagint, which we have now, they translated *Faciam,* and not *Faciamus:* that God said here, *I* will make, in the singular, and not, Let *us* make man, in the plurall, lest that plurall word might have misled King *Ptolomee* to thinke, that the *Jews* had a plurall Religion, and worshipped divers Gods. So good an evidence doe they confesse this text to be, for some kinde of plurality in the Godhead.
>
> Here then God notified the Trinity; and here first, for though we accept an intimation of the Trinity, in the first line of the Bible, where *Moses* joynes a plurall name, *Elohim,* with a singular Verbe, *Bara;* and so in construction it is *Creavit dii,* Gods created heaven, and earth: yet besides that, that is rather a mysterious collection, then an evident conclusion of a plurality of Persons....God says, *Let us make man to our Image,* And could he say so to Angels? Are Angels and God all one? Or is that that is like an Angell, therefore like God? It was *Sua Ratio, Suum verbum, Sua sapientia,* says that Father [Saint Basil], God spake to his own word, and wisdome, to his own purpose, and goodnesse....
>
> If there were no more intended in this plural expression, *us,* but, (as some have conceived) that God spake here in the person of a Prince, and Soveraigne Lord, and therefore spake as Princes doe, in the plural, We command, and We forbid, yet Saint *Gregories* caution would justly fall upon it, *Reverenter pensandum est,* it requires a reverend consideration, if it be but so. For, God speakes so, like a King, in the plural, but seldome, but five times, (in my account) in all the Scriptures; and in all five, in cases of important consequence....
>
> So he speakes in our text; not onely as the Lord our King, intimating his providence, and administration; but as the Lord our maker, and then a maker so, as that he made us in a councell, *Faciamus,* Let us; and that that he speakes, as in councell, is another argu-

ment for reverence. For what interest, or freedome soever I have by his favour, with any Counseller of State; yet I should surely use another manner of behaviour towards him, at the Councell Table, then at his owne Table. So does there belong another manner of consideration to this plurality in God, to this meeting in Councell, to this intimation of a Trinity, then to those other actions in which God is presented to us, singly, as one God. (*Sermons* 9:57–60)

Donne joins the exegetical and theological debate by first citing the Greek Septuagint,[18] bringing to the attention of his auditory the story of its divinely inspired, yet polemically-fraught origin (table 34). In doing so, he not only draws them into that interchange among Jews, Greeks, and Christians marked out by Andrewes, but also raises a potent question about the reliability of biblical translations, a concern to which he returns often in his sermons. Thus, for example, in his sermon on Psalm 144:15, Donne evaluates the Septuagint, writing that that "which we call *Sinistram Interpretationem,* is that sense of these words, which arise from the first Translators of the Bible, the *Septuagint,* and those Fathers which followed them; which, though it bee not an ill way, is not the best, because it is not according to the letter" (*Sermons* 3:74). Donne quite correctly echoes the talmudic narrative,[19] which demonstrates the heightened awareness of the Septuagint translators concerning the need for self-censorship; thus they translate "we will make man" as "I shall make man" in order to remove support (as Rashi explains) from "the sects [that] heretically said that it was two powers" (commentary to Babylonian Talmud—see fig. 8).[20] Naturally Donne makes use of this narrative to establish the Jews' (reluctant) recognition of "plurality in the Godhead." Yet what is most intriguing is the way in which the talmudic passage interweaves divine inspiration and polemics—revealing, as it were, God's guidance ("placed advice") as the source for preserving the intended meaning of the biblical text within the dispute over Trinitarianism.

This has significant consequences for reading the subsequent passages in Donne's sermon, particularly his extended exegetical discussion of Genesis 1:1 and 1:26, in which he takes care

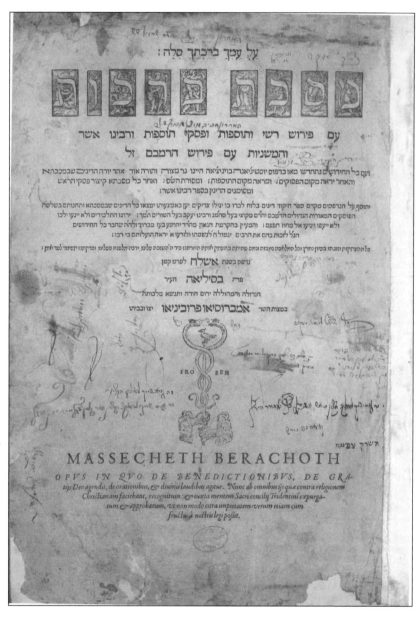

Fig. 8. Title page of *The Babylonian Talmud* (1578). Reproduced by permission of the National Library of Israel.

to instruct his royal auditory on the grammatical problems and the theological solution. Indeed, these passages are cited at length above because they reproduce the various, alternative answers to the grammatical problems cited in the Jewish exegetical tradition. Thus Donne proposes and readily disposes of the possibility of God speaking to angels, adapting Rashi's solution to present instead a God consulting with himself in the plurality of "his own word, and wisdome," of "his own purpose, and goodnesse." Subsequently, Donne brings forward the image of God as a King, raised in Genesis *Rabbah*, who (by speaking in the idiomatic "Royal Plurall") obligates a "reverend consideration" as a "prince, and Soveraigne Lord." Finally, Donne echoes Rashi's lesson about the "proper conduct and the virtue of humility," re-directing the Jewish exegete's lesson to include the King's subjects, who "should surely use another manner of behaviour towards him, at the Councell Table, then at his owne Table."

It is this more inclusive admonition that suggests Donne's own heightened awareness of a need for self-censorship in the King's presence. In these passages Donne is particularly diplomatic; following his difficulty with King Charles and Bishop Laud over his April 1627 sermon (on Mark 4:24),[21] he chooses on this occasion to employ a strategy that is described by Marla Lunderberg as presenting "an ideal which is aligned—for the most part—with a patron's ideals, voicing his own stance by adding to the patron's model something outside of the patron's ideal" (98). In this instance, it is the particular concept of a God creating "in Councell" that is added to the basic ideal of Trinitarianism. In fact, the theological concept takes on a decidedly political significance, as Donne applies Rashi's moral lesson to the contemporary seventeenth century debate about monarchical rule. Reflecting on the hermeneutic gap in the Hebrew Bible—Is God singular or multiple? Is the divine creation of man the act of God alone?—Donne transforms the Jewish-Christian polemics over this text into an admonition to King Charles and his subjects about the importance of consultation, conveying to his audience the same lesson which the various Jewish commentaries make available.

Despite his polemic tone, which he shares with Andrewes and Gibbens, Donne is intent on cautiously making use of an accessible exegetical tradition to unify a divisive, quarreling church and state. Establishing his authority as an educated and careful reader of the Bible, Donne ultimately turns this text into a subtle warning within the context of what Tom Cain perceives as his alarm at the "Arminians' almost mystic advocacy of the king's absolute power" (97).[22] Extending the discussion of the Prebend sermons, Donne on this later occasion not only makes this exegetical tradition transparent to his royal auditory—encouraging both him and his subjects to accept the preacher's homiletic authority—but also sets up the Trinitarian nature of God as a pattern for political behavior. Recognition of the complex exegetical tradition illustrates the particular way in which Donne responds to the equally complex political situation. Offering his auditory the common ground of Trinitarianism, he unifies his Christian auditory against the Jewish concept of God's nature, thus affording them the opportunity to take a cautious stand against the King's embattled Arminianism—a stand which is not only subtle, but almost incontrovertible in its appeal to both monarchic rule and parliamentary behavior based on a pattern of divine counsel. This sermon is indeed "an excellent example of Donne applying this Trinitarian theology within a particular historical/political situation" (Jeffrey Johnson 16), its rhetorical and theological effectiveness illuminated by situating Donne within the intertwined exegetical tradition that offers him the opportunity to evade the King's often censorious eye while arguing for a resolution of the explosive political situation.

Etymology of Names

In part 2 of this sermon on Genesis 1:26, entitled "*Occidens*" ("West"), Donne turns his attention to the nature of a "man that is but *Adam,* the Earth" (*Sermons* 9:61). He writes in *Essayes in Divinity* that "names are to instruct us, and express natures and essences" (27), thereby continuing a tradition reflected in the phrase from Genesis 2:7—***adam** 'afar min-ha-**adamah*** ("man, dust from the earth")—and evidenced in Jerome's etymological dictionary, *Liber Interpretationis Hebraicorum Nominum,* which demonstrates the belief that "there is a latent meaning in biblical names, which aids in understanding the deeds of those named" (Limor and Raz-Krakozkin 24). The significance of Hebrew biblical names clearly fascinates Donne, who saw that they could be used to great advantage in defining the nature of God—singular or plural (*Eloha/Elohim*), present or future (Jehovah/YHWH as "I Am That I Am," "I Am Who I Am," or "I Will Be What I Will Be")—as well as that of the various characters populating the biblical narrative in Genesis, such as "*Cain* [קַיִן], the first man, [who] had his name from possession [קָנִיתִי]; but the second, *Habel* [הֶבֶל] from vacuity, from vanity [הֶבֶל *havel*], from vanishing" (*Sermons* 3:50).[23] Moreover, Donne designates the inherent relationship between the divine and the human by explaining at the end of his second court sermon on Genesis 1:26 that "the *Cabalists* expresse our nearnesse to God, in that state, in that note, that the name of man, and the name of God, *Adam,* and *Jehovah,* in their numeral letters, are alike, and equall" (*Sermons* 9:89–90). His rare direct citing of the Kabbalah[24] is manifestly correct; for through an elaborate numerological calculation (*Gematria*), the numerical value of the Hebrew letters in "Adam" can indeed be considered equivalent to that of the names of the Hebrew letters in the Tetragrammaton.[25]

Donne shares this fascination with names with Lancelot Andrewes, as is readily apparent from the latter's discussion of the compound Hebrew name *Immanuel* (literally: *'im,* "with"; *nu,* "us"; el, "God"). In his 1614 Christmas sermon on Isaiah 7:14 ("Behold, a Virgine shall conceive and beare a Sonne, and shall call his name Immanuel"), "Preached before the KINGS MAJESTIE, at *White-hall*" (*XCVI Sermons* 72), Andrewes explains:

And, now, to look into the *Name*. It is compounded, and to be taken in peeces. First, into *Immanu*, and *El:* Of which, *El*, (the latter) is the more prinicpall by farr: for, *El* is GOD.... And, not GOD, every way; but (as the force of the word is) GOD, in His full strength and vertue: GOD, *cum plenitudine potestasis* (as we say) with all that ever He can do: And that is enough, I am sure.

For the other, *Immanu* [marginal note: *Immanu, Nobiscum:* wherein *Anu, Nobis*]: though *El* be the more principall, yet, I cannot tell, whether it, or *Immanu*, do more concerne us. For, as in *El*, is might: So, in *Immanu*, is our right, to His might, and to all He hath, or is worth: By that word, we hold; therefore, we to lay hold of it. The very standing of it, thus before; thus, in the first place, toucheth us somewhat. The first thing ever, that we look for, is *Nos, Nobis*, and *Noster* the Possessives: For, they do *mittere in possessionem*, put us in possession. We looke for it first; and lo, it stands heer first: *Nobiscum*, first; and then, *Deus*, after.

. . . .

This *Immanu* is a Compound againe: we may take it, in sunder, into *Nobis*, and *cum:* And so then we have three peeces.[1] *El*, the mighty GOD:[2] and *Anu*, we, poore we; (Poore indeed, if we have all the world beside, if we have not Him to be *with us;*)[3] And *Im*, which is *cum*, And that *cum*, in the midst betweene *nobis* and *Deus*, GOD and Us; to couple God and *us:* thereby to conveigh the things of one, to the other. (*XCVI Sermons* 75)

Noam Reisner has written of the third passage that the "religious metaphor behind this famous example of scriptural wordplay demonstrates the governing principle behind Andrewes' conception of sermons as liturgical copulatives...to bring man and God together through what is effectively a form of 'textual sacrament'" (673–74). This move from the etymology of the Hebrew name to the sermon's theology was more thoroughly developed in the two preceding passages, in which Andrewes makes available to his auditory issues of Hebrew etymology and grammar by transposing them onto Latin. In the first instance he unfolds the literal meaning of the term *El* by building upon the possible root of *El* as (*eiyal*) "power, strength" (Even-Shoshan 1:57; 1:70), writing of God "in His full strength and vertue...*cum plenitudine potestatis.*" In this Andrewes looks forward both to Minsheu's *Ductor in*

Linguas, which explains that the "grammarians *think that these words derive from the root,* איל ejal, *i.e. strength*" (217),[26] as well as to Donne's second Prebend sermon, which explains that "*Elohim* is *Deus fortis,* The mighty, The powerfull God" (*Sermons* 7:66).

The etymological and homonymic point is used (admittedly somewhat enigmatically) by both preachers to instruct their respective auditories in the divine attributes. Presenting a progressively custodial meaning of Latin words as respectively nominative (*Nos,* "we"), dative (*Nobis,* "to us") and possessive (*Noster,* "our/ours"), Andrewes's pedagogical tone establishes the semantic, theological lesson about the human claim to God's "might, and to all He hath, or is worth"—strengthened by his explanation of *anu* as the Latin dative *nobis.*[27] In these examples of a dedicated, perhaps somewhat dogged, focus on the grammatical and syntactical structure of the Hebrew name as possessing inherent meaning, Andrewes takes a step toward that Donnean iconic rendering of language (*ḥatah* as "withdrawne" from "straightness"; '*avon* as "crooked" and "pervert") as "something quite other than an incidental or a transparent system of notations...in short, substantial *res,* things opaque and self-sustaining" (Judith Anderson 191–92).

This concept of language is put to particularly good use in Donne's elaboration on the four names of man. In two passages, respectively from his Lincoln Inn's sermon on the Penitential Psalm 38:3 and the first sermon on Genesis 1:26, Donne designates the inherent misery of the human condition. Although they are very similar in content, these passages are quoted at length in order to clarify the different ways in which Donne adapts his Hebrew scholarship to different auditories and occasions:

> [Penitential Psalm 38:3]: In all those names that the Holy Ghost hath given man, he hath declared him miserable, for, *Adam,* (by which name God calls him, and Eve too [marginal note: Genesis 5:2])[28] signifies but *Redness,* but a *Blushing:* and whether we consider their low materials, it was but *earth,* or the *redness* of that

earth, as they stained it with their own blood, and the blood of all their posterity, and as they drew another more precious blood, the blood of the Messias upon it, every way *both* may be Adam, both may *blush*. So God called that pair, our first Parents, man in that root, *Adam:* But the first name, by which God called man in generall, *mankinde*, is Ish, *Therefore shall a man leave his Father, &* c. [marginal note: Genesis 2:24]. And *Ish*, is but *à sonitu, à rugitu:* Man hath his name from *crying*, and the occasion of crying, misery, testified in his entrance into the world, for he is born crying; and our very Laws presume, that if he be alive, he will cry, and if he be not heard cry, conclude him to be born dead. And where man is called *Gheber*, (as he is often) which is derived from *Greatness*, man is but great so, as that word signifies; it signifies a Giant, an *oppressour*, Great in power, and in a delight to doe great mischiefs upon others, or *Great*, as he is a *Great mark*, and easily hit by others. But man has a fourth name too in Scripture, *Enosh*, and that signifies nothing but *misery*. (*Sermons* 2:78–79)

[Gen. 1:26]: I remember foure names, by which man is often called in the Scriptures: and of those foure, three doe absolutely carry misery in their significations: Three to one against any man, that he is miserable. One name of Man is *Ish;* and that they derive *à Sonitu;* Man is but a voice, but a sound, but a noise, he begins the noise himselfe, when he comes crying into the world; and when he goes out, perchance friends celebrate, perchance enemies calumniate him, with a diverse voice, a diverse noise. A melancholique man, is but a groaning; a sportfull man, but a song; an active man, but a Trumpet; a mighty man, but a thunderclap: Every man but *Ish,* but a sound, but a noyse. Another name is *Enosh*. *Enosh* is meer Calamity, misery, depression. It is indeed most properly Oblivion. And so the word is most elegantly used by David, *Quid est homo?* where the name of man, is *Enosh* [marginal note: Psalm 8:4]: And so, that which we translate *What is man, that thou art mindefull of him?* is indeed, *What is forgetfulnesse, that thou shouldest remember it?* That thou shouldest thinke of that man, whom all the world hath forgotten? First, man is but a voice, but a sound. But because fame, and honour may come within that name of a sound, of a voice; therefore he is overtaken with another dampe: man is but oblivion: his fame, his name shall be forgotten. One name man hath, that hath some taste of greatnesse, and power in it, *Gheber*. And yet, I that am that man, says the Prophet, (for there that name of man Gheber is used) *I am the man, that hath seen affliction, by the rod of Gods wrath* [marginal note: Lamentations 3:1]. Man, *Ish*, is so miserable, as that he afflicts himselfe, cryes, and whines out his own time. And man, *Enosh*, so miserable, as that others afflict him, and bury him in ignominious oblivion; And man, that is *Gheber*, the greatest, and powerfullest of men, is yet but that man, that may possibly, nay that may justly see affliction by the rod of Gods wrath, and from *Gheber* be made *Adam*, which is the fourth name of man, indeed the first name of man, the name in this text, and the name to which every man must refer himselfe, and call himselfe by, Earth, and red Earth. (*Sermons* 9:61–62)

Each of these four names presents a different perspective on human nature, whereby "man is conceived as both strong and weak, as a member of the human race and of the family unit, and as an individual: *Adam* in the collective sense of 'men, human beings'; *Ish* as 'husband,' 'male,' 'individual'; *Gever* as an adult male; and *Enosh* as a collective denoting the human race, and as an antithesis to God connoting frail, mortal man" (Abrahams 446). Donne's particular application of these names stresses various psychological and theological meanings that are generated out of the words as that very "*res*, things opaque and self-sustaining." He accomplishes this by quite correctly developing various etymological relationships (tables 35 and 36): *adam*, formed from *adamah*, "earth" (with the Latin *homo/humo*, "human/humus," reproducing the Hebrew etymology) is, in Minsheu's explanation, "earthly, red or bloudie, from Hebrew Dam, i.e. blood"; *ish* is developed through what Evelyn Simpson describes as "probably some fancy etymology,"[29] which nonetheless is actually alluded to in Even-Shoshan's twenty-first century Hebrew dictionary which refers the reader to the root *ush*, "noise";[30] *gever* (echoed in Udall) is formed from the root *gvr*, "strong"; and *enosh* is formed (echoing Minsheu) from the root *anash*, "suffer from a desparate illness."[31]

Of primary interest is how Donne adapts his discussion of biblical names to the two different homiletic situations of Lincoln's

Table 35. Names of Man

Adam	Ish
209. *dictl. ab. Heb.* אדם Adam, *i. subrufus fuit, vel* אדמה Adamah, *i. rubra terra, ex quo illo formatus, sicut* homo ab humo…Adam, *the man*, i. earthly, red *or* bloudie, *ab Hebr.* דם Dam, *i. sanguis* (Minsheu. *Ductoris in Linguas* 14).	אִישׁ *ish* (Moabite and Phoenician אש ash, and in plural אשמ 'shm; Arabic: אֱנָשׁ *ins*, אֱנָשָׁן *insan*; Aramaic: אֱנָשׁ *enash*; close to אֱנוֹשׁ 'enosh; from which the regular plural: אֲנָשִׁים 'anashim; see also אוש *ush*). Man, human being (Even-Shoshan 1:65).
[The English noun Adam] is derived from Hebrew אדם, Adam, i.e., he was red, or אדמה Adamah, i.e., red earth, from which he was made, that is to say human from humus…Adam the man, i.e., earthly, red or bloudie, from Hebrew דם Dam, i.e., blood.	אוש *ush* (Aramaic: אֲוַשׁ *avash* "noise," "tumult") (Even-Shoshan 1:38).

Table 36. Names of Man

Gever	Enosh
גָּבַר He prevailed. גֶּבֶר A strongman (Udall, *Hebrue Dictionaire* 23).	Enos also has a meaning of its own, being in the Greek language interpreted "forgetful."…It is written at least in a certain prophet "What is man, that Thou art mindful of him? Or the son of man, that Thou visitest him?" [Ps. 8:4] For which the Hebrew, in the first naming of "man," contains the word "Enos": as if he said more plainly, "What is this forgetful one, that Thou, O God, rememberest him, forgetful though he is?" (Eusebius, book 11, chapter 6).
גֶּבֶר *gever* (See: גבר *gvr*; Aramaic: גְּבַר *gevar*, גַּבְרָא *gavra*); man, human being, male (Even-Shoshan 1:229).	
גבר *gvr* (Akkadian: gapru, "strong"; Aramaic: גְּבַר *gevar*; Arabic: גַ'בַּר *jabara*, "compel") (Even-Shoshan 1:229).	

Table 36 (*cont.*)

Gever	Enosh
	3766. Enosch, filius Seth, ut constat Geneseos quarto, à vitae miserijs & aerumnis nomen traxit; אנש Anasch, enim verbum doloris est, & significant aegrotare, morbo desperato laborare, hinc אנוש Enosch, & omnem etiam hominem significat utpote misereum, mortalem & brevis aevi, varijsque subjectum calamitatibus, vere ut cum Poeta dicamus. Eheu nos miseros quam totus homuncio nil est. Ab Enosch fit B. T. Mensch, i. homo, quasi ensch. ¶ Guich. Minsheu. (*Ductor in Linguas* 174).
	Enosch, son [of] Seth, according to Genesis 4, took his name from the miseries and pains of life; from *Anash*, which is in fact a verb of suffering, and it means to suffer from a desperate illness, so [therefore] *Enosh* means every man that it is miserable, mortal and short-lived, subject to many sorts of calamities, so that we say with the poet, "Alas, poor us, miserable man is nothing."[32] From Enosch it becomes B. [Belgick or Low Dutch] T. [Teutonick, German] Mensch, i.e., mensch like ensch. ¶ Guich].[33]

Inn and the Caroline court. As such, these passages can be set against two other sermons, namely those preached at the Jacobean court (in 1619) and at St. Dunstan's (between 1624 and 1631), in which Donne explains the biblical phrases *mi gever,* "what man" (Ps. 89:48) and *ani ha-gever,* "I am the man" (Lamen. 3:1). In these instances he organizes the names to compose a "hierarchy of terms for man, [that moves] from the least in dignity...to the highest [*Ishe, Adam, Enos, Gheber*]" (Nelson 209),[34] emphasizing, however, humankind's ultimate fate as being (in the words of the sermon on Lamen. 3:1) "thrown down into the pit of misery, and submitted to all afflictions" (*Sermons* 10:198). In the Lincoln's Inn and Court sermons, however, these lists (respectively: *Adam, Ish, Gheber, Enosh;* and *Ish, Enosh, Gheber, Adam*) comprise both a scholarly note and a dramatic aside by which the preacher draws his auditory into a more detailed consideration of the various legal, moral and existential implications of the biblical names.

Such implications are drawn directly out of the etymological meanings of these names. Donne indeed confirms the misery of humankind by playing on the lexical meaning of *gever* as "strong"; thus he explains in the first sermon that this name signifies "a delight to doe great mischiefs" or a *"Great mark"* for wounding, further explaining in the second that "the greatest, and powerfullest of men...may justly see affliction by the rod of Gods wrath." Citing Lamentations 3:1 in his sermon on Genesis 1:26, Donne invokes the authority of the biblical text; the first-person statement "I am the man [*gever*] that hath seen affliction" contributes a personal dimension to this tension between pride sustained by lexical meaning and its overturning by personal flaws and divine judgment. Furthermore, Donne's discussion of the name *Adam* reinforces this focus on humankind's ultimate misery. In both the Lincoln's Inn and Court sermons his explanation of the name *Adam* resonates with the combined meanings of *adamah,* "earth" and *dam,* "blood," to signify not only humankind's inherent lowly state (created from the "low materials" of the earth) but most notably its shame (expressed in the

"Redness" of "Blushing" and in the "red Earth") at the sin that
necessitated the sacrifice of the "Messias." Moreover, in its dual
meaning this name vividly brings to mind images of blood-soaked
earth, thereby sustaining its own essential, substantial signification of human nature.

What is even more fascinating is the way in which Donne develops meaning out of the two etymologically more complex names,
Ish and *Enosh*. In the first instance, Donne transforms a contemporary legal definition of life through his explanation of the name
ish. Certainly attuned to his auditory of lawyers at Lincoln's Inn,
Donne cites the law applied, for example, in Edward Coke's *The
First Part of the Institutes of the Lawes of England:* "And some
have said, that he shall not be tenant by the curtesie, unless the
childe which he hath by his wife be heard crie; for by the cry
it is proved that the child was born alive" (book 1, chapter 4,
p. 29a).[35] Drawing out the very substance of the name as "noise"
or "crying," Donne transposes this legal discussion onto both an
existential and moral plane, at once evoking the anxious moment
of birth and the subsequent relief upon hearing the child's cry, as
well as the misery of its inherent state of sin.

Turning once again to this name *ish* in his court sermon,
Donne on this occasion balances the scene of childbirth against
the deathbed scene so vividly evoked in "A Valediction Forbidding
Mourning" — "As vertuous men pass mildly away, / And whis-
per to their soules, to goe, / Whilst some of their sad friends doe
say, / The breath goes now, and some say, no" (*Poems* 42). In
doing so, Donne emphasizes the name's capacity to forge what
John Freccero has noted as "the association between breath-
ing and speaking and the importance of both as symbols of the
soul [which] are as old as the Bible" (358 n. 59), an association
deepened by Freccero's citing of *Targum Onkelos*'s interpretive
translation of Genesis 2:7.[36] For the *Targum* comments on the
biblical verse (God "breathed into his nostrils the breath of life;
and man became a living soule") as meaning God "breathed upon
his face the breath of life (*nishmita de-hayei*) and it became in

man a speaking spirit (*ruah memalela*)" (*Biblia Rabbinica* 1:17);
it is this connection that is reflected in and sharpened by Donne's
catalog, interweaving as it does psychological characteristics
("melancholique," "mighty") with particularly dramatic sounds
("groaning," "Trumpet," "thunderclap").

Finally, Donne takes special care in this court sermon to inter-
weave two alternative explanations for the name *Enosh:* the more
prevalent "meer Calamity, misery, depression" with the meaning
"Oblivion." Only a sophisticated auditory or reader of this sermon will recognize, however, the exegetical tradition underlying
Donne's preaching, a tradition that fully demonstrates the ongo-
ing desire by readers of the Bible to provide meanings for biblical
names. Thus the preacher's citing of two alternative translations
of Genesis 1:26 (*ma-enosh*, "What is man / What is forgetfulness")
distinctly echoes the explanation presented in the fourth century
Praeparatio Evangelica composed by Eusebius of Caesarea (table
36).[37] Moreover, as Steven Fraade and George Brooke have suggested, such a clarification of the name *Enosh* is to be considered
part of a "Jewish-Christian interpretive tradition" (Brooke 259) in
which attention to homonymous words enables a reader to provide (doubtful) inherent meanings for biblical names: either as
derived from the Aramaic verb *inshai*, "forget" (Jastrow 2:939);[38]
or derived from the Septuagint translation of Genesis 4:26—"And
he named his name Enos; this one hoped [ἤλπισεν, *êlpisen*] to call
upon the name of *the* Lord God" (*Apostolic Bible* 6)—by which
the Greek word *epilêsmon*, "forgetful," is read as a pun on (ἤλπισεν)
êlpisen, "hoped."[39]

To what use does Donne put this specific exegetical tradition?
He has previously introduced the list of names with the performative "I remember," thereby asserting in this illocutionary
act (Searle 65–68) his authority as biblical scholar and preacher.
Particularly in the case of the names *ish* and *enosh*, Donne uses
this authority to turn linguistic witticisms into a serious lesson
for his royal auditory on the ultimate vacuity of human existence;

drawing out lexical meaning into both metaphor and destiny, he writes of man as "but a voice, but a sound," adding that "his fame, his name shall be forgotten," and that others will "bury him in ignominious oblivion." Carefully couching his lesson within the considerations of biblical history and hermeneutics, Donne is thus able to instruct Charles I to deliberate not upon the political lesson set up in the previous, first sermon on Genesis 1:26, but rather upon the psychological and moral consequences to be drawn from the various names of man.

Conclusion

In its discussion of Donne's Christian Hebraism, this book quite fittingly opens and concludes with the English monarchy; these two episodes (Henry VIII's "Great Matter," Charles I and Arminianism) delineate that period which has been called the "pre-history of English Hebraic learning" and also demonstrate its interest in biblical exegesis and hermeneutics. The variety of issues raised here about Christian Hebraism—its highly inter-textual dimension, its extensive use of Jewish sources, its adaptation to distinct theological, cultural and political purposes and circumstances—retain significance for the modern reader of the Hebrew Bible. Indeed, a modern occasion highlights precisely this significance, and serves as a touchstone for the ways in which late twentieth century Jews and Christians respond to the biblical text.

This occasion was the 1995 "A Time of Healing" prayer service, convened a few days after the bombing of the Murrah Federal Building in Oklahoma City. Held in the very public space of the state fairgrounds arena, and covered in live television broadcasts, this service was necessarily addressed to a large, widespread and heterogeneous auditory. This aspect of the service is very much evident in the choice of speakers: state and federal officials were followed by various religious leaders. Standing in front of their auditory, many of these speakers chose to cite from the Bible, couching their attempts to solace within a shared religious and textual tradition.

Within this framework, what stands out is the distinctively different ways in which the Christian and Jewish speakers choose their biblical passages and adapt them to the public, official ceremony of mourning. President Clinton, like the other Christian speakers, cites from the Psalms to provide a deeply personal tone:

> this morning before [Hillary and I] got on the plane to come here, at the White House, we planted a tree in honor of the children of Oklahoma. It was a dogwood with its wonderful spring flower and its deep, enduring roots. It embodies the lesson of the Psalms—that the life of a good person is like a tree whose leaf does not wither [Ps. 1:3].[40]

This image of a personal hope and consolation is echoed by both Archbishop Eusebius J. Beltran and Reverent Billy Graham. The Archbishop has chosen to recite Psalm 23, which reads, "The Lord *is* my shepheard, I shall not want.... Yea though I walke through the valley of the shadowe of death, I will feare no evill: for thou *art* with me, in the presence of mine enemies," while the preacher cites Psalm 147:3, saying that God "heals the broken-hearted, He binds up the wounds. And so with this service today, we stand together to say: Let the healing begin!"

In his turn, Rabbi Packman highlights a communal ritual of mourning by citing from *Eikhah,* the book of Lamentations, which commemorates the ancient destructions of the Temple in Jerusalem. Striking a parallel, he says:

> But one city came back, in greater splendor, in greater holiness, in greater togetherness, and it was named Jerusalem. And so our city, our community, our Oklahoma City will come back—in greater closeness, with greater beauty, in greater love...."Restore us to yourself, O Lord, That we may be restored. Renew our days as of old" [Lamen. 5:21].

Traditionally read by Jews on the fast day of *Tisha Ba-Av* (the ninth day of the Jewish month of *Av*), the prayer service encompasses the individual's agony within a national prayer for renewal. This traditional Jewish reading of the book of Lamentations is further highlighted when juxtaposed with Donne's own response to this biblical text. For what Raymond-Jean Frontain says of Donne's poetic translation *The Lamentations of Jeremy* (Donne, *Poems* 372–86) points back to the Christian emphasis on the personal and the individual (rather than the Jewish emphasis on the communal); Frontain comments insightfully that "seventeenth-century divines emphasized that the individual can learn from Lamentations how to grieve and accept loss, and I suspect that it was in private devotional use that the text appealed to Donne most" (137).[41]

Understanding these unique ways in which a reader of the Hebrew Bible rewrites this text out of a specific religious tradition can therefore modulate a modern reader's engagement with Donne's preaching on the Hebrew Bible. As he navigates his way through his times and circumstances, Donne as Christian Hebraist adapts the Jewish exegetical tradition to his immediate theological and political concerns. The way from Henry VIII's "Great Matter," through the political tensions preceding the English civil war and finally to a contemporary American response to a terrorist attack is at once a loaded and fascinating one, which ultimately confirms and maintains the Hebrew Bible at the very vortex of responses to national as well as theological situations.

Appendix
Hebrew and Aramaic Texts

Introduction

דניאל. ה׳.ה״: בַּהּ שַׁעֲתָה נפקו (נְפַקָה) אֶצְבְּעָן דִּי יַד אֱנָשׁ וְכָתְבָן לָקֲבֵל נֶבְרַשְׁתָּא עַל גִּירָא דִּי כְתַל הֵיכְלָא דִּי מַלְכָּא וּמַלְכָּא חָזֵה פַּס יְדָא דִּי כָתְבָה

דניאל. ה׳.כ״ה-כ״ח: [כ״ה] וּדְנָה כְתָבָא דִּי רְשִׁים מְנֵא מְנֵא תְּקֵל וּפַרְסִין [כ״ו] דְּנָה פְּשַׁר מִלְתָא מְנֵא מְנָה אֱלָהָא מַלְכוּתָךְ וְהַשְׁלְמַהּ [כז] תְּקֵל תְּקִילְתָּ בְּמֹאזַנְיָא וְהִשְׁתְּכַחַתְּ חַסִּיר [כ״ח] פְּרֵס פְּרִיסַת מַלְכוּתָךְ וִיהִיבַת לְמָדַי וּפָרָס

חבקוק. ב׳.ב׳: וַיַּעֲנֵנִי יְהוָה וַיֹּאמֶר כְּתוֹב חָזוֹן וּבָאֵר עַל הַלֻּחוֹת לְמַעַן יָרוּץ קוֹרֵא בוֹ

Chapter One. Christian Hebraism: Sources and Strategies

בראשית ל״ח.ח׳: וַיֹּאמֶר יְהוּדָה לְאוֹנָן בֹּא אֶל אֵשֶׁת אָחִיךָ וְיַבֵּם אֹתָהּ וְהָקֵם זֶרַע לְאָחִיךָ
אבן עזרא: ויבם אותה. טעמו אחר שאתה יבמה הראה היבום וזהו בא אל אשת אחיך

ויקרא י״ח.ט״ז: עֶרְוַת אֵשֶׁת אָחִיךָ לֹא תְגַלֵּה עֶרְוַת אָחִיךָ הִוא

דברים כ״ה.ה׳: כִּי יֵשְׁבוּ אַחִים יַחְדָּו וּמֵת אַחַד מֵהֶם וּבֵן אֵין לוֹ לֹא תִהְיֶה אֵשֶׁת הַמֵּת הַחוּצָה לְאִישׁ זָר יְבָמָהּ יָבֹא עָלֶיהָ וּלְקָחָהּ לוֹ לְאִשָּׁה וְיִבְּמָהּ
אבן עזרא: כִּי יֵשְׁבוּ אַחִים יַחְדָּו. גם הם אמרו כי אינם אחים ממש כי אם קרובים והביאו ראיה מבועז ולא אמרו כלום כי אין שם זכר יבום כי אם גאולה ומה טעם להזכיר יחדו ואם הם היו במדינה אחת או בחצר אחד או שהיו אוהבים זה את זה ואמר כי הנה הכתוב אמר ויבמה וזה אות כי איננה יבמה כי אם בשם כמו שבה יבמתך והנה נואלו ונסכלו כי הנה מפורש בבני יהודה ויבם אותה והוא יבמה גם יבמתך בעבור היותן לשני אחים וכל איש ידע דעת כי המצות שנתנו למשה שהם מצות לא תעשה לא היו אסורות קודם לכן. ואילו היה אדם מונע עצמו מהן קודם משה לא היה הדבר רע בעיני השם אף כי שכתב כי את כל התועבות האל עשו אנשי הארץ אשר לפניכם

171

ולא מצאנו נביא שהזהירם והנה הכתוב אמר על אונן שלא נתן זרע לאחיו, וירע בעיני
ה' על כן אנחנו נסמוך על הקבלה שהם אחים ממש
ובן אין לו. כי אם יש לו בן אין צורך כי היא אסורה

רות א'.ט'ז': וַתֹּאמֶר הִנֵּה שָׁבָה יְבִמְתֵּךְ אֶל עַמָּהּ וְאֶל אֱלֹהֶיהָ שׁוּבִי אַחֲרֵי יְבִמְתֵּךְ
אבן עזרא : *שבה יבמתך* . מגזרת יבמה כבר פירשנוהו בתורה

ויקרא כ"ה.כ"ה': כִּי-יָמוּךְ אָחִיךָ וּמָכַר מֵאֲחֻזָּתוֹ וּבָא גֹאֲלוֹ הַקָּרֹב אֵלָיו וְגָאַל אֵת מִמְכַּר אָחִיו
תהילים נ"א.ט': תְּחַטְּאֵנִי בְאֵזוֹב וְאֶטְהָר תְּכַבְּסֵנִי וּמִשֶּׁלֶג אַלְבִּין

שמות י"ב.כ"ב: וּלְקַחְתֶּם אֲגֻדַּת אֵזוֹב וּטְבַלְתֶּם בַּדָּם אֲשֶׁר בַּסַּף וְהִגַּעְתֶּם אֶל הַמַּשְׁקוֹף
וְאֶל שְׁתֵּי הַמְּזוּזֹת מִן הַדָּם אֲשֶׁר בַּסָּף וְאַתֶּם לֹא תֵצְאוּ אִישׁ מִפֶּתַח בֵּיתוֹ עַד בֹּקֶר
אבן עזרא: [*אזוב*]. והגאון פי' האזוב בלשון ערבי זעת"ר ובלשון לעז אוריג"נ והוא
עשב נכבד במיני מטעמים. וזה לא יתכן, כי הכתוב אמר על האזוב אשר יצא בקיר
ולא ידעתי מהו

שמואל א' ז'.ו': וַיִּקָּבְצוּ מִצְפָּתָה וַיִּשְׁאֲבוּ מַיִם וַיִּשְׁפְּכוּ לִפְנֵי יְהוָה וַיָּצוּמוּ בַּיּוֹם הַהוּא וַיֹּאמְרוּ
שָׁם חָטָאנוּ לַיהוָה וַיִּשְׁפֹּט שְׁמוּאֵל אֶת בְּנֵי יִשְׂרָאֵל בַּמִּצְפָּה
תרגום יונתן: וְאִתְכְּנִישׁוּ לְמִצְפֵּי וּשְׁפִיכוּ לִבְּהוֹן בִּתְיוּבְתָּא כְּמַיָּא קֳדָם יְיָ וְצָמוּ בְּיוֹמָא הַהוּא
וַאֲמָרוּ תַּמָּן חַבְנָא קֳדָם יְיָ וְדָן שְׁמוּאֵל יַת בְּנֵי יִשְׂרָאֵל בְּמִצְפַּיָּא
רש"י: *וישאבו מים וישפכו.* תרגם יונתן ושפיכו לבהון בתיובתא כמיא קדם ה' ולפי
משמעו אינו אלא סימן הכנעה הרי אנו לפניך כמים הללו הנשפכין
רד"ק: *וישאבו מים וישפכו לפני ה'.* תרגום יונתן ושפיכו לבהון בתיובתא כמיא קדם ה'
ויתכן לפרש ששפכו מים לפני ה' סימן לכפרת עונות על דרך כמים עברו תזכור

שמות ד'.י"ג: וַיֹּאמֶר בִּי אֲדֹנָי שְׁלַח נָא בְּיַד תִּשְׁלָח.
רש"י: *ביד תשלח.* ביד מי שאתה רגיל לשלוח והוא אהרן ד"א ביד אחר ביד אחר שתרצה
לשלוח שאין סופי להכניסם לארץ ולהיות גואלם לעתיד יש לך שלוחים הרבה

איוב ט"ז.י"ח: אֶרֶץ אַל תְּכַסִּי דָמִי וְאַל יְהִי מָקוֹם לְזַעֲקָתִי
אבן עזרא: *ארץ אל תכסי דמי*. כמו און אם ראיתי בלבי לא ישמע ה' אכן שמע אלהים
ה' וכן ותפלתי זכה ואת ארץ אם אכזב אל תכסי דמי

משלי כ"ה.כ"ב: כִּי גֶחָלִים אַתָּה חֹתֶה עַל-רֹאשׁוֹ וַיהוָה יְשַׁלֶּם-לָךְ
אבן עזרא: *כי גחלים.* בזכרו המאכל והמשקה שנתת לו תשרפנו כאילו גחלים הבאת
על ראשו לשרפו וישמור מעשות לך רע
רלב"ג: *כי גחלים.* כי זה הענין קשה לו כאילו אתה חותה גחלים על ראשו לשרפו מרוב
בשתו על הטוב שיקבל ממך תחת הרעה אשר גמלך וה' ישלם לך טובה תחת הטובה
אשר גמלת אותו

Chapter Two. The Penitential Psalm 6: Notes and Margins

תהילים ו'.ה': שׁוּבָה יְהוָה חַלְּצָה נַפְשִׁי הוֹשִׁיעֵנִי לְמַעַן חַסְדֶּךָ
רש"י: *שובה ה'.* מחרונך
אבן עזרא: *שובה ה'.* שׁוּבָה - שישוב מחרון אפו

יחזקאל ט'.ד': וַיֹּאמֶר יְהוָה אֵלָו, עֲבֹר בְּתוֹךְ הָעִיר בְּתוֹךְ יְרוּשָׁלָ͏ם וְהִתְוִיתָ תָּו עַל-מִצְחוֹת
הָאֲנָשִׁים הַנֶּאֱנָחִים וְהַנֶּאֱנָקִים עַל כָּל-הַתּוֹעֵבוֹת הַנַּעֲשׂוֹת בְּתוֹכָהּ.

רד״ק: *והתוית תו*. ורבותינו ז״ל פי׳ תיו האות הנקראת תי״ו אמר לו הקדוש ברוך הוא לגבריאל כתוב על מצחן של צדיקים תי״ו של דיו ועל מצחן של רשעים תי״ו של דם

תהילים ו.ח׳: עָשְׁשָׁה מִכַּעַס עֵינִי עָתְקָה, בְּכָל-צוֹרְרָי

רש״י: *עששה*. ל׳ עששית עין שמאורה כהה ודומה לו כאלו הוא רואה דרך זכוכית שכנגד עיניו ומנחם פירשו לשון רקבון כמו ועצמי עששו וכן כל לשון עש

אבן עזרא: *עששה*. מגזרת עש יאכלם

רד״ק: *עששה*. מגזרת עש יאכלם כאילו אמר רקבה

ישעיהו נ׳.ט׳: הֵן אֲדֹנָי יְהוָה יַעֲזָר-לִי, מִי-הוּא יַרְשִׁיעֵנִי הֵן כֻּלָּם כַּבֶּגֶד יִבְלוּ עָשׁ יֹאכְלֵם

רש״י: *עש*. תולע׳ הבגדים

Chapter Three. The Penitential Psalm 32: The Sacred Philology of Sin

תהילים ק״ו.כ״ט-ל׳: וַיַּכְעִיסוּ בְּמַעַלְלֵיהֶם וַתִּפְרָץ בָּם מַגֵּפָה. וַיַּעֲמֹד פִּינְחָס וַיְפַלֵּל וַתֵּעָצַר הַמַּגֵּפָה

אבן עזרא [ל׳]: *ויעמד, ויפלל* עשה דין כמו עון פלילי

במדבר כ״ה.ז׳-ח׳: [ז] וַיַּרְא פִּינְחָס בֶּן אֶלְעָזָר בֶּן אַהֲרֹן הַכֹּהֵן וַיָּקָם מִתּוֹךְ הָעֵדָה וַיִּקַּח רֹמַח בְּיָדוֹ [ח׳] וַיָּבֹא אַחַר אִישׁ יִשְׂרָאֵל אֶל הַקֻּבָּה וַיִּדְקֹר אֶת שְׁנֵיהֶם אֵת אִישׁ יִשְׂרָאֵל וְאֶת הָאִשָּׁה אֶל קֳבָתָהּ וַתֵּעָצַר הַמַּגֵּפָה מֵעַל בְּנֵי יִשְׂרָאֵל

תהילים ל״ב.א׳: לְדָוִד מַשְׂכִּיל אַשְׁרֵי נְשׂוּי פֶּשַׁע כְּסוּי חֲטָאָה.

תהילים ל״ב. ב׳: אַשְׁרֵי אָדָם לֹא יַחְשֹׁב יְהוָה לוֹ עָוֹן וְאֵין בְּרוּחוֹ רְמִיָּה

רד״ק: *אשרי אדם לא יחשוב ה׳ לו עון*. כי זכר שלש מדרגות שהצדיקים הם בהן והחל במדרגה התחתונה והוא *נשוי פשע* והוא שחטא והעוה ועבר עבירות ואחר כן חזר בתשובה שלימה ונסלח לו. *כסוי חטאה* שיש לו זכיות וצדקות הרבה ואין לו כי אם חטא קטן והוא כסוי ואינו נראה בתוך צדקותיו דומה כמו גרעין דוחן בתוך סאה של חטים שמתכסה הגרעינה בהם שאינה נראית. *לא יחשוב ה׳ לו עון* זה שלא חטא כלל ואפילו על לבו לא עלה

בראשית ד׳.י״ג: וַיֹּאמֶר קַיִן אֶל יְהוֶה גָּדוֹל עֲוֹנִי מִנְּשֹׂא

רש״י: *גדול עוני מנשוא*. בתמיה, אתה טוען עליונים ותחתונים, ועוני אי אפשר לטעון

אבן עזרא: *גדול עוני מנשוא*. על דעת כל המפרשים שהודה חטאו ופי׳ נשוא כטעם סלוח כמו נושא עון ולפי דעתו שהעברים יקראו העקב שכר, והעונש הרע הבא בעבור העון חטאת וכן כי לא שלם עון האמורי אם יקרך עון ויגדל עון בת עמי והטעם כי זה העונש גדול לא אוכל לסבלו ויורה על אמיתת זה הפי׳ הפסוק הבא אחריו

תהילים ל״ב.ו׳: עַל זֹאת יִתְפַּלֵּל כָּל חָסִיד אֵלֶיךָ לְעֵת מְצֹא רַק לְשֵׁטֶף מַיִם רַבִּים אֵלָיו לֹא יַגִּיעוּ רש״י: *רק לשטף מים רבים אשר לא יגיעו אליו*. שלא יפול ביד האומות שהם כמים שוטפים וכן מצינו שהתפלל דוד על זאת ואמר נפלה נא ביד ה׳ כי רבים רחמיו וביד אדם אל אפולה

Chapter Four. The Literal Sense: Moralized Grammar

אבן עזרא: הקדמה לתורה

זה ספר היָשר לאברהם השָר, ובעבותות הדקדוק נקשר

ובעיני הדעת יכשר, וכל תומכו מאושר

…

הדרך החמישית, מוסד פירושי עליה אשית, והיא היָשרה בעיני, נכח פני ד', אשר
ממנה לבדו אירא, ולא אשא פנים בתורה, ואחפש היטיב דקדוק כל מלה בכל מאדי,
ואחר כן אפרשנה כפי אשר תשיג ידי

תהילים ל׳׳ח.ג׳: כִּי חִצֶּיךָ נִחֲתוּ בִי וַתִּנְחַת עָלַי יָדֶךָ

אבן עזרא: כי, נחתו. בנין נפעל כמו ננחתו מגזרת ותנח' עלי ידך והטעם תחלואים
ומכאובים כחצים

רד׳׳ק: כי חצִיך. החליים שהם כחצים. נחתו בי. מבנין נפעל משפטו בתשלומו ננחתו
ולולא החי׳׳ת שהיא גרונית היה נדגש כמו נצבו נגשו

תהילים צ׳׳א.ה׳: לֹא תִירָא מִפַּחַד לָיְלָה מֵחֵץ יָעוּף יוֹמָם

תרגום: לָא תִדְחַל מִן דְלוּחָה דְמַזִיקֵי דְאָזְלִין בְּלֵילְיָא מִן גִירְרָא דְמַלְאָךְ מוֹתָא דְשָׁרֵי בִּימָמָא

אבן עזרא: לא מפחד לילה. מקורו' לילה ולא מקורות היום שיעופו כחצים כאשר יפרש

תהילים צ׳׳א.ו׳: מִדֶּבֶר בָּאֹפֶל יַהֲלֹךְ מִקֶּטֶב יָשׁוּד צָהֳרָיִם

אבן עזרא: מדבר. כי רוב הדבר בלילה הוא אם היתה הסבה קור ואם מחום יהיה
ביום צהרים

איכה ג׳.י׳׳ג: הֵבִיא בְּכִלְיוֹתָי בְּנֵי אַשְׁפָּתוֹ

רש׳׳י: בני אשפתו. חצים שנותנין בתוך אשפה

אבן עזרא: אשפתו. דימה האשפה לבטן ההרה

איוב מ׳׳א.כ׳: לֹא יַבְרִיחֶנּוּ בֶן קָשֶׁת לְקַשׁ נֶהְפְּכוּ לוֹ אַבְנֵי קָלַע

רש׳׳י: לא יבריחנו בן קשת. לא יברח מפני בעל קשת

אבן עזרא: בן קשת. הוא החץ

תהילים ס׳׳ד.י׳׳א: וְיִתְהַלְלוּ כָּל יִשְׁרֵי לֵב

רש׳׳י: ויתהללו כל ישרי לב. יתפארו על יושר לבם וישתבחו בעצמם כי בטוחים הם
שהקב׳׳ה בעזרתם

שמואל א׳. כ׳׳ו. י׳׳ב: וַיִּקַּח דָּוִד אֶת-הַחֲנִית וְאֶת-צַפַּחַת הַמַּיִם, מֵרַאֲשֹׁתֵי שָׁאוּל, וַיֵּלְכוּ,
לָהֶם; וְאֵין רֹאֶה וְאֵין יוֹדֵעַ וְאֵין מֵקִיץ, כִּי כֻלָּם יְשֵׁנִים--כִּי תַּרְדֵּמַת יְהוָה, נָפְלָה עֲלֵיהֶם

רד׳׳ק כי תרדמת ה'. הסמיכות הוא לאחד משני פנים או פירושו תרדמה גדולה כי
הדבר שרוצה להגדילו סומך אותו לאל יתברך כמו מאפליה שלהבת יה כהררי אל עיר
גדולה לאלהים ותהי לחרדת אלהים או פירושו להודיע כי התרדמה היתה סבה מאת
האל כדי שלא ירגישו בדוד ובאבישי בקחתם הצפחת והחנית

Chapter Five. The Literal Sense: Genesis

בְּרֵאשִׁית א׳.א׳: בְּרֵאשִׁית בָּרָא אֱלֹהִים אֵת הַשָּׁמַיִם וְאֵת הָאָרֶץ
תלמוד בבלי מסכת מגילה [דף ט׳ עמוד א׳]: מעשה בתלמי המלך שכינס שבעים
ושנים זקנים, והכניסן בשבעים ושנים בתים, ולא גילה להם על מה הכינסן. ונכנס אצל
כל אחד ואחד ואמר להם: כתבו לי תורת משה רבכם. נתן הקדוש ברוך הוא בלב כל
אחד ואחד עצה, והסכימו כולן לדעת אחת וכתבו לו...אעשה אדם בצלם ובדמות
אבן עזרא: אלהים. אחר שמצאנו אלוה ידענו כי אלהים לשון רבים ושרש זה מדרך
הלשון כי כל לשון יש לו דרך כבוד וכבוד לשון לועז, שיאמר הקטן לנכח הגדול לשון
רבים ובלשון ישמעאל דרך שידבר הגדול כמו המלך בלשון רבים. ובלשון הקדש
דרך כבוד לומר על הגדול לשון רבים כמו אדנים ובעלים

בְּרֵאשִׁית א׳.כ׳ו׳: וַיֹּאמֶר אֱלֹהִים נַעֲשֶׂה אָדָם בְּצַלְמֵנוּ כִּדְמוּתֵנוּ וְיִרְדּוּ בִדְגַת הַיָּם וּבְעוֹף
הַשָּׁמַיִם וּבַבְּהֵמָה וּבְכָל הָאָרֶץ וּבְכָל הָרֶמֶשׂ הָרֹמֵשׂ עַל הָאָרֶץ
בראשית רבה [פרשה ח׳.ג׳]. וַיֹּאמֶר אלהים נעשה אדם. במי נמלך רבי יהושע בשם
ר׳ לוי אמר במלאכת השמים והארץ נמלך משל למלך שהיו לו ב׳ סנקליטים ולא היה
עושה דבר חוץ מדעתן, רבי שמואל בר נחמן אמר במעשה כל יום ויום נמלך, משל
למלך שהיה לו סנקתדרון ולא היה עושה דבר חוץ מדעתו
רש״י: נעשה אדם. ענותנותו של הקב״ה למדנו מכאן לפי שהאדם בדמות המלאכים
ויתקנאו בו לפיכך נמלך בהם וכשהוא דן את המלכים הוא נמלך בפמליא שלו שכן
מצינו באחאב שאמר לו מיכה ראיתי את ה׳ יושב על כסאו וכל צבא השמים עומד עליו
מימינו ומשמאלו וכי יש ימין ושמאל לפניו אלא אלו מימינים לזכות ואלו משמאילין
לחובה. וכן בגזרת עירין פתגמא ובמאמר קדישין שאלתא אף כאן בפמליא שלו נמלך
ונטל רשות, אמר להם יש בעליונים כדמותי אם אין בתחתונים כדמותי הרי יש קנאה
במעשה בראשית
נעשה אדם. אף על פי שלא סייעוהו ביצירתו ויש מקום למינים לרדות לא נמנע הכתוב
מללמד דרך ארץ ומדת ענוה שיהא הגדול נמלך ונוטל רשות מן הקטן ואם כתב
אעשה אדם לא למדנו שיהא מדבר עם בית דינו אלא עם עצמו, ותשובת המינים כתב
בצדו ויברא אלהים את האדם ולא כתב ויבראו

Notes

Notes to Introduction

1. The term "Chaldeans" designates members of an ethnic group that became the ruling class of the Neo-Babylonian Empire and southern Mesopotamia in the middle of the first millennium BCE. In the *Book of Daniel* this name "appears as a technical term for astrologers" (Anson Rainey, "Chaldea, Chaldeans").

2. The prophet Daniel explains this phrase as follows: "MENE, God hath numbered thy kingdome, and finished it. TEKEL, thou art weighed in the balances, and art found wanting. PERES, thy kingdome is divided, and given to the Medes and Persians" (Dan. 5:26–8). For his part, Donne develops this into the following explanation: "Thou art waighed, Thou art found too light, Thou art divided, separated from the face of God" (*Sermons* 5:361). For an explication of this Aramaic phrase, see Daniel Boyarin and Moshe Zeidner, "Mene, Mene, Tekel, U-farsin."

3. The citation from Habakkuk 2:2 is noted by Simpson and Potter in their edition. The two marginal notes on Daniel are not evident in the *XXVI Sermons*, but do appear in various manuscript versions (e.g., The St. Paul's Cathedral Manuscript; *Sermons* 3:410).

4. 1 Timothy 3:16 reads: "And without controversie, great is the mystery of godliness: God was manifest in the flesh, justified in the Spirit, seene of Angels, preached unto the Gentiles, beleeved on in the world, received up into glory."

5. Paul Stanwood suggests that "Donne probably preached a series on the penitential psalms, of which we possess only about one-half of the whole course" ("Donne's Earliest Sermons" 366). There is thus extant only a single sermon on Psalm 51, while no sermons on Psalms 102, 130 and 143 are extant.

6. Stanwood argues for the earlier dating ("Donne's Earliest Sermons"), while the emphasis on the parochial (re-)preaching is a recent contribution made by *The Oxford Edition of the Sermons of John Donne.* The discussion of these particular sermons will appear in vol. 9, "Parochial Sermons: St. Dunstan's-in-the-West," ed. Arnold Hunt. During her long discussion (1913–62) concerning the dating of the series on the Penitential Psalm 6, Evelyn Simpson changed her mind at various times. Throughout, she accepts the 1628 dating from *LXXX Sermons* ("Preached to the King at White-hall, upon the occasion of the Fast April 5. 1628"; 535) for the sermon on verses 6:6–7. In the first phase (Spearing, "A Chronological Arrangement") Simpson uses this to date the entire series to 1627–1628. In the second phase (*A Study of the Prose Works* 1924, 1948), she dates the sermons on verses 6:1–5 between 1615 and 1619, based on intertextual connections with the (pre-1615) *Essayes in Divinity* (leaving the sermon on verses 6:8–10 undated). In the third and final phase (*Sermons:* 5:30; 6:1–2), she dates all the sermons (except for the one on verses 6:6–7) to 1623, based on intertextual connections with Donne's 1623 letter to Ker (following a letter from I. A. Shapiro; OSB MSS 90, Box 2, Folder 68; see also I. A. Shapiro, ("Donne's Sermon Dates" 55).

7. The first five sermons have been dated to the spring of 1618, while the final one has been tentatively redated to winter 1620. These datings are recent emendations (compare the dating of the final sermon in *Sermons* 2:13–14) suggested in the *Oxford Edition of the Sermons of John Donne.* The discussion of these particular sermons will appear in vol. 4, "Sermons Preached at the Inns of Court," ed. Emma Rhatigan.

8. This dating is a recent emendation suggested in the *Oxford Edition of the Sermons of John Donne.* The discussion of these particular sermons will appear in vol. 12, "Sermons Preached in St. Paul's Cathedral," ed. Mary Ann Lund.

9. The fifth sermon is undated in *LXXX Sermons;* Janel Mueller dates it between May and June of 1627 (*Donne's Prebend Sermons* 331–37), while Evelyn Simpson dates it between November and December of 1627 (*Sermons* 8:11).

10. Mueller acknowledges that "I owe much to Professor Coert Rylaarsdam of the Divinity School of the University of Chicago for his assistance with Donne's Hebrew" ("Preface" xi).

11. This essay was first published in 1913 under Simpson's birth name of Spearing, and then reprinted in revised form in both editions of *The Prose Works of John Donne* (1924, 340–55; 1948, 339–56). For further development of this argument, see also Spearing, "Donne's Sermons, and their Relation to his Poetry"; and Simpson, "The Biographical Value of Donne's Sermons."

12. Donne was installed as Dean on November 22, 1621; his resignation from his readership at Lincoln's Inn was recorded, however, only in early 1622 (David Colclough, "Donne, John"). In the Simpson and Potter edition Donne's ecclesiastical career is divided into: an early period, 1615 to 1621; a middle period, 1622 to mid-1627; and a final period, mid-1627 to 1631 (*Sermons* 8:33). Focusing on Donne's time at St. Paul's Cathedral, Janel Mueller proposes a different division: early years, late 1621 to late 1623; middle years, mid-1624 to mid-1627; late years, mid-1627 to March 1631 ("Introduction" 3, 58).

13. See Hugh Adlington, "Preaching the Holy Ghost: John Donne's Whitsunday Sermons"; Dayton Haskin, "John Donne and the Cultural Contradictions of Christmas"; Elizabeth Hodgson, *Gender and the Sacred Self in John Donne*; Jeffrey Johnson, *The Theology of John Donne*; Lindsay Mann, "Misogyny and Libertinism: Donne's Marriage Sermons"; Maria Salenius, "True Purification"; and Robert Whalen, "Sacramentalizing the Word."

14. For further discussion of the Christian tradition of the Penitential Psalms, see Eamon Duffy, *The Stripping of the Altars* (368–69); Roman Dubinski, "Donne's Holy Sonnets"; and Hannibal Hamlin, *Psalm Culture* (173–74).

15. For discussion of the Prebendary system and of Donne as Prebendary of Chiswick, see R. C. Bald, *John Donne* (389–405); and Jessopp, *John Donne* (141).

16. These two pairs are printed in succession in *Fifty Sermons*, and are considered to be part of a series of sermons that do not survive. For further discussion, see *Sermons* 2:39–42; *Sermons* 3:6–10; and Shami, "Squint-Eyed, Left-Handed."

17. For the dating of the sermons on 1 Timothy 1:15, see Peter McCullough, "Donne as Preacher at Court (184–85). The two sermons on Ecclesiastes 5:13–14 were printed in *XXVI Sermons* as two sermons but with only one number (No. 10); McCullough proposes that they were actually preached as "a two-part sermon on the same text on two different days" ("Donne as Preacher at Court" 185). Finally, McCullough dates the two sermons on Ezekiel 34:19 between 1622 and 1625 ("Donne as Preacher at Court" 186), that is during the reign of King James.

18. Throughout his sermons on the Penitential Psalm 6, Donne relates to the division of the psalmic text into three rhetorical and thematic parts, "Deprecatory, Postulatory and Gratulatory"; see *Sermons:* 5:329 (verse 6:1); 5:338 (verses 6:2–3); 5:364–65 (verses 6:4–5); 6:40–1 (verses 6:8–10); and 8:194 (verses 6:6–7). Regarding the Penitential Psalm 38, Donne divides the psalmic text into deprecatory (38:1) and postulatory prayers (38:21–22), and into the reasons for these prayers (in his sermon on verse 38:9): "intrinsecall, arisinge from consideration of

himself" (38:2–10); and "extrinsecall, in the behavior and disposition of others towards him (verses 11–20)" (*Sermons* 2:144); see also *Sermons* 2:51 (verse 38:2).

19. Throughout his sermons on the Penitential Psalm 32, Donne reiterates the meaning of its title, *maskil*, as meaning "giving instruction." See *Sermons* 9:251 (32:1–2); 9:274–75 (32:3–4); 9:350–51 (32:8); and 9:382 (32:9).

20. Donne reiterates this in subsequent sermons of the Prebend series. See *Sermons*: 7:51–52 (second Prebend, on verse 63:7); 7:237 (third Prebend, on verse 64:10); and 7:301 (fourth Prebend, on verse 65:5).

Notes to Chapter One

1. For discussion of Christian Hebraic scholarship in these Bibles, see David Daiches, *The King James Version*; Stanley Greenslade, "English Versions of the Bible"; Basil Hall, "Biblical Scholarship"; and G. Lloyd Jones, *The Discovery of Hebrew* (115–43).

2. For discussion of Hebraic scholarship in the Sidneian psalms, see Chanita Goodblatt, "High Holy Muse"; Theodore Steinberg, "The Sidneys and the Psalms"; and Seth Weiner, "Sidney and the Rabbis." For brief discussions of Hebraic scholarship in Andrewes's sermons, see Horton Davies, "Ten Characteristics" (116–17); and Noam Reisner, "Textual Sacraments" (673–76). For further discussion of this topic in other writers, see Sanford Budick, "Milton's Joban Phoenix"; Harold Fisch, "Hebraic Style" and *Jerusalem and Albion*; Noam Flinker, *The Song of Songs*; Jason Rosenblatt, *Torah and Law in Paradise Lost* and *Renaissance England's Chief Rabbi*; Jeffrey Shoulson, *Milton and the Rabbis*; and Golda Werman, *Milton and Midrash*.

3. The Complutensian Polyglot (*Biblia Sacra Polyglotta*) was printed in Alcalá de Henares, Spain, by the University of Complutum between 1514 and 1517, while the Antwerp or Royal Polyglot was printed between 1569 and 1584 and was partially funded by Philip II of Spain (hence the name). Each Polyglot contained the Hebrew text, the Vulgate, the Greek Septuagint with its Latin translation, and the *Targum* with its Latin translation. For discussion of these Polyglots, see Basil Hall, "Biblical Scholarship" (50–55); Katz, "The Prehistoric English Bible" (4–9, 23–24); and Pelikan, *The Reformation of the Bible* (109–10). Donne makes a direct reference to both of them in his sermon on Proverbs 25:16 (*Sermons* 3:232), calling the Antwerp or royal edition by the name "Kings" (Allen, "Dean Donne" 210, n. 2; Goodblatt, "Vetus"). He writes:

> In the sixt Chapter of this booke, when *Solomon* had sent us to the *Ant*, to learne wisedome, betweene the eight verse and the ninth, he sends us to another schoole, to the Bee: *Vade ad Apem &*

disce quomodo operationem venerabilem facit, "Goe to the Bee, and learne how reverend and mysterious a worke she workes." For, though S. *Hierome* acknowledge, that in his time, this verse was not in the Hebrew text, yet it hath ever been in many Copies of the Septuagint, and though it be now left out in the Complutense Bible, and that which they call the Kings, yet it is in that still, which they value above all, the Vatican. (*Sermons* 3:231–32)

4. The 1525 (second) *Biblia Rabbinica* became the *textus receptus,* "the standard form of the Masoretic text for subsequent scholarship by both Jews and Christians" (Pelikan, *The Reformation of the Bible* 106). The *Biblia Rabbinica* contains various rabbinic commentaries (hence the name), the *Masorah* (critical notes on the biblical text) and the *Targum.* For a discussion of Renaissance familiarity with the *Biblia Rabbinica,* as well as with the Masorah, see D. C. Allen, *Noah* (49–55); Martin Elsky, *Authorizing Speech* (134–37); and Fisch, "Hebraic Style." Both Allen ("Dean Donne" 219) and Simpson (*Sermons* 9:307 and 314) suggest that Donne read the *Biblia Rabbinica* in which these commentaries were readily found, but he himself makes no direct mention of this book.

5. Henry himself had originally been intended and educated for the Church (Gardiner xx n. 15). Abraham Woodhead elaborates: "For King *Henry* was designed by his Father for a Church-man: and during the life of his Elder Brother, was educated in Learning, and not unstudied in School Divinity. Lord *Herbert's Hist.* p. 2" (111). In this prior source, Edward Herbert writes: "His [Henry's] education was accurate, being destined (as a credible Author affirmes) to the Archbishoprick of *Canterbury,* during the life of his elder brother Prince *Arthur*" (2).

6. A series of tracts written by the hand of Henry or by his scholars— *Henricus Octavious* 1529, *Censuræ* or *Determinations* 1531, *A Glasse of the Truthe* 1532 — attempted to solve the King's problem (John Guy, "Thomas Cromwell" 153–58; Virginia Murphy, "Introduction"). They did so by raising a variety of legal and ecclesiastical issues, ranging from the legal status of Pope Julius II's original dispensation for Henry and Catherine to marry, to the force of Old Testament law after the gospel, to the status of Leviticus as divine or ecclesiastical law. For further discussion, see J. J. Scarisbrick, *Henry VIII* (164–65), Guy Bedouelle, "The Consultations of the Universities and Scholars" (23–24); David Katz, "Jewish Advocates" (19); and Jason Rosenblatt, "Hamlet" (35–36).

7. Using his modern knowledge of Jewish sources as well as of ancient Semitic languages, Chaim Cohen has proven that Ibn Ezra is indeed correct in his resolution of various philological and legal conundrums ("Biblical Institution"): the Deuteronomic *ahim* refers to biological brothers who naturally live together, rather than to the more general, alternative meaning of "kinsman, son of the same family or nation" (Even-Shoshan 1:43); *yevam* is the biological brother as brother-in-law;

and Boaz as kinsman does not participate in a Levirate marriage, but rather redeems the land of Elimelekh, Ruth's father-in-law and his kinsman (following Leviticus 25:25, which reads: "If thy brother be waxen poor, and hath sold away *some* of his possession, and if any of his kin come to redeem it, then shall he redeem that which his brother sold."

8. The Karaites were a Jewish sect which appeared in the middle of the ninth century, and which recognized "the Scriptures as the sole and direct source of law, to the exclusion of the Oral Law as it is embodied in the talmudic-rabbinic tradition" (Daniel Lasker, Eli Citonne and Haggai Ben-Shammai, "Karaites"). For discussion of the importance of Karaites for Reformation Protestants, see J. van den Berg, "Proto-Protestants"; Daniel Lasker, "Karaism and Christian Hebraism"; and Jeffrey Shoulson, *Milton and the Rabbis*.

9. In this argument, Henry relied on the authority of Robert Wakefield, the first salaried Hebrew lecturer at Cambridge University, who argued that "the true signification of the Hebrew word [*yevam*] was any near, male relative ('cousin' in the sixteenth-century sense)" (Rex, "Controversy" 173). For a discussion of Wakefield's knowledge of Hebrew, see G. Lloyd Jones, "Introduction."

10. Pope Julius II desired to preserve the dynastic continuity of Catholic Christendom by granting a dispensation for Henry and Catherine to marry — in his words, "that peace and harmony flourish between individual Christians and especially between Catholic Kings and Princes" (Cajetan, *Cajetan Responds* 177).

11. For discussion of this *Respublica Litterarum Sacrarum* as a "textual community" see Jeffrey Shoulson, "Proprietie in this Hebrew Poesy" (359–60); and Debora Shuger, *The Renaissance Bible* (13–17)].

12. This discussion of the medieval Jewish exegetes summarizes and integrates the following sources: "Ibn Ezra, Abraham: As Grammarian"; Avraham Grossman, "The School of Literal Jewish Exegesis"; Mayer Gruber, "Solomon ben Isaac"; Hailperin, *Rashi and the Christiam Scholars*; Frank Manuel, *The Broken Staff*; Erwin Rosenthal, "Rashi and the English Bible"; and Frank Talmage, "Apples of Gold."

13. Donne also makes mention in several places of "Rabbi Moses," known as Maimonides or Rambam (*Rabbi Moses ben Maimon*, 1135–1204). Unlike Rashi, Ibn Ezra and Kimhi, however, Maimonides "wrote no line by line commentary on the Bible" (Manuel 138), rather incorporating such commentary into his works. In her discussion of Donne's Spanish studies, Simpson cites his reference to Maimonides ("Donne's Spanish Authors" 184). Donne directly mentions Maimonides in several places: in the sermon on 2 Corinthians 4:6: "It is sufficiently expressed by *Rabbi Moses*, In *Creatione Dicta sunt voluntates*; In the act of Creation, the Will of GOD, was the Word of God" (*Sermons* 4:102); in the sermon on John 10:10:

There is *defatigatio in intellectualibus,* sayes the saddest and soundest of the Hebrew Rabbins [marginal note: R. Moses], the soule may be tired, as well as the body, and the understanding dazeled, as well as the eye. It is a good note of the same Rabbi, upon those words of Solomon, *fill not thy selfe with hony, lest thou vomit it* [marginal note: Proverbs 25.16], that it is not said, that if thou beest cloyd with it, thou maist be distasted, disaffected towards it after, but thou maist vomit it, and a vomit works so, as that it does not onely bring up that which was then, but that also which was formerly taken. (*Sermons* 9:134)

And again in the sermon on John 10:10: "yet it is a good peece of counsaile, which that Rabbi [marginal note: Moses] whom I named before, gives, *Ne redarguas ea falsitatis, de quorum contrariis nulla est demonstratio,* Be not apt to call any opinion false, or hereticall, or damnable, the contrary whereof cannot be evidently proved" (*Sermons* 9:139); and in the sermon on the Penitential Psalm 32:7: "*Thy Teachers shall not bee removed into a corner any more, but thine eye shall see thy Teachers* [marginal note: Esay 30.20], which in the Originall (as is appliably to our present purpose, noted by *Rabbi Moses*) is, *Non erunt Doctores tui alati,* Thy Teachers shall have no wings, They shall never flie from thee" (*Sermons* 9:348). Donne also refers to Maimonides in *Essayes in Divinity:* "*Rabbi Moses,* call'd the *Egyptian,* but a *Spaniard. A Mose ad Mosem non surrexit qualis Moses* [marginal note: Drus. in Not. ad nomen Tetra]" (13). This phrase is translated by Robert Wakefield as: "from Moses [the lawgiver] until [the time of] Moses there has been no one like Moses [Maimonides]" (*On the Three Languages* 190). Donne cites this adage from Johann Clemens Drusius's book, *Tetragrammata sive de Nomine Dei proprio quod Tetragrammata vocant* (Tetragrammaton: Which is to say concerning the proper name of God, which they call Tetragrammaton; 1604), which he owned (Keynes 268). For a discussion of this adage in Jewish sources, see Isadore Twersky, "The Figure of Maimonides."

14. For further discussion of John Dee, see Noam Flinker, "Odyssean Return"; G. Lloyd Jones, *The Discovery of Hebrew in Tudor England* (168–74); and Frances A. Yates, *The Occult Philosophy.* The two appendices (II and III) noted by Goldish are to be found in Jones, *The Discovery of Hebrew in Tudor England* (275–90).

15. Layfield worked at Westminster on Genesis to 2 Kings inclusive (Alfred Pollard, *Records of the English Bible* 49). Donne writes that I "aske you leave to make this which I am fain to call my good day, so much truly good, as to spend the rest of it with D. *Layfield,* who is, upon my summons, at this hour come to me" (*Letters* 171).

16. Donne writes that "Mr *Alabaster* hath got of the King the Deans best Living" (*Letters* 168); Bald suggests that Donne "could have known

him ever since 1596, when he had been Essex's chaplain on the Cadiz expedition" (282).

17. Allen uses this term in a letter to Simpson, dated January 27, 1949 (OSB MSS 90, Box 1, Folder 1), in which he writes about his own oversight of Hebrew words.

18. Certain aspects of this indexing have been upgraded through computer technology, and are available in the online collection of Donne's sermons (http://www.lib.byu.edu/donne).

19. Despite her painstaking work in compiling the "List of Hebrew Words on Which Donne Comments in the Sermons" (*Sermons* 10:329–44), Simpson does miss various entries, for example, Donne's reference to the Hebrew word *kevosim* as a homonymic term for "lambs" and "clean clothes" (Goodblatt, "Intertextual Discourse" 33–34). Other missed entries include: "We read [Judg. 20:16] that in the Tribe of Benjamin [בְּנְיָמִין] which is, by interpretation *Filius dextræ*, The Son of the right hand" (*Sermons* 6:114); "But the true roote of the word mercy, through all the Prophets, is *Racham* [רְחַם]" (*Sermons* 6:170); "The word which Solomon uses there [Ecclesiastes 10:20] is Iadang [יָדַע]" (*Sermons* 7:408); "*They wept,* sayes the text, there was their present remedy; and they called the name of the place *Bochim,* Teares [בְּכִים; Judges 2:5], that there might be a permanent testimony of that expressing of their repentance" (*Sermons* 8:200); "Those Translators use that word for *Napal* [נָפַל]. *Napal* is *Ruere, Postrare,* to throw down, to deject our selves, to admit any undervalue, any exinanition, any evacuation of our selves, so we may advance this great work. *I fell down before the Lord,* says *Moses* of himself [Deut. 9:18]" (*Sermons* 10:123); "the *word* (the word is *Nasang* [נָסַע]) signifies but a *journey* [Exod. 17:1]" (*Sermons* 10:234).

20. Rev. Professor D. C. Simpson (1883–1955) was Reader in Semitic Languages and Old Testament, Oriel Professor of Interpretation of Holy Scriptures, and Fellow of Oriel College, Oxford. He was the author of *Pentateuchal Studies* (1914) and *Pentateuchal Criticism* (1924), as well as editor of *The Psalmist Essays* (1926).

21. This essay is particularly important, presaging as it does Eugene Kintgen's important study of *Reading in Tudor England*, published more than 50 years later. For both Kintgen and Allen are interested in designating the "underlying interpretive strategies" of "reading in a religious setting" (Kintgen 105), emphasizing aspects of multiple significations, analysis of elements such as grammar and syntax, and comparative semantics or intertextuality (Allen 212–13; Kintgen 99–139).

22. D. C. Allen subsequently states that "in slightly more than a hundred places, Donne refers to the Hebrew Bible" (212). In her more inclusive "Report of Work Done on *The Sermons of John Donne* from June 1 to December 1, 1958" (as she edited this twentieth century, ten-volume edition) Simpson writes that: "We have concluded that Donne took much

more interest in Hebrew than in Greek, and we have collected nearly two hundred passages in which he discusses the meaning of about a hundred and fifty Hebrew words" (OSB MSS 90, Box 3, Folder 78). Simpson somewhat rephrases this statement in her edition of the *Sermons*, when she writes, "Donne knew a certain amount of Hebrew, and made use of it in approximately 140 passages of his *Sermons*" (*Sermons* 10:306).

23. Anthony Grafton calls Allen (1904–1972) one of the "great individualists of an older generation" ("Colloquy Live"). Allen's knowledge of Hebrew is also demonstrated in his essay "Some Theories of the Growth and Origin of Language in Milton's Age," as well as in his book *The Legend of Noah*.

24. For further discussion, see the two essays by David Katz: "Babel Revers'd" and "The Language of Adam."

25. For further discussion see Bernard Casper, *An Introduction to Jewish Bible Commentary*; Chaim Cohen, "Elements of *Peshat*"; Avraham Grossman, "The School of Literal Jewish Exegesis"; and Elazar Touitou, "The Exegetical Method of Rashbam."

26. For another, highly interesting example of this tradition, see Anthony Grafton's demonstration (*Defenders* 126–28) that Joseph Justus Scaliger—one of the greatest Christian Hebraists of his time (Shuger, *Renaissance Bible* 34)—based the discussion about the dating of the Jewish New Year in his 1583 *Opus Novum de Emendatione Temporarum* not on the Babylonian Talmud, which is the original source, but rather on the 1527 work *Kalendarium Hebraicum* by the Christian Hebraist Sebastian Münster.

27. Donne donated his copy of this Bible to the Library of Lincoln's Inn when he resigned his Readership in February 1621/2 (Keynes 279; *Sermons* 2:2–3); he cites Lyre in various prose works, including the *Sermons*, *Biathanatos*, *Essayes in Divinity* and *Pseudo-Martyr* (*Sermons* 10:395).

28. In his sermon on John 14:2, Donne writes: "one Author [marginal note: Munster]...pronounces that Hell cannot possibly be above three thousand miles in compasse" (*Sermons* 7:137). In his sermon on Lamentations 4:20, Donne cites Santes Pagnino directly: "*The Spirit of God, sufflabat,* saith *Pagnins* translation" (*Sermons* 4:251).

29. See Evelyn Simpson's "List of Medieval and Renaissance Commentators and Controversialists Quoted by Donne in the Sermons and Other Main Prose Works" (*Sermons* 10:387–401).

30. For a more complete discussion of Donne's use of Christian Hebraism in this sermon, see Chanita Goodblatt's essays "Intertextual Discourse" and "Jewish Literal Meaning." This undated sermon is printed as number 64 in *LXXX Sermons*. It can tentatively be dated as having been preached on February 13, 1624, perhaps at Whitehall, thus forming part of one of Donne's series of Lenten sermons. This dating

is a recent conclusion reached in *The Oxford Edition of the Sermons of John Donne* (16 vols.), gen. ed. Peter McCullough, forthcoming from Oxford University Press. The discussion of this sermon will appear in volume 2, "Sermons Preached at the Jacobean Courts, 1619–1625," ed. Hugh Adlington.

31. This service was held before the principal Mass on Sundays and on holy or feast days. As Philip George explains, it had a two-fold significance: "First, it was used to cleanse metaphorically a new church or altar and to cleanse the church and altar before Mass. Second, it was used to remind parishioners of the waters of their baptism, helping them to recall in quiet meditation that in baptism Christ had cleansed them from their inherited sin" (15).

32. The term *Rabbin* is the English plural equivalent of the Aramaic word *Rabban*, "Rabbi, teacher," particularly used in Palestine in the first and second centuries.

33. Donne writes, "In this doe S. *Ambrose,* and *Augustine,* and *Hierome* agree, that Hyssop hath vertue in it proper for the lungs, in which part, as it is the furnace of breath, they place the seat of pride and opposition against the Truth" (*Sermons* 5:308).

34. Ibn Ezra writes this commentary on Exodus 12:22: "And ye shall take a bunch of hysope, and dip it in the blood that *is* in the bason, and strike the lintel and the two side postes with the blood that is in the bason." Donne himself refers to this passage in subsequent lines of his sermon (*Sermons* 5:309). Sa`adiah Ga'on (882–942), cited by Ibn Ezra, was the first to write a Hebrew grammar and dictionary, and so "introduced philology as a definite department of rabbinic scholarship and established a new method of Bible-study based on accurate scientific investigation of the text" (Casper 45).

35. Matthiolus was the author of one of the most widely read books on botany, *Commentarii in Sex Libros Pedacii Dioscorides* (Rhodus, "Mattioli").

36. Donne owned a copy of the first, 1617 edition of Minsheu's dictionary. See Minsheu, *Catalogue,* where Donne's name is listed as "Doctor *Dunne* Chaplaine *to the K Majest*" (1); and Geoffrey Keynes's *Bibliography,* which lists the book as item number L123 (272).

37. Both Paul Stanwood ("Donne's Earliest Sermons") and I. A. Shapiro ("Sermon Dates") posit an early dating (1616–22) and venue (Lincoln's Inn), arguing that the first 64 lines as well as the last 40 lines of this text were composed specifically for the occasion of the Fast, and most probably attached to an earlier sermon preached on Psalm 6:6–7. As Jeffrey Johnson writes, this posited re-use of the sermon makes it, however, "no less poignant or applicable for this historical moment" (*The Theology of John Donne* 50–51 n. 35).

38. There are three versions of the *Targum* (literally meaning "translation"): *Targum* (attributed to) *Onkelos* on the first part of the Hebrew Bible, the Pentateuch; *Targum Jonathan* (attributed to Jonathan ben Uzziel) written on the second part of the Hebrew Bible, the Prophets; and *Targum*, written on the third part of the Hebrew Bible, the Hagiographa. The final redaction of these versions was made beginning in the fifth century CE. For further discussion of the various editions of the *Targum*, see Bernard Grossfeld and S. David Sperling, "Bible. Aramaic: The *Targumim*."

39. For a discussion of the move from the spoken to the written sermon, see John Sparrow's essay, "John Donne and Contemporary Preachers," as well as David Edwards's comment that "it seems probable that this scholarly apparatus was enlarged when he wrote out sermons for the printer, but equally probable that he took not a few quotations with him into the pulpit" (302). For further discussion of Donne's preparation of his sermons for publication, see *Sermons* 1:46–47; and Stanwood, "John Donne's Sermon Notes" 75–76.

40. For a general discussion of Donne's use of the *Targum*, see *Sermons* 10:312–14.

41. Dr. Rabbi Israel Otto Lehman (1912–2001) was a German-educated scholar who worked at Oxford University after leaving Germany and before moving to Hebrew Union College in Cincinnati; "his knowledge of philology, linguistics and manuscript orthography was stunning" ("Texas Christian University"). I would like to thank Michael Segal for his assistance in obtaining this information. In a letter to Mabel Potter (George Potter's widow) dated May 8, 1956, Evelyn Simpson explains:

> After much consultation with theological professors in Oxford, Nab. Oziel has been run to earth by Professor C. A. Simpson who consulted a certain Rabbi Lehmann, who says that he must be "Rabbi Uzziel, i.e. the Targum Jonathan ben Uzziel." He thinks that Donne used the Targum on 1 Sam. 7.6 through Nicholas de Lyra on 1 Reg. 7.4 (Vulg.), who explains: "hoc fecerunt in signum humiliationis.... Jonathan filius Oziel maximae reputationis apud Hebraeos, hoc exponit de conversione cordium ad Deum, et sic per istas aquas intelliguntur lacrymae contritionis exeuntes a corde." This would have made a fine note, but as the book must have been printed off by now, I shall hope to include it in Vol. X, when I discuss the minor authorities used by Donne. (OSB MSS 90, Box 4, Folder 101)

42. As her daughter Mary Fleay attests, Evelyn Simpson "did not study the Hebrew language. She had access to Hebrew scholars at Oxford University & would have consulted them" (personal correspondence,

April 22, 2003); D. C. Simpson himself writes to Evelyn Simpson that "you are not a Hebraist" (OSB MSS 90, Box 2, Folder 69). Simpson therefore consulted several scholars on matters of Hebrew, specifically D. C. Simpson in the years 1949–55; Rev. Dr. C. A. Simpson, Dean of Christ Church, Oxford, in the years 1955–60; and Rev. J. R. Porter, Chaplain and Dean of Oriel College, Oxford, in the years 1960–1961 (*Sermons* 2:vi; *Sermons* 10:xi, 311–12; 329; Evelyn Simpson, letter of August 13, 1955, OSB MSS, Box 4, Folder 100; *Report on Donne's Sermons December 1, 1959 to June 1, 1960*; OSB MSS 90, Box 3, Folder 79). George Potter, the co-editor of the *Sermons*, also consulted with various Hebrew scholars: Walter J. Fischel of the University of California, Santa Cruz; William Popper of the University of California, Berkeley; Francis R. Johnson of Stanford University (*Sermons* 2:vi; Donne, *A Sermon Preached* vi); and Henry L. F. Lutz of the University of California, Berkeley (George Potter's letter to Evelyn Simpson, October 15, 1952; OSB MSS 90, Box 2, Folder 47).

43. Daiches asserts that "there is strong evidence for concluding that the Gen[eva] B[ible] translators were the first of the English translators to make considerable use at first hand of the Hebrew commentary of David Kimchi" (180). Greenslade, however, suggests that these translators "may have known him [Kimhi] only through Pagninus" (157). Daiches further explains about the translators of the King James Bible that Kimhi "was the only Jewish commentator whom they used continuously" (153) and that his commentary "was regarded by Christian scholars of the time as the work of the most competent of the Jewish grammarians and which consequently enjoyed tremendous prestige among them" (173). Donne mentions Kimhi directly only in *The Courtier's Library*, and then with a slightly changed name. This is in entry number 7 (cited from the most recent translation): "Peace in Jerusalem; or The Settlement of the most passionate disagreement between Rabbi Simeon Kimchi and Onkelos, On whether a human body composed (may God forbid) from the consumption of pig flesh will be put away, annihilated, or purified on the Resurrection, by the most enlighted Doctor Reuchlin" (Piers Brown, "Hac Ex Consilio" 861).

44. For discussion of the difference between simile and metaphor, see Joseph Glicksohn and Chanita Goodblatt, "Metaphor and Gestalt"; and Goodblatt and Glicksohn, "Metaphor Comprehension as Problem Solving."

45. The Franciscan Johann Wild (1497–1554), who was better known by his Latin name Ferus. He composed commentaries on nearly all the parts of the Hebrew Bible, as well as on the Gospels, the Acts, and several of the Epistles (Cleary; *Sermons* 10:393).

46. Donne mentions Rashi directly in two other places. The first instance is in *Essayes in Divinity*: "And *Jeremy*, as though they did not

else concur with God in his purpose to restore them to greatnesse, when they were in Babylon, sayes to them, *Nolite esse pauci Numero* [marginal note Jer. 29.6]. Upon this love of God, to see his people prosper, sayes *Rabbi Solomon, Ut homo habens peculium:* or, As a man which hath a Stock of cattell which he loves, reckons them every day, so doth God his people" (60); Rashi, however, did not write this commentary on Jeremiah 29:6, and so its source is not easily identifiable. The second instance is in the sermon on Psalm 2:12: "Amongst the Jews, *Rabbi Solomon* reads it [*nashqu-bar;* "Kisse the Sonne"], *Armamini disciplina, Arme your selves with knowledge* (*Sermons* 3:315).

47. This sermon is listed in the *LXXX Folio* as the first of a series of "Sermons Preached in Lent." Its dating is, however, somewhat problematic; see Simpson's discussion (*Sermons* 9:26–28).

48. Donne directly mentions Ibn Ezra in two other sermons. The first instance is in his sermon on 1 Timothy 3:16: "*Aben-Ezra*, and some Rabbins mistake this matter so much, as to deny that any person in the Old Testament ever speakes of himself in the plural number, *Nos, We*" (*Sermons* 3:221). Donne does not, however, cite the source from which he obtained this information. The second instance is in his sermon on Romans 12:20: "So much good God intends him in this phrase [*thou shalt heap coales of fire on his head;* Prov. 25:22], and so much good he intends us, that *si non incendant,* if these coales do not purge him, *si non injiciant pudorem,* if they do not kindle a shame in him" [marginal note: *Aben Ezra; Levi Gherson*]" (*Sermons* 3:387). In their commentaries on Proverbs 25:22, Ibn Ezra and the fourteenth century Jewish astronomer, philosopher and biblical commentator Levi ben Gershom (Touati and Goldstein) write (*Biblia Rabbinica* 4:179): "When he [your enemy] remembers the food and drink that you gave him, you will burn him as if you put coals on his head to burn him, and he will be careful not to do you harm" (Ibn Ezra); "This is a difficult matter for him, as if you heap coals on his head to burn him, because from his great shame over the goodness that he will receive from you in place of the evil that he caused you, and God will reward you with goodness for the goodness that you have done to him" (Levi ben Gershom).

49. Donne calls the *Targum* "the Chalde Paraphrase" due to the accepted, though mistaken, belief that the language spoken in Chaldea (southern Mesopotamia) in the days of the prophet Daniel was Aramaic (Rainey 562; *Sermons* 10:312).

50. Holtby notes the complicated relationship among Donne's sources in this passage, tracing out parallel passages in Donne's sermon, Bolduc's commentary and uncited commentaries on the book of Job by Lapide and the Spanish Jesuit Gasper Sanctius (Sanchez). Simpson explains in a letter (dated May 8, 1956) that the information about this passage arrived too late for printing with the sermon. This letter and the archival notes

(dated May 3–4, 1956) are to be found in OSB MSS 90, Box 1, Folder 22; OSB MSS 90, Box 4, Folder 101; and OSB MSS 90, Box. 5, Folder 121.

Notes to Chapter Two

1. This entry from Burley's manuscript volume is cited from Paul Stanwood, "John Donne's Sermon Notes" (79).

2. The single sermon that Burley heard on the Penitential Psalm 6:4–5 was published in *LXXX Sermons* as two separate texts (nos. 52 and 53). Burley also subsequently records lines from a sermon that Donne preached on Colossians 1:24.

3. The date of Burley's notes can well be taken as reflecting the practice of preaching the same sermon to different audiences (*Sermons* 10:408–09). This certainly applies to the sermon on Colossians 1:24, in consequence of the privileging of its Folio title, "Preached at Lincolns Inne" (*Fifty Sermons* 128) between 1616 and 1621. The parochial (re-) preaching (of a possible Lincoln's Inn series on the Penitential Psalm 6) will be emphasized in *The Oxford Edition of the Sermons of John Donne*, gen. ed. Peter McCullough, forthcoming from Oxford University Press.

4. I. A. Shapiro persuasively argues that Burley heard the sermons preached ("John Burley"); the alternative possibility raised by Stanwood that he copied directly from Donne's own sermon notes ("John Donne's Sermon Notes" 76–77) seems less likely. As to the venue of Donne's preaching, Stanwood ("John Donne's Sermon Notes" 76) and I. A. Shapiro ("John Burley's Notes") raise two possibilities: the chapel at Chelsea College, and the Chelsea parish church.

5. David Norton cites Donne's "explicit sense of delight in style" (150) over the Hebrew words *Iashabu* ("returne") and *Ieboshu* ("be ashamed"), while his discussion of the various meanings of word *Shamang* (*audit, Credit,* Affecting, Effecting or *Respondet,* Publication or *Divulgat*) intensifies those cited in Udall's *Hebrue Dictionaire*—"*He heard, he hearkened unto. . . . he convocated. . . . A hearing, a report*" (162).

6. In this instance, however, Donne's explanation is erroneous, for the final *heh* is here rather a sign of the long (or cohortative) imperative (Charles Augustus Briggs and Emilie Grace Briggs. *A Critical and Exegetical Commentary* 1:49).

7. Donne follows contemporary practice in his transliteration of the Hebrew guttural letter ע *ayin* as *ng* (*Sermons* 10:309, 329); see also Udall's explanation of the letter *ayin* as an "aspirated mute" that is pronounced "Gnain" (*Hebrue Grammar* 9). See, for example, Minsheu's entry: "6496. **Jesus,** *the name of our blessed saviour*...from Hebrew יֵשׁוּעַ jeschuang, to יָשַׁע jeschang, that is to say, salvation" (*Ductoris in Linguas* 376).

8. It seems that Donne is confusing the Hebrew roots פלל *pll* and פלג *plg*.

9. In Donne's introduction to his discussion of verse 6:1 ("O Lord, rebuke me not in Thine anger, neither chasten me in thy displeasure; cited in table 1) he directly mentions the Bibles he has consulted: "For the words themselves, all our three Translations retaine the two first words, to *Rebuke* and to *Chasten;* neither that which we call the *Bishops Bible* nor that which we call the *Geneva Bible,* and that which wee may call the *Kings,* depart from those two first words" (*Sermons* 5:332).

10. Donne also discusses this passage in his sermon on the Penitential Psalm 32:5. He writes: "*Those words, In multitudine virtutis tuae, Through the greatnesse of thy power, thine enemies shall submit* [marginal note: Psalm 66:3], S. *Jerome,* and the Septuagint before, and *Tremellius* after and all that binde themselves to the Hebrew letter, reade it thus, *Mentientur tibi inimici tui,* when thy power is shewed upon them, when thy hand lies upon them, *thine enemies will lie unto thee,* They will counterfait a confession, they will acknowledge some sins, but yet *operiunt,* they hide, they cover others" (*Sermons* 9:301).

11. This is one of "The Rules to be Observed in the Translation of the Bible," and complies directly with William Barlow's report of the 1604 Hampton Court Conference (of which Donne himself owed a copy; Geoffrey Keynes, *A Bibliography* 264): "Whereuppon his Highnesse [King James I] wished that some especiall paines shoulde bee taken in that behalfe for one uniforme translation...Marie, withall, hee gave this caveat (uppon a worde cast out by my Lorde of London) that no Marginall Notes shoulde bee added, having found in them which are annexed to the Geneva translation (which he saw in a Bible given him by an English lady) some Notes very partiall, untrue, seditious, and savouring too much of dangerous and trayterous conceites. As for example, the first chapter of Exodus and the nineteenth verse, where the marginall Note alloweth Disobedience unto Kings. And 2 Chro. 15.16. the note taxeth *Asa* for deposing his mother, only, & not killing her" (William Barlow, *The Summe and Substance of the Conference* 46–47).

12. For a discussion of this aspect of the *Essayes in Divinity,* see Michael Hall, "Searching and Not Finding"; Arthur Marotti, *John Donne: Coterie Poet,* 261–68.

13. Respectively: Galatin, *De Arcanis Catholicae Veritatis;* Drusius, *Tetragrammata sive de Nomine Dei proprio quod Tetragrammata Vocant;* Genebrard, *Eisagōgē...ad Legenda & Intelligenda Hebraeorum & Orientalium sine Punctis Scripta;* Rainolds, *De Romanae Ecclesiae Idolatria.*

14. *Essayes in Divinity* was published in 1651, 20 years after Donne's death, by his son. For discussion of the dating and publication of the *Essayes,* see Michael Hall, "Searching and Not Finding" (423); Clayon Lein, "John Donne" (129); and Anthony Raspa, "Introduction" (xvi–xxii).

15. Simpson also cites another, more general discussion of God's name that appears both in *Essayes in Divinity* (27–28) and in the sermon on verse 6:1 (*Sermons* 5:322–23), as well as the shared discussion of the Hebrew title צָפְנַת פַּעְנֵחַ *Tsafnat Pa'aneah*, "creator of life" (*Tanakh* 66) in the sermon on verse 6:4–5 (*Essayes in Divinity* 53; *Sermons* 5:378).

16. Donne's discussion of the philological and exegetical history of the Tetragrammaton is quite correct; for further discussion, see B. W. Anderson, "God, Names of"; and Louis Hartman and S. David Sperling, "God, Names of: YHWH." Donne also demonstrates interest in the three different names of God, as for example in his second Prebend sermon:

> The Names of God, which are most frequent in the Scriptures, are these three, *Elohim*, and *Adonai*, and *Jehovah*; and to assure us of his Power to deliver us, two of these three are Names of Power. *Elohim* is *Deus fortis*, The mighty, The powerfull God: And (which deserves a particular consideration) *Elohim* is a plurall Name; it is not *Deus fortis*, but *Dii fortes*, powerfull Gods. God is al kinde of Gods....The second Name of God, is a Name of power too, *Adonai*. For, *Adonai* is *Dominus*, the Lord, such a Lord, as is Lord and Propietary of all his creatures, and all creatures are his creatures....But then, his third Name, and Name which hee chooses to himselfe, and in the signification of which Name, hee employes *Moses*, for the reliefe of his people under Pharaoh, that Name *Jehovah*, is not a Name of Power, but onely of Essence, of Being, of Subsistence, and yet in the vertue of that Name, God relieved his people. (*Sermons* 7:66)

In this explanation Donne echoes Minsheu's *Ductor in Linguas* (217):

> 5445. *God.* L. *etiam* Jehóua, *ab Heb:* יהוה Joheueh, *ab* הוה hauah, *fuit.* Apocal. 1.4. ο ων και ο ην και ο ερχομενος, i. qui est, & qui erat, & qui venturus est. *Taliter autem appareat ex consonantibus* הוה huh *participium praesens,* הוה houeh, *ens,* & *tertia persona singularis praeteriti in conjugatione* kal, הוה hauah, i. *fuit,* & הוהי huhi *conficiant tertiam personam singularem futuri in* kal יהוה Joheueh, *erit....*Deus *quoque appellatur* אלוה Eloahh, אלוהים Elohim, & אל El. *Quas voces* Grammatici *derivant à radice* איל ejal, i. *fortitudo....Vocatur etiam* אדני Adonai, *Domini mei, ab* אדן edhen, i. *basis.* [Latin *also* Jehóua, *from Hebrew:* יהוה Jehouah, *from* הוה hauah, *was.* Apocalypse 1:4. *ho on kai, ho en kai, ho erchomenos,* i.e., "that is, and that was, and that who is to come." *Of such a kind appears from the consonants* הוה huh *present participle,* הוה houeh, *ing,* & (from) the third person singular of the past tense *in the (Hebrew verb) conjugation* kal, הוה hauah, i.e., *was,* & הוהי huhi *he will bring about the third person singular future*

in kal יהוה Joheueh, *he will be....* God *is also called* אלוה Elohah,
אלוהים Elohim, & אל El. The grammarians *think that these words
derive from the root,* איל ejal, *i.e., strength....He is also called* אדני
Adonai, *My Lord, from* אדן edhen, i.e., basis].

17. In his prose works, Donne cites Reuchlin in five different places:
in the two instances discussed in this chapter (in *Essayes in Divinity*
and in his sermon on verses 6:6–7); again in the *Essayes,* when he writes
(98) of "the Cabalists (as one which understood them well, observes)
[marginal note: Reuch. de Arte Cabal 1.1]"; in *Biathanatos,* "for, as one
notes, the serpent counseled, the woman helped, and Adam perpetrated
[marginal note: Reuchlin De verbo mirifico, li. 2, cap. 14]" (116); and in
The Courtier's Library (cited from the most recent translation): "7. Peace
in Jerusalem; or The Settlement of the most passionate disagreement
between Rabbi Simeon Kimchi and Onkelos, On whether a human body
composed (may God forbid) from the consumption of pig flesh will be put
away, annihilated, or purified on the Resurrection, by the most enlighted
Doctor Reuchlin" (Piers Brown, "Hac Ex Consilio" 861).

18. Both Simpson (*Essays in Divinity* 24) and Raspa (*Essayes in
Divinity* 137) correct Donne's citation, pointing to book 2 rather than
book 1.

19. For thought-provoking, though sparse, accounts of Donne's use
of the Kabbalah, see Philip Beitchman, *Alchemy of the Word* (126–27,
165); Joseph Blau, "The Diffusion of the Christian Interpretation of the
Cabala" (162); and Beth Newman, "John Donne and the Cabala."

20. Donne explicitly cites the form *hiph`il* in his sermon on Galatians
3:27: "But as it was in *Adams Clothing* there [marginal note: Genesis
3:21], so must it be in our spirituall putting on of Christ. The word used
there, *Labash,* doth not signifie that God cloathed *Adam,* nor that *Adam*
cloathed himselfe; but as the *Grammarians* call it, it is in *Hiphil* [*va-
yalbisheim*] and it signified *Induere fecit eos;* God caused them to be
cloathed, or God caused them to cloath themselves (*Sermons* 5:155).

21. As explained in *Gesenius' Hebrew Grammar* (116): "This simple
form is called *Qal* (קל light, because it has no formative additions). He
further explains that the "*meaning of Hiph`il* is primarily...causative
of *Qal,* e.g., יָצָא *to go forth,* Hiph. *to bring forth, to lead forth, to draw
forth*" (144). See the discussions on "God, Names of" by B. W. Anderson,
and by Louis Hartman and S. David Sperling, as well as the essay by
A. J. Maas, "Jehovah."

22. For a detailed discussion of Reuchlin's involvement in controversy over the use of Jewish books, see Erika Rummel, *The Case Against
Johann Reuchlin.*

23. The complete explanation of these annotations reads: "we have
also indevored bothe by the diligent reading of the best commentaries,

and also by the conference with the godly and learned brethren, to gather brief annotations upon all the hard places aswel for the understanding of suche wordes as are obscure, and for the declaration of the text, as for the application of the same as may moste apperteine to Gods glorie and editication of his Churche" ("To the Reader," *The [Geneva] Bible and Holy Scriptures* iiii[v]).

24. The marginal note in the Geneva Bible is marked by the sign ‖, which is explained thus: "Yet lest ether the simple shulde be discouraged, or the malicious have any occasion of just cavillation, seing some translations read after one sort, and some after another, whereas all may serve to good purpose and edification, we have in the margent noted that diversitie of speache or reading which may also seme agreeable to the mynde of the holy Gost and proper for our language with this marke ‖" ("To the Reader," *The [Geneva] Bible and Holy Scriptures*, iiii[r]). The marginal note in the King James Bible is marked by the sign †; in both the 1599 Geneva Bible and in the 1611 King James Bible this replaces the sign "which was used in the 1560 Geneva Bible, and which is explained as follows:" where as the Ebrewe speache semed hardly to agre with ours, we have noted it in the margent after this sort, "using that which was more intelligible" ("To the Reader," *The [Geneva] Bible and Holy Scriptures* iiii[r]).

25. Kimhi is quoting the Rabbis from the Babylonian Talmud: "For Rabbi Aha the son of Rabbi Hanina said... The Holy, blessed be He, said to the [the angel] Gabriel, 'Go and set a *tav* of ink upon the foreheads of the righteous, that the destroying angels may have no power over them, and a *tav* of blood upon the forehead of the wicked, that the destroying angels may have power over them'" (Tractate of *Shabbath*, p. 55, side 1; Soncino 253).

26. This term is taken from the Vulgate Bible, 6:8, *Turbatus est a furore oculus meus* (*Biblia Sacra Polyglotta.* n. pag.), which means "my eye is trubled for furie" (*The Holie [Doway] Bible* 2:24).

27. Rashi cites Menahem ben Saruq, a tenth century Spanish-Jewish grammarian, who composed the Hebrew dictionary *Mahberet Menahem*. See Angel Sáenz-Badillos, "Early Hebraists in Spain." Rashi has a similar commentary on Psalm 31:10, which reads: "'*asheshah*...is a cognate of [the noun] *'ashashit* 'lantern.' [The expression 'my eyes are wasted' refers to the situation] in which a person places a glass before his eyes to see something through the glass, [and] the appearance of that object is not clear" (*Rashi's Commentary* 293).

28. As the *OED* explains: "In early use the word moth seems to have been used for the larva of these insects [the clothes moth]. From the 16th cent. it primarily denoted the adult, and any similar nocturnal insect, often under the misapprehension that all such insects attack clothes. The true clothes moths are now included in the family Tineidae."

29. For a recent discussion of this issue see Clare Costley, "David, Bathsheba, and the Penitential Psalms."

Notes to Chapter Three

1. Simpson wrote this letter, dated February 22, 1958, to Mabel Potter, the widow of coeditor George Potter (OSB MSS 90, Box 4, Folder 102).

2. Shuger's discussion of "philosophical exegesis" in her book *The Renaissance Bible* is cited in Pelikan's chapter "Exegesis and Hermeneutics (23 n. 1). She has perceptively formulated the change in the philological method of biblical scholarship between the mid-fifteenth and mid-seventeenth centuries as a "crucial reorientation of exegesis from patristics to orientalism" (25); her subsequent comment explains that various "late Renaissance exegetes tend to view individual words less in terms of either theology or lexical meaning—the fixed relation between signifier and signified—than as elements in a culturally specific discursive system, whether the Hebraic penal code or ritual practice" (26–27).

3. As D. C. Allen acknowledges, "Donne's usual method of definition [of Hebrew words] may be best illustrated by his analysis of the Thirty-second Psalm" ("Dean Donne" 214).

4. See for example Daniel Doerksen, "Preaching Pastor"; Peter McCullough, "Donne and Andrewes"; Winfried Schleiner, *The Imagery of John Donne's Sermons* (182–89); and Joan Webber, "Celebration of Word and World in Lancelot Andrewes' Style."

5. In *Records of the English Bible*, Andrewes is listed as one of the group of scholars working at Westminster on the "*Penteteuchon*, The Story from *Joshua* to the first Book of *Chronicles*, exclusive" (Pollard 49). For further discussion, see the essays by Peter McCullough: "Andrewes, Lancelot" and *Sermons at Court* (147–55).

6. This sermon is printed in *XCVI Sermons* in a section entitled "Certaine Sermons Preached at Sundry Times, upon Several Occasions," which is numbered separately at the end of the volume.

7. The Bishops' Bible reads: "Thus they provoked him unto anger with their owne inventions: and the plague was great among them. Then stoode up Phinees, and prayed: and so the plague ceased" (*The Holie [Bishops'] Bible*. Thirde Part. xli[v]). The Geneva Bible reads: "Thus they provoked *him* unto angre with their owne inventions, and the plague brake in upon them. But Phinehás stode up, and executed judgement, and the plague was staied" ("The Olde Testament" 258r).

8. The Hebrew word תִּפְרָץ *tifrats* means literally "broke out" (*Tanakh* 1236), as it is translated (in parentheses) by the Geneva Bible. It does, however, also carry the connotation of "become great," explained by

Kimhi as "a great plague" (241). Though Andrewes takes care to set out the perceived ambiguity of this word, as well as of the Hebrew word תֵּעָצַר *tei'atsar*, "was ceased (or, stayed)," he does not discuss them in the sermon. In addition, subsequently in the sermon Andrewes also cites the Hebrew word *Deber*: "And indeed, the very name of the *Plague* doth tel us as much. For דֶּבֶר *Deber* in *hebrew* sheweth, there is a [דָּבָר] reason, there is a *cause*, why it commeth" (*XCVI Sermons* 161).

9. *Pi'el* is a verb form whose meaning is *"to busy oneself eagerly* with the action indicated by the stem. This [is an] intensifying of the idea of the stem" (*Gesenius' Hebrew Grammar* 141).

10. See also the sermon on the Penitential Psalm 32:8, "I will instruct thee [אַשְׂכִּילְךָ *askilkha*]": "the Originall there is somewhat more than our Translation reaches to; It is there, *Intelligere faciam te, I will make thee understand*" (*Sermons* 9:351). As in the phrase "an instruction [מַשְׂכִּיל *maskil*] to David," which opens the Penitential Psalm 32, this term can be understood in its causative verb form *Hiph'il*, as "imparting understanding" (Franz Delitzch, *Biblical Commentary* 1:394). Donne explicitly cites the form *hiph'il* in his sermon on Galatians 3:27: "But as it was in *Adams Clothing* there [marginal note: Genesis 3:21], so must it be in our spirituall putting on of Christ. The word used there, *Labash*, doth not signifie that God cloathed *Adam*, nor that *Adam* cloathed himselfe; but as the *Grammarians* call it, it is in *Hiphil* [וַיַּלְבִּשֵׁם *va-yalbisheim*] and it signified *Induere fecit eos*; God caused them to be cloathed, or God caused them to cloath themselves (*Sermons* 5:155).

11. Andrewes's attention to the particular circumstance of the pestilence certainly contributes to the relevance of this sermon, which is emphasized by its reprinting seven years later during the plague season of 1636 (*A Sermon of the Pestilence*). Andrewes had preached this sermon while residing in Chiswick, in retreat from the 1603 plague in London (David Hutt, "Sermon at Matins"). Furthermore, he very probably repreached an earlier version, published only in the 1657 *Apospasmatia Sacra*, which contains "the impressively full notes of over 100 sermons preached by Andrewes at St. Giles and St. Paul's between 1590 and 1601" (McCullough, "Introduction" xviii). These particular notes are included in the section entitled "Lectures Preached in the Parish Church of St. Giles without Cripple-gate London"; one can readily assume that the sermon on Psalm 106 was originally preached during the plague season of 1593.

12. It is interesting to note that the earlier (1593) St. Giles version confines itself to calling Phinehes a "Priest" (*Apospasmatia Sacra* 655); it reads: "First, *Phinehas* prayer, that is the prayer of the Priest.... The prayer of the just avails much, but especially of the elders and Priests.... So, then, the wrath of God will cease, if people cease to sinne; or if *Phinehas*, the *Magistrate*, begin to punish sinne in the people.... The wrath of God

for our sinnes being the cause of this plague, we must appease him with prayer and repentance. If we fail to do this, the devotions of the Priest, and the zeale of the Magistrate, must look to it, else the plague cannot but still increase" (*Apospasmatia Sacra* 655–56).

13. For further discussion of Andrewes's "gathering of various Scriptural elements" (315) see Peter McCullough, "Lancelot Andrewes and Language." I would like to thank McCullough for his assistance in correcting typescript errors in the marginal notes. These biblical passages read (*The [Geneva] Bible and Holy Scriptures*):

> 2 Corinthians 7:11: "For beholde, this thing that ye have bene godly sorie, what great care it hathe wroght in you: yea, what clearing of your selves: yea, *what* indignacion: yea, *what* feare: yea, *how* great desire: yea, *what* a zeale: yea, *what* punishment: in all things ye have shewed your selves, that ye are pure in this matter" ("The Newe Testament" 85r).

> 1 Corinthians 9:27: "But I beat downe my bodie, & bring it into subjection, lest by any meanes after that I have preached to other, I my self shulde be reproved" ("The New Testament" 79v);

> 1 Corinthians 11:31: "For if we wolde judge our selves, we shulde not be judged." ("The New Testament" 80v).

14. Not surprisingly, this pattern expresses the structure of the psalmic text itself, which has been conceived as moving from God's grace (32:1–2), to the confession of sin (32:3–5) and prayer for God's deliverance (32:6–7), and finally to instruction (32:8–10) and celebration (32:11). See particularly the nineteenth century scholar Franz Delitzsch's *Biblical Commentary* (1:392–400), and the twentieth century *International Critical Commentary* (1:276–84).

15. See John Chamberlin's of discussion these verses within the Christian tradition, which reads them as a move from "transgression" as original sin, to "sin" as actual venial sin, and finally to "iniquity" as actual mortal sin (146).

16. See chapter 2, note 26 regarding the transliteration of the Hebrew guttural letter ע *ayin* as *ng*.

17. The twenty-first century Hebrew dictionary by Even-Shoshan lists the root of *heit* as the Akkadian term *hatu* (2:543), while Strong's nineteenth century biblical dictionary explains that it is from "a primitive root; properly, to miss; hence (figuratively and generally) to sin" (entry 2398). Yet there is some basis for Donne's mistake; for the Hebrew term *natah* drops its initial letter *nun* in various verb conjugations (*Gesenius' Hebrew Grammar* 217).

18. For a discussion of Donne's indebtedness to Pererius's commentaries see *Sermons* 8:393–96, 10:367–69.

19. I would like to thank Graham Roebuck for calling my attention to this letter in his response to my paper presented at the 1997 John Donne Society Conference.

20. In this instance *Niph`al* comprises a reflexive form of *qal* (*Gesenius' Hebrew Grammar* 137).

21. The first four letters are addressed "To the worthiest Lady Mrs. Bridget White," the daughter of John White of Hampshire who married Sir Henry Kingsmill in 1610. When John Donne Jr. published his father's *Biathanatos* in 1647, he sent her a copy. See R. E. Bennett, "Donne's Letters" 133–34; and Ronald Fritze, "Kingsmill family."

22. This passage reads: "Those things which God dissolves at once, as he shall so the Sun, and Moon, and those bodies at the last conflagration, he never intends to reunite again; but in those things which he takes in pieces, as he doth man, and wife, in those divorces by death, and in single persons, by the divorce of body and soul, God hath another purpose to make them up again" (*Letters to Severall Persons of Honour* 7).

23. This is an important passage for Donne, as he returns to it throughout his sermons. For other examples, see his sermon on the Penitential Psalm 32:5: "The word is the same here, in *Davids* sweetnesse, as in *Cains* bitternesse, *Gnavon;* and we cannot tell whether *Cain* speake there [marginal note: Genesis 4:13] of a punishment too great to be borne, or a sin too great to be pardoned" (*Sermons* 9:313); on the Penitential Psalm 32:6: "For, *This,* as appears in the words immediately before the Text, is, *The forgiveness of the punishment, and of the iniquity of our sinne*" (*Sermons* 9:323); on the Penitential Psalm 32:10: "So they are great to them, as *Cains* punishment was to him, greater then he could beare, because he could not ease himself upon the consideration of Gods purpose, in laying that punishment upon him" (*Sermons* 9:396); on the Penitential Psalm 38:3: "When *Cain* says, *My sin is greater then can be forgiven* [marginal note: Genesis 4], that word *Gnavon* is ambiguous, it may be sinne, it may bee punishment, and wee know not whether his impatience grew out of the horrour of his sinne, or the weight of his punishment" (*Sermons* 2:88); on the Penitential Psalm 38:4: "for wee cannot tell by the construction and origination of the words, whether *Cain* said, *My sin is greater then can bee pardoned,* or, *my punishment is greater then can bee borne*" (*Sermons* 2:125); on Proverbs 22:11 (March 24, 1616/17): "And then, *Cains major iniquitas* (my sin is too great for God to forgive) is not worse than this *minor iniquitas,* My sin is too little for God to consider" (*Sermons* 1:189); the sermon on Isaiah 50:1 (February 24, 1625/6): "*Cain* cryes out, that his punishment is greater then he can beare" (*Sermons* 7:83); and the sermon on Genesis 1:26 (April 1629): "All Christian expositors read those words of *Cain, My sin is greater then can be pardoned,* positively; and so they are evident words of desperation. The Jews read them with an interrogation, *Are my sinnes greater, then*

can be pardoned? And so they are words of compunction, and repentance" (*Sermons* 9:71).

24. Andrewes became Dean of Westminster Abbey in 1601, and removed not only himself but also the Westminster School to Chiswick during the 1603 plague season (McCullough, "Lancelot Andrewes").

25. For further discussion of conceptual metaphors in Renaissance and early modern texts, see for example, Elizabeth Bradburn, "Bodily Metaphor"; Donald Freeman, "Catch[ing] the Nearest Way" and "The Rack Dislimns'"; and Mark Turner and Gilles Fauconnier, "A Mechanism of Creativity" (414–16).

26. D. C. Allen cites the reference to Lamentations ("Dean Donne" 215), in which the term *sakotah*, "cover'st," is used.

27. See also the following two sermons: (on John 11:21) "God hath made two Testaments, two Wills; And in both, he hath declared his Power, and his Will, to give this new life after death, in this world. To the Widows sonne of *Zarephtha*, he bequeaths new life; and to the Shunamites sonne, he gives the same legacy, in the Old Testament" (*Sermons* 7:258); (on Heb. 11:35) "The other example in this point, is that *Shunamite*, whose dead son restored to life. . . . that Mother, in the body of the Chapter, who having, by *Elisha's* prayers, obtained a Son of God, after she was past hope, and that Son being dead in her lap, in her also, (as in the former example) we may consider, how Passion and Faith may consist together" (*Sermons* 7:382).

28. Donne recognizes the significance of the Hebrew term for heavy, *tikhbad*, for he explains in two other sermons: on the Penitential Psalm 38:4, "In the Originall language, the same word, that is here, a burden, *Chabad*, signifies *honour* and *wealth*, as well as a *burden*" (*Sermons* 2:129); on Proverbs 14:31, "*Cabad*, this *honouring of God*. The word does properly signifie *Augere, Ampliare*, To enlarge God, to amplifie, to dilate God" (*Sermons* 8:288).

29. Isaiah reads literally: "For the waters of Dimon shalbe full of blood."

30. For a discussion of these various movements, see J. P. Kirsch, "Simonians"; and N. A. Weber, "Anabaptists" and "Waldenses." In his sermon on Revelation 1:17, for example, Donne explicitly mentions the Anabaptists: "Well, then, they to whom these waters belong, have Christ in his Church to lead them; and therefore they need not stay, till they can come *alone*; till they be of age and years of discretion, as the *Anabaptists* say" (*Sermons* 5:109).

31. Donne cites Augustine throughout his sermons (see the discussion in *Sermons* 10:376–86). He cites Cassiodorus in two sermons, namely those on Amos 5:18: "That clause which the Chancellors had in their Patents under the Romaine Emperours, *Ut praerogativam gerat conscientiae nostrae* [marginal note: Cassiodorus], is in our commis-

sion too, for God hath put his conscience into his Church" (*Sermons* 2:361); and on Romans 12:20: "(And then God does hunger and thirst, in this sense, in the members of his mysticall body,) neither is that onely intended in that place [Ps. 50:12] of the Psalme (though Cassiodore take it so) (*Sermons* 3:385).

Notes to Chapter Four

I would like to thank Eugene Hill for permission to use his phrase as the title of my chapter.

1. Tyndale's *The Pentateuch* was published in 1530. Regarding Tyndale's knowledge of Hebrew, see David Daniell, "Introduction" (xiii–xvii); Gerald Hammond, "William Tyndale's Pentateuch"; G. Lloyd Jones, *The Discovery of Hebrew* (115–23); and Dahlia Karpman, "William Tyndale's Response."

2. During the first five years of Hebrew printing (1475–80), the *Five Megillot* (Ruth, Song of Songs, Ecclesiastes, Lamentations and Esther) was printed in Bologna, containing the commentaries of both Rashi and Ibn Ezra. Ibn Ezra's *Commentaries on the Pentateuch* were first printed separately at Naples in 1488, and then were included in a 1522 edition of the Hebrew Bible, printed at Istanbul. For further discussion, see *The Bibliography of the Hebrew Book*; Joseph Cohen, "The Beginning of Hebrew Printing" (104–05); and Harris Fletcher, *Milton's Rabbinical Readings* (64).

3. Jones notes several possible sources for the Latin translations, specifically the sixteenth century Christian Hebraists Sebastian Münster, Santes Pagnino, and Leo Jud ("The Bridge Builders," in *The Discovery of Hebrew* 39–55).

4. David Daiches puts particular emphasis on Edward Lively (1545–1605), Regius Professor of Hebrew at Cambridge (*The King James Version* 144, 153). Jones discusses, for example, William Alley, Bishop of Exeter and a translator of the Bishops' Bible (1510/11–70), and John Rainolds (1549–1607), president of Corpus Christi College, Oxford, and a translator of the King James Bible (*The Discovery of Hebrew* 159–63).

5. In his study of *Milton's Rabbinical Readings*, Harris Fletcher suggests that there are echoes in Milton's *De Doctrinia Christiana* of Ibn Ezra's "Introduction" (61 n. 1; 62 n. 1). It is not clear, however, whether they came directly from the "Introduction" or from an intermediate Latin commentary (as suggested by Maurice Kelley, "Milton, Ibn Ezra, and Wollebius").

6. The essay itself is composed entirely in the "rhymed-prose fashionable among the Jewish and Muslim literati of the day" (Brener, *Judah Halevi* 29).

7. For further discussion, see Chaim Cohen, "Elements of *Peshat*"; and Uriel Simon, "Abraham Ibn Ezra." It is interesting to note that in his third Prebend Sermon, Donne correctly explains the dual meaning of the Hebrew word יָשָׁר *yashar*, found in the term *yishrei-leiv*, "the upright in heart": "For, the word of this Text, *Iashar* signifies *Rectitudinem* ["upright"], and *Planiciem* ["level"]; It signifies a direct way...the Angels way to heaven upon *Jacobs* ladder, was a straight, a direct way. And then it signifies, as a direct and straight, so a plaine, a smooth, and even way" (*Sermons* 7:244).

8. These "paths" are: the introduction of secular, foreign learning by the *Ge'onim* (heads of the Babylonian-Jewish academies during between the sixth to eleventh centuries), the rejection of rabbinic tradition by the Karaites, the adoption of Christian allegory, and the sole reliance on collections of Midrash (homiletic interpretations of the Bible). For further discussion of Ibn Ezra and of these different influences, see David Biale, "Exegesis and Philosophy in the Writings of Abraham Ibn Ezra"; Bernard Casper, *An Introduction to Jewish Bible Commentary* (68–69); and Irene Lancaster, *Deconstructing the Bible*.

9. This reference to Barthes is not fortuitous. For as Bruce Holsinger argues, "Barthes himself was preoccupied with the four levels of scripture and their critical implications for structuralist reading practices during the years immediately preceding the publication of *S/Z*"; consequently, a "concentrated preoccupation with medieval habits of mind inspired Barthes's working through of the 'multiple text'" ("The Four Senses" 167, 172).

10. For discussions of Donne's second Prebend sermon (on Ps. 63:7), acclaimed by Evelyn Simpson as "one of Donne's finest discourses" (*Sermons* 7:2), see Gale Carrithers, *Donne at Sermons* (160–67); Judith Anderson, *Words that Matter* (189–230); Winifred Crombie, "To Enter in These Bonds"; Paul Harland, "Dramatic Technique" (714–16); William Rooney, "Donne's 'Second Prebend Sermon'"; and Paul Stanwood, "Word and Sacrament" (44–45).

11. See also Donne's concern with time and tense in his sermon on the Penitential Psalm 32:7:

> That as God himselfe is eternall and cannot bee considered in the distinction of times, so hath that language in which God hath spoken in his written word, the Hebrew, the least consideration of Time of any other language. Evermore in expressing the mercies of God to man, it is an indifferent thing to the holy Ghost whether he speak in the present, or in the future, or in the time that is past: what mercies soever he hath given us, he will give us over againe; And whatsoever he hath done, and will doe, hee is alwayes ready to doe at the present. (*Sermons* 9:335)

12. For further discussion of Donne's use of the threefold (and occa-
sionally fourfold) method of exegesis, see Walter Davis, "Meditation,
Typology"; Helen Gardner, "The Historical Sense"; William Mueller,
John Donne: Preacher (89–92); Dennis Quinn, "John Donne's Principles"
(322–26); and Winfried Schleiner, *The Imagery of John Donne's Sermons*
(185–200). Earlier studies of Donne's sermons have also mentioned, albeit
in passing, his use of the fourth, allegorical sense; see Herbert Umbach,
"The Rhetoric of Donne's Sermons" (357); and Ruth Wallerstein, *Studies
in Seventeenth-Century Poetic* (72–73).

The four Christian "senses" are reflected in the four Jewish "senses,"
which are called by the mnemonic *Pardes* ("orchard"): *Peshat* ("literal"),
Remez ("moral"), *Derash* ("allegorical"); and *Sod* ("mystical"). For further discussion of these "senses" in both Jewish and Christian exegesis, see Roland Bainton, "The Bible" (24–27); Harry Caplan, "The Four
Senses"; Bernard Casper, *An Introduction to Jewish Bible Commentary*
(30–35); Beryl Smalley, *The Study of the Bible* (214–63); and Frank
Talmage, "Apples of Gold" (114–16).

13. For further discussion of these aspects of grace, see Jeffrey Johnson,
The Theology of John Donne 123–27.

14. Tense in biblical Hebrew is related (as in other Semitic languages)
not to "time-distinction" but rather to "the kind of action" (Chomsky,
Hebrew 162), regarded by the speaker as either *perfect*, that is, completed,
or *imperfect*, that is, continuous (*Gesenius' Hebrew Grammar* 309–19).

15. Donne develops several explicit and implicit intertextual connections among the five Prebend sermons: the image of weights and measures in the first and second ones (*Sermons* 6:294–95, 305–09; 7:53–57);
the map of heaven as being made of "two Hemisphears too, two half
heavens; Halfe will be Joy, and halfe will be Glory" in the second and
third ones (*Sermons* 7:69; 7:237–38); and the catalogue of God's names
in the second and fifth (*Sermons* 7:66; 8:128). For further discussion,
see Judith Anderson, *Words that Matter* (190–93); and Janel Mueller,
"Introduction" (50, 54, 64–65).

16. Shuger cites John Carey's discussion in *John Donne: Life, Mind
and Art*, in which he writes that "it is God's destructive power that
Donne particularly relishes dwelling on. . . . It is God as killer and pulver-
izer that Donne celebrates" (109).

17. Another interesting example of Donne's attention to Hebrew
grammatical form is to be found in his discussion of the word אַשְׁרֵי
ashrei, "blessed," about which Chamberlin notes that "the ambivalence
of the word's grammatical category matches the ambivalence of the idea"
(*Increase and Multiply* 141): "Divines themselves, and those who are
best exercised in the language of the Holy Ghost, the Originall tongue
of this Text, cannot give us a cleare Grammaticall understanding, of this
first word, in which *David* expresses this Blessednesse, *Ashrei*, which is

here Translated *Blessed*. They cannot tell, whether it be an Adverb (And then it is *Bene Viro*, Well is it for that man, A pathetique, a vehement acclamation, Happily, Blessedly is that man provided for) Or whether it be a Plurall Noune, (and then it is *Beatitudines*, such a Blessednesse as includes many, all blessednesses in it)" (*Sermons* 9:255). Donne's marking out of *ashrei* as a plural noun, though incorrect, seems to be based on the Hebrew masculine plural noun in the "construct state," itself being in a close connection with a second noun to express the genitive case, such as *benei David*, "the sons of David" (*Gesenius' Hebrew Grammar* 247, 414).

18. The strength of this image has attracted the attention of Joan Webber, who notes "the driving insistence upon this single symbol" (*Contrary Music* 169), and of Winfriẹd Schleiner, who writes about words "that are in this way invested with a particular meaning and that acquire a certain symbolic character will no doubt stick in the memory of the hearer" (*The Imagery of John Donne's Sermons* 168).

19. In this instance *Niph`al* comprises the passive of the causative verb form *Hiph`il* (*Gesenius' Hebrew Grammar* 138), endowing it with the meaning of a result or consequence. Ibn Ezra's discussion of the verb *ni'atu* is based on the acknowledgement that a reader of the Bible who is conversant with Hebrew grammar would expect the passive *niph`al* form of the root *nht* ("descend" or "come down") to be created by the addition of the grammatical prefix "n"—that is, *nin'atu* rather than *ni'atu*.

20. The term *ben-qeshet* is accented in the Hebrew biblical text as *ven-qashet*, because of the genitive relationship between the two nouns (*Gesenius' Hebrew Grammar* 415–16).

21. Evelyn Simpson mistakenly states that this is Donne's "one reference to Wyclif's translation" (*Sermons* 10:324). Yet there is at least one other reference, evident in his sermon on the Penitential Psalm 32:10 ("Many sorrowes *shall be* to the wicked"): "That these sorrowes are determinable by no time; for in the Originall, there is neither that which our first Translation inserted, (*Shall come*) *Sorrowes shall come to the wicked*, lest the wicked might say, Let it goe as it came, if I know how it came, what occasioned the sorrow, I know how to overcome it...." (*Sermons* 9:392).

22. The different readings of the Hebrew term *yithalelu* are generated by the reader's syntactical and grammatical expectations concerning the biblical text. On the one hand, the inherent syntactic parallelism of the psalmic verse (the two active verbs "shall be glad" and "shall trust" of the first part) invites the subsequent translation of the third verb *yithalelu* as the active form *yehallu* "shall glory." On the other hand, the verb form *yithalelu*, as the reflexive or passive *hitpa`el* form (*Gesenius' Hebrew Grammar* 149–50) literally means "they shall praise themselves" or "they shall be praised."

23. The name of the morning star, the planet Venus, is termed in Hebrew *heileil ben-shahar*, "Lucifer, sonne of the morning" (Isa. 14:12).

24. As is noted in *Gesenius' Hebrew Grammar*, "Hebrew possesses no special form either for the comparative or superlative of the adjective" (429). Thus John Udall explains that one may, for example, add the word מְאֹד *me`od*, "very," "greatly," "much" to create a superlative ("Hebrue Grammar" 181).

25. The preceding verses read as follows:

> 26:8: Then said Abishai to David, God hath delivered thine enemie into thine hand this day: now therefore let mee smite him, I pray thee, with *the* speare, and I will not *smite* him the second time.
> 26:9: And David sayd to Abishai, Destroy him not: for who can stretch forth his hand against the LORDS Annointed, and be guilt-lesse?
> 26:10: David said furthermore, as the LORD liveth, the LORD shall smite him, or his day shall come to die, or hee shall descend into battell, and perish.
> 26:11: The LORD forbid that I should stretch foorth mine hand against the LORDS Annointed; but I pray three, take thou now the speare that is at his bolster, and the cruse of water, and let us goe.

26. In private correspondence, Chaim Cohen has verified that modern dictionaries of biblical Hebrew list the different meanings of *hll* as being derived, however, from different roots, and so they are simply homonymic. See, for example, the general Hebrew dictionary Even-Shoshan (see table 8).

27. These passages read:

> Psalm 75:4: "I said unto the [**holel**im] fooles, Deale not [*taholu*] foolishly."
> Isaiah 44:25: "[That] maketh diviners [*yeholel*] mad."
> Job 12:17: "[He] maketh the Judges [*yeholel*] fooles."

28. Udall's complete entry reads: "צוּר He besieged, or straitened. צַר straitninge, straitens. צָרָה Oppression. צִיר tribulation, a hinge. צַר, צוּר a rocke. צוּרֹת Rockes. צוּר, צוּרָה A forme. מְצוֹר, מָצוֹר, מְצוּרָה Distresse, perplexion" ("Hebrue Dictionaire" 128).

29. They are, however, basically correct in their understanding of the Hebrew lexicon as being based on consonantal roots. For example, from the root חשב *ḥshv*, which has a basic meaning of "think," are derived words such as "consider," "intend," "calculate," and "computer." A fuller account of this aspect of the Hebrew lexicon is available in "Etymology, or the Part of Speech" (*Gesenius' Hebrew Grammar* 99–104).

30. See Geoffrey Sampson's discussion of the distinction between "philology" or "historical, diachonric linguistics" of the nineteenth cen-

tury (applicable also to Donne's discussion) and the "synchronic linguistics" developed in the twentieth century (*Schools of Linguistics* 13–33).

Notes to Chapter Five

1. These sciences included modern prehistory, paleontology and ethnology. For further discussion see particularly the chapters in *The Legend of Noah* entitled "Science and the Universality of the Flood" (92–112) and "The Migrations of Men and the Plantation of America" (113–36).

2. For further discussion see R. Hassel Jr., "Donne's 'Ignatius His Conclave' and the New Astronomy"; Catherine Martin, "*The Advancement of Learning* and the Decay of the World"; and Avihu Zakai, "All Coherence Gone."

3. Donne also preaches another five sermons on various episodes from the book of Genesis: he draws out in 1618 (possible) implications for the reign of James I (Gen. 32:10); appeals in 1619 for a new chapel at Lincoln's Inn (Gen. 28:16–17); instructs in 1620 on God's judgment (Gen. 18:25); celebrates in 1624 the Feast of Circumcision/New Year's Day (Gen. 17:24); and finally, as Evelyn Simpson writes (*Sermons* 10:25–26), reflects in 1624 on his own "love of paradox, exemplified in the Serpent" (Gen. 3:14).

4. While there is no specific date recorded for this sermon in the folio of *Fifty Sermons*, Simpson and Potter in their edition use manuscript and biographical evidence to date it as having been preached at the wedding of Sir Francis Nethersole shortly before February 12, 1620.

5. Donne writes, "And then, that that is made here, is but *Adjutorium*, but an accessory, not a principall; but a *Helper*. First the wife must be so *much*, she must *Helpe*; and then she must be *no more*, she must *not Governe*. But she cannot be that, except she have that quality, which God intended in the first woman, *Adjutorium simile sibi*, a helper *fit for him*" (*Sermons* 2:337). For further discussion of this sermon see Elizabeth Hodgson, *Gender and the Sacred Self* (89–92); and Lindsay Mann, "Misogyny and Libertinism."

6. Ibn Ezra cites Psalm 114:7, "the presence of the God [*Eloha*] of Jacob." Donne cites: Job 12:4, "I am *as* one mocked of his neighbour, *who* calleth upon God [*Eloha*]"; and Job 36:2, "I *have* yet to speake on Gods [*Eloha*] behalfe."

7. These sources include the twelfth century Italian theologian Peter Lombard, Nicholas of Lyre, and the sixteenth century Italian Franciscan Peter Galatin[us], who support a Trinitarian reading, with Calvin and Cajetan opposing. See particularly Raspa's detailed annotation of Donne's drawing out of these exegetical lines of debate in his edition of Donne's *Essayes* (*Essayes in Divinity* 140–43).

8. For a discussion of the complex issue of Donne's attitudes toward Jews see Chanita Goodblatt, "From 'Tav' to the Cross" (229–33); Jeanne Shami, "Donne, Anti-Jewish Rhetoric and the English Church"; and James Shapiro, *Shakespeare and the Jews*.

9. For further discussion of these issues see Paul Harland, "Donne's Political Intervention"; Jeffrey Johnson, *The Theology of John Donne* (16–27); and Alan Smith, *The Emergence of a Nation State* (268–84).

10. In the biblical text, the "conversive" letter *vav* (pronounced here as *va*) turns the biblical future tense into the past tense (Yitshak Livni and Moshe Kokhba, *Hebrew Grammar* 49–51).

11. For example, in the first Prebend sermon Donne writes, "For howsoever when they two are compared together, with one another, it may admit discourse and disputation, whether men of high degree, or of low degree doe most violate the lawes of God; that is, whether prosperity or adversity make men most obnoxious to sin, yet, when they come to bee compared, not with one another, but both with God, this asseveration, this *surely* reaches to both; *Surely, The man of low degree is vanity*, and, as *Surely, The man of high degree is a lie* [Prebend Psalm 62:9] (*Sermons* 6:295). Similarly, in the second Prebend sermon Donne writes: "the Almighty God himselfe onely knowes the waight of this affliction, and except hee put in that *pondus gloriae* [2 Cor. 4:17], that exceeding weight of an eternall glory, with his owne hand, into the other scale, we are waighed downe, we are swallowed up, irreparably, irrevocably, irrecoverably, irremediably" (*Sermons* 7:57).

12. For further discussion of the Christian-Jewish polemic regarding the Trinitarian nature of God, see Philip Almond, *Adam and Eve* 14–15; Herman Hailperin, *Rashi and the Christian Scholars* 43–46; Daniel Lasker, "Major Themes" 115–18; and John Skinner, *A Critical and Exegetical Commentary* 30–31.

13. In *De Opificio Mundi* Philo actually writes: "For this reason it is only in the case of the genesis of the human being that he [Moses] states that God said *let us make*, which reveals the enlistment of others as collaborators, so that whenever the human being acts rightly in decisions and actions that are beyond reproach, these can be assigned to God's account as universal Director, whereas in the case of their opposite they can be attributed to others who are subordinate to him" (§75, p. 66).

Donne cites Philo on the creation of humankind in his Whitehall sermon on Matthew 19:17 (March 4, 1625): "And he, whom they call so often *Platonem Hebraeorum*, the Jews *Plato*, that is, *Philo Judaeus*, sayes well, *Nihil boni sterile creavit Deus*; God hath made nothing, in which he hath not imprinted, and from which he hath not produced some good: He follows it so far, (and justly) as to say, that God does good, where that good does no good" (*Sermons* 6:236–37).

14. Gibbens (fl. 1601–02) was a Church of England clergyman. Only one volume of his commentary ("The first part of the first Tome") was published, covering the first fourteen chapters of Genesis (Leachman, "Gibbens, Nicholas").

15. Ibn Ezra echoes Rashi in explaining that "God said to the angels 'Let us make man, we will deal with him and not the waters and the earth'" (*Biblia Rabbinica* 16; *Ibn Ezra's Commentary on the Pentateuch: Genesis* 45). As G. M. G. Teugels explains, however, "after the rabbinic period, Jewish scholars such as Sa`adia Gaon [882–942] distanced themselves from the idea that God discussed creation, or even created, together with the angels, because they saw in it indeed a dangerous, polytheistic, interpretation in view of Christian interpretations of the verse" (110 n. 13).

16. *Genesis Rabbah* is an exegetical Midrash, a compilation of rabbinic homilies that provides a running commentary (chapter by chapter, verse by verse, and at times word by word) on this biblical book. Redacted in Palestine in the fifth century CE, it was first published in Istanbul in 1512, with many later reissues. For further discussion see *The Bibliography of the Hebrew Book*; Moshe Herr, "Genesis Rabbah" and "Midrash"; and Jacob Neusner, *Genesis and Judaism*. For an extended discussion of Genesis Rabbah within the context of seventeenth century English literature, see Jeffrey Shoulson, *Milton and the Rabbis*.

17. See Leonard Greenspoon, "Bible Translations. Greek: The Septuagint."

18. The Septuagint ("Seventy"), along with its Latin translation, was available to Donne in the Complutensian and Antwerp Polyglots. He mentions the Septuagint in over 20 places throughout his sermons; one can quite readily consult both *John Donne Sermons: Electronic Archives*, and Troy Reeves, *Index to Proper Names* (133–34), as well as the discussion in Allen, "Dean Donne" (210–11), and in *Sermons* 10:316–17.

19. The Talmud is a series of commentaries "geared, specifically, towards an understanding of a Jew's legal and moral responsibilities as proclaimed in the Bible and discussed, commented upon, and interpreted by the rabbis and scholars over a period of 1,000 years—from Ezra, who lived about 450 BCE, up until the end of the sixth century C.E." (Alfred Kolatch, *Who's Who in the Talmud* 5). As David Katz explains, "It was only several generations later, by the outbreak of the English Civil War in the 1640s, that English scholars were ready to expand their interests in any sort of systematic way to include other aspects of Jewish tradition, both the kabbalah (Jewish mysticism) and the Talmud (the 'oral' law)" ("Abendana Brothers" 30). Donne does refer to the Talmud several times, specifically in the sermon on 1 Timothy 1:15: "That the will of God must be revealed somewhere, and then he receives this for that

Gospell, rather then the Alcoran of the Turks, rather then the Talmud of the Jewes" (*Sermons* 1:298); the sermon on Job 19:26: "That they doe so now, appears out of the doctrine of their *Talmud,* where we find that *onely the Jews* shall rise againe, but all the Gentiles shall perish, body and soule together" (*Sermons* 3:93); the sermon on 1 Timothy 3:16: "To say, if I consider the *Talmud,* Christ may as well be the *Messias,* as any whom the Jews place their marks upon" (*Sermons* 3:215); the sermon on 2 Corinthians 1:3: "And hence is it, that in the Talmud of the Jews, and in the Alcoran of the Turks, though they both oppose the Trinity, yet when they handle not that point, there fall often from them, as cleare confessions of the three Persons" (*Sermons* 3:264); the sermon on Acts 23:6–7: "For so, in the Talmud it selfe, the difference is expresly put; *Sacerdos magnus judicat & judicatur,* The High Priest, the greatest Prelate in the Clergy, may have place in this Councel....But then of the King, it is as expressly said, of this Councel, in that Talmud, *Nec judicat, nec judicatur,* The King sits in Judgement upon no man" (*Sermons* 9:164).

20. The illustration of the Talmud printed in this chapter is taken from Ambrosius Froben's heavily censored Basel Talmud (1578–1580). He employed both a Catholic and a Protestant censor, who "between them produced a thoroughly butchered Talmud edition, which was not well received by Jewish customers but could be produced legally and sold within the German empire" (Burnett, "The Regulation of Hebrew Printing" 338).

21. Bishop Laud and King Charles requested to see Donne's sermon after it was preached, since in it he indirectly criticized the King and Queen Henrietta Maria. For further discussion of this episode see Annabel Patterson, *Censorship and Interpretation* (100–05); *Sermons* 7:38–43; and Joshua Scodel, "John Donne and the Religious Politics of the Mean" (63–70).

22. For further discussion of Donne's complex attitude toward Arminianism, see Achsah Guibbory, "Donne's Religion"; and Jeanne Shami, "Labels, Controversy."

23. See also Donne's discussion of *"Lamech,* who had two wives, the first was *Adah,* and *Adah* signifies *Coetum, congregationem* [*eida* as 'community, assembly, herd']; there is company enough, society enough in a wife: His other wife was but *Zillah,* and *Zillah* is but *umbra,* but a shadow [*tzel,* 'shadow'], but a *ghost,* that will *terrifie* at last" (Gen. 2:18; *Sermons* 2:344). This etymological explanation echoes in part the one given by Rashi, who writes: "Ada: She is [the wife] for procreation because she is repulsive to him and taken away from him. 'Ada' in [Aramaic] translation means 'turn away.' Tzilla: She is [the wife] for sexual relations because she sits always in his shadow" (*Biblia Rabbinica* 1:22; *Pentateuch: Genesis* 20).

24. Donne's generally critical attitude toward the Kabbalah is evident in the *Essayes in Divinity,* when he writes that "Cabalistick learning seems to most *Occupatissima vanitas,* I will forbear the observations, both of *Picus* [Giovanni Pico della Mirandola] in his *Heptaplus,* and in the [*Scripturam Sacram*] *Problemata* of *Francis George*" (*Essayes* 12–13; note 117). Donne also parodies these Christian Kabbalists in the following entries from *The Courtier's Library:* "6. That the Book of Tobit is canonical. In which, drawing upon the Rabbis and the other more obscure Theologians, the hairs on the tail of the dog are counted and from their different turns and combinations letters are put together to create amazing words. By Francis George, the Venetian….8. The Judeo-Christian Pythagoras, in which 99 and 66 are shown to be the same number if the page is turned upside down, by the more than angelic Giovanni Pico Della Mirandola" (Piers Brown, "Hac Ex Consilio" 861).

25. This numerological calculation (45) is as follows (see Derovan, Scholem, and Idel, "Gematria" 426; and Scholem, Garb, and Idel, "Kabbalah" 643):

אדם *Adam:* 40 = ם ;4 = ד ;1 = א
יהוה *YHWH:* יוד *yod* = 20 [4 = ד ;6 = ו ;10 = י]
הא *heh* = 6 [1 = א ;5 = ה]
ואו *vav* = 13 [6 = ו ;1 = א ;6 = ו]
הא *heh* = 6 [1 = א ;5 = ה]

26. Minsheu writes in Latin: *"Quas voces* Grammatici *derivant à radice* איל ejal, *i. fortitudo."*

27. Andrewes considers the particle `*immanu* as being formed from the preposition `*im* and the (elided) pronoun *anu,* "we." But it is actually formed by the addition of the pronominal suffix *nu,* "us" (first person, plural) to the preposition *'im,* "with" (*Gesenius' Hebrew Grammar* 300–01).

28. Genesis 5:2 reads: "Male and female created hee them, and blessed them, and called their name Adam, in the day when they were created."

29. Cited from the page proofs for "List of Hebrew Words"; OSB MSS 90, Box 5, Folder 116.

30. The two Hebrew letters ו *vav* and · *yod* function as consonantal vowels (much as "u" and "i" in English) and are often interchangeable (Gesenius 26, 67–68). In his twentieth century dictionary Eliezer Ben Yehuda summarizes discussion of the etymology of the word *ish,* concluding that it is related etymologically to *enosh* (197). Yet he does make mention of the (rejected) possibility that *ish* was formed from a presently unknown root *ush,* meaning "become strong."

31. This etymological relationship between *enosh* and *anash* is not certain. Strong's nineteenth century Hebrew dictionary confirms Donne's

explanation, writing that *enosh* (entry 582) is from *anash*, "a primitive root; to be frail, feeble, or (figuratively) melancholy:—desparate(-ly wicked), incurable, sick, woeful" (entry 605). Even-Shoshan's twenty-first century Hebrew dictionary, however, cites these two words as rather being formed from homonymic roots: *enosh* from the Aramaic word *enash*, "men" (1:92); and *anash* from the Ugaritic word *ansh*, "weaken" (1:97).

32. Minsheu cites from Petronius, *Satyricon*, chapter 5:24.

33. Minsheu cites from Estienne Guichard's sixteenth century *L'harmonie éytmologigue des langues* (James Rosier, "The Source and Methods," 71).

34. In the first passage (Ps. 89:48), Donne writes, "Every man does; *Mi Gheber*, sayes the Originall; It is not *Ishe*, which is the first name of man, in the Scriptures, and signifies nothing but a *sound*, a voyce, a word....It is not *Adam*, which is another name of man, and signifies nothing but *red earth*....It is not *Enos*, which is also a third name of man, and signifies nothing a *wretched and miserable creature*....but it is *Mi Gheber, Quis vir;* which is the word always signifying a man accomplished in all excellencies....and yet *Mi Gheber, Quid homo,* this man must see death" (*Sermons* 2:200). Much in the same manner, Donne writes in the second passage (Lamen. 3:1), "*Gheber, vir, I am the man* [that has seen affliction]. At first, man is called *Ishe;* a word, which their Grammarians derive *à sonitu*, from a voice....Another name of man is *Adam*, and *Adam* is no more but *earth*, and *red earth*....*Enosh* signifies *aegrum, calamitosum*, a person naturally subject to, and actually possest with all kindes of infirmities....But when man is presented in this Text, in this fourth and great name, *Gheber*, which denotes excellency...And then, in this heighth, this heighth of vertue and merit, of wealth and treasure, of command and power, of favour and acclamation, is thrown down into the pit of misery, and submitted to all afflictions, what man can hope to be exempted?" (*Sermons* 10:197–98).

35. I would like to thank Andrew Zurcher of Queen's College, Cambridge for his assistance in locating this source.

36. Freccero cites *Targum Onkelos* in its Latin translation (*Factus est spiritum loquentem*) from Augustine Calmet's eighteenth century *Commentarius Literalis.*

37. Though Donne perhaps does not obtain this information directly from Eusebius, he does cite him in various places in his sermons; see *Sermons* 10:345; *John Donne Sermons: Electronic Archives;* and Troy Reeves, *Index to Proper Names* 72.

38. The nineteenth century German scholar Max Grünbaum cites the Aramaic phrase *liba de-inshai inshai*, "once the heart forgets [*inshai*], its remains forgotten [*inshai*]" (Babylonian Talmud, Tractate of Sanhedrin, p. 35, side 1; Soncino 223)—translated by him as "the heart of the person [*inshai*], forgets [*inshai*]"—to propose that the Aramaic *inshai*, "forget"

and the Hebrew word *enosh*, "human" are related alliteratively and thus semantically (24–25).

39. Genesis 4:26 reads most literally: "And he called his name Enosh, then was begun to call by name the Lord [yhwh] [*va-yiqra et-shemo enosh az huḥal liqro be-shem adonai*]." The Septuagint's translation of the Hebrew verb הוּחַל *huḥal*, "was begun," as "hoped" is presumably based on the erroneous assumption that this verb is formed from the root יחל *yḥl*, "hope" rather than from the root חלל *ḥll*, "begin" (Even-Shoshan 2:565).

40. Psalm 1:3 reads: "And he shalbe like a tree planted by the rivers of water, that bringeth foorth his fruit in his season, his leafe also shall not wither, and whatsoever he doeth, shall prosper."

41. Discussions of "The Lamentations of Jeremy" have focused primarily on the issue of its dating, as well as on Donne's use of various sources for his work in translating the biblical text; see particularly John Klause, "The Two Occasions of Donne's *Lamentations of Jeremy*"; Ted-Larry Pebworth, "John Donne's 'Lamentations'"; and Graham Roebuck, "Donne's *Lamentations of Jeremy* Reconsidered."

BIBLIOGRAPHY

Primary Sources

Ainsworth, Henry. *The Book of Psalmes: Englished both in Prose and Metre*. Amsterdam: Giles Thorp, 1612.

Alabaster, William. *Schindleri Lexicon Pentaglotton*. London: William Jones, 1635.

Andrewes, Lancelot. *Apospasmatia Sacra, or A Collection of Posthumous and Orphan Lectures*. London: H. Moseley, A. Crooke. D. Pakeman, L. Fawne, R. Royston, and N. Ekins, 1657.

———. *Holy Devotions, with Directions to Pray also a Brief Exposition upon The Lords Prayer, The Creed, The Ten Commandements, The 7 Penitential Psalms, The 7 Psalms of Thanksgiving: Together with a Letanie*. London: A. Seile, 1663.

———. *A Sermon of the Pestilence Preached at Chiswick, 1603*. London: Richard Badger, 1636.

———. *XCVI Sermons*. London: Richard Badger, 1629.

The Apostolic Bible: Genesis. Ed. and trans. Charles Van der Pool. April 2006. Available at http://www.apostolicbible.com; accessed March 30, 2008.

Augustine, Saint. *Sancti Aurelii Augustini Hipponensis Episcopi Enarrationes in Psalmos*. In *Patrologia Latina*, vol. 36, ed. Jacques-Paul Migne. Paris: 1844–55.

————. *Expositions on the Book of Psalms, by S. Augustine, Bishop of Hippo.* Ed. A. Cleveland Coxe. A Select Library of the Nicene and Post-Nicene Fathers of the Christian Church, vol. 8. Grand Rapids: Wm. B. Eerdmans, 1956.

————. *Expositions on the Book of Psalms, by S. Augustine, Bishop of Hippo.* Trans. J. Tweed, T. Scratton, H. M. Wilkins, and H. Walford. 6 vols. Oxford: John Henry Parker, 1847–57.

The Babylonian Talmud. Ed. Rabbi Dr. I. Epstein. London: Soncino Press. "Tractate of *Megillah,*" vol. 2, part 8, trans. Maurice Simon, 1938. "Tractate of *Sanhedrin,*" vol. 4, part 5, trans. Jacob Shachter and H. Freedman, 1935. "Tractate of *Shabbath,*" vol. 2, part 1, trans. H. Freedman, 1938.

Baynes, Ralph. *Prima Rudimenta in Linguam Hebraem.* Paris: Christian Wechel, 1550.

Biblia Rabbinica. A reprint of the 1525 Venice edition. 4 vols. Ed. Jacob Ben Hayim Ibn Adoniya. Jerusalem: Makor, 1972.

Biblia Sacra: Juxta Vulgatam Clementinam. Paris: Desclée, 1927.

Biblia Sacra Polyglotta. Ed. Diego López de Zuñiga. Alcalá de Henares: Arnaldi Guillelmi de Brocario, 1514–17.

The [Geneva] Bible and Holy Scriptures Conteyned in the Olde and New Testament. Geneva: Rouland Hall, 1560.

The Booke of Common Prayer. London: Robert Barker, 1605.

Cajetan, Tommaso de Vio Gaetani. *Cajetan Responds: A Reader in Reformation Controversy.* Ed. and trans. Jared Wicks. Washington, D.C.: The Catholic University of America Press, 1978.

————. *In Librum Job Commentarii.* Romae: Antonij Bladi, 1535.

Calvin, John. *Commentaries on the First Twenty Chapters of the Book of the Prophet Ezekiel.* Vol. 1. Trans. Thomas Meyers. Edinburgh: Calvin Translation Society, 1849. Christian Classics Ethereal Library November 24, 1999. Available at http://www.ccel.org/ccel/calvin/calcom22.html; accessed November 7, 2005.

————. *Commentary on The Book of Psalms.* Translated from the original Latin, and collated with the author's French version, by the Rev. James Anderson. 5 vols. Grand Rapids: Wm. B. Eerdmans, 1949.

————. *The Psalmes of David and Others: With M. John Calvin's Commentaries.* London: Lucas Harison and George Byshop, 1571.

Cassiodorus [Senator], Flavius Magnus Aurelius. *In Psalterium Expositio.* In *Patrologia Latina,* vol. 70, ed. Jacques-Paul Migne. Paris, 1844–55.

Coke, Edward. *The First Part of the Institutes of the Lawes of England.* London: Adam Islip, 1628.

Coverdale, Miles. *Biblia the Byble, that is the Holy Scryptures of the Olde and New Testament, Faithfully Translated in to Engylishe.* Southwark: J. Nycolson, 1535.

Donne, John. *Biathanatos: A Modern-Spelling Edition.* Ed. Michael Rudick and M. Pabst Battin. New York: Garland, 1982.

———. *Donne's Prebend Sermons.* Ed. Janel M. Mueller. Cambridge, Mass.: Harvard University Press, 1971.

———. *Essays in Divinity.* Ed. Evelyn M. Simpson. Oxford: The Clarendon Press, 1952.

———. *Essayes in Divinity.* Ed. Anthony Raspa. Montreal: McGill-Queen's University Press, 2001.

———. *Fifty Sermons Preached by that Learned and Reverend Divine John Donne.* Vol. 2. London: J. Marriot and R. Royston, 1649.

———. *John Donne Sermons: Electronic Archives.* Ed. Kimberly Johnson. Brigham Young University, 2005. Available at http://www.lib.byu.edu/dlib/donne.

———. *John Donne's Sermons on the Psalms and Gospels.* Ed. Evelyn M. Simpson. Berkeley and Los Angeles: University of California Press, 1963.

———. *Letters to Severall Persons of Honour: Written by John Donne.* London: Richard Marriot, 1651.

———. *LXXX Sermons Preached by that Learned and Reverend Divine John Donne.* London: Richard Royston and Richard Marriot, 1640.

———. *Poems by J. D. with Elegies on the Authors Death.* London: John Marriot, 1635.

———. *The Sermons of John Donne.* 10 vols. Ed. Evelyn M. Simpson and George R. Potter. Berkeley and Los Angeles: University of California Press, 1953–62.

———. *XXVI Sermons (Never before Published) Preached by that Learned and Reverend Divine John Donne.* London: Thomas Newcomb, 1661.

Eusebius of Caesarea. *Praeparatio Evangelica* [*Preparation for the Gospel*]. Ed. Roger Pearse and trans. E. H. Gifford. Oxford: E Typographico Academico, 1903. Available at http://www.tertullian.org/fathers/eusebius; accessed March 29, 2008.

Genesis Rabbah: The Judaic Commentary to the Book of Genesis. A New American Translation. Vol. 1, Parshiyyot One through Thirty-Three on Genesis 1:1 to 8:14. Trans. Jacob Neusner. Atlanta: Scholars Press, 1985.

Gibbens, Nicholas. *Questions and Disputations concerning the Holy Scriptures.* London: Felix Kyngston, 1602.

Gregory I. *Sancti Gregorii Magni Romani Pontificus Moralium Libri, Sive Expositio in Librum B. Job.* In *Patrologia Latina,* vol. 75, Ed. Jacques-Paul Migne. Paris: 1844–55.

Henry VIII, King of England. A *Glasse of the Truthe: A Dialogue Between a Lawyer and a Divine Concerning Henry VIII's Proposed Divorce from Catherine of Aragon.* London: Thomas Berthelet, 1532.

The Holie [Bishops'] Bible. London: Richard Jugge, 1572.

The Holie [Doway] Bible. Faithfully Translated into English, out of the Authentical Latin, by the English College of Doway. Two Tomes. Doway: Lawrence Kellam, 1609–10.

The Holy [King James] Bible, Conteyning the Old Testament, and the New: Newly Translated out of the Originall tongues: & with the former Translations diligently compared and reuised by his Majesties Speciall Comandement. Appointed to be read in the Churches. London: Robert Barker, 1611.

The Holy [Wycliffe] Bible, Containing the Old and New Testaments, with the Apocryphal Books, in the Earliest Emglish Versions made from the Latin Vulgate by John Wycliffe and his Followers. Ed. Josiah Forshall. Oxford: Oxford University Press, 1850. Available at http://www.sbible.boom.ru/wyc/wycle.htm; accessed August 14, 2004.

Ibn Ezra, Abraham ben Meir. *The Commentary of Abraham ibn Ezra on the Pentateuch: Deuteronomy.* Trans. Jay F. Shachter. Hoboken, N.J.: Ktav, 2003.

———. *Commentaries on the Pentateuch* [Hebrew]. Vol. 1. Ed. Asher Vizer. Jerusalem: Ha-Rav Kook Institute, 1976.

———. *Ibn Ezra's Commentary on the Pentateuch.* Vols. 1–2, Genesis and Exodus. Trans. H. Norman Strickman and Arthur M. Silver. New York: Menorah, 1988 and 1996.

Jerome. *Commentariorum in Hiezechielem.* Ed. Franciscus Glorie. Turnholti: Brepols, 1964.

Kimhi, David. *The Complete Commentary on the Psalms* [Hebrew]. Ed. Avraham Darom. Jerusalem: Mossad Harav Kook, 1967.

Luther, Martin. *Luther's Works:* Vols. 1–8, *Lectures on Genesis*. Ed. Jaroslav Pelikan. St. Louis: Concordia, 1955–86.

Lyre, Nicholas de. *Biblia Sacra cum Glossis, Interlineari et Ordinaria: Nicolai Lyrani Postilla*. Venice: N.p., 1588.

Milton, John. *Paradise Lost*. Ed. Merritt Y. Hughes. Indianapolis: Bobbs-Merrill, 1962.

Minsheu, John. *A Catalogue and True Note of the Names of Such Persons Which (Upon Good Liking They Have to the Worke Being a Great Helpe to Memorie) Have Received the Etymologicall Dictionarie of XI Languages*. London: John Brown, 1617.

———. *Ductor in Linguas, The Guide into Tongues*. London: John Brown, 1617.

———. *Ductoris in Linguas, The Guide into Tongues*. 2nd ed. London: John Haviland, 1625.

Miqra'ot Gedolot. Vol. 5, *Prophets*. Jerusalem: B. Brokhman, 2001.

Otsrot Yisra'el [The treasures of Israel]. The Responsa Project, version 2.0. Ramat-Gan: Bar-Ilan University, 1972–2005.

Philo of Alexandria. *On the Creation of the Cosmos according to Moses* [*De Opificio Mundi*]. Trans. David T. Runia. Leiden: Brill, 2001.

The Psalter or Psalmes of David, Corrected and Poyneted as Thei Shalbe Song in Churches after the Translacion of the Greate Bible. London: Richard Grafton, 1549.

Rashi (Rabbi Solomon Ben Isaac). *Pentateuch with Rashi's Commentary*. Vols. 1–2, Genesis and Exodus. Translated into English and annotated by M. Rosenbaum and A. M. Silbermann, in collaboration with A. Blashki and L. Joseph. Jerusalem: Silbermann Family.

———. *Rashi's Commentary on Psalms*. Translation, introduction, and notes by Mayer I. Gruber. Leiden: Brill, 2004.

Reuchlin, Johannes. *De Rudimentis Hebraicis*. Pforzheim, 1506.

———. *De Verbo Mirifico*. In *Samtliche Werke*, vol. 1.1. Stuttgart-Bad Cannstatt: Frommann-Holzboog, 1996.

———. *In Septem Psalmos Poenitentiales*. Tübingin, 1512.

Schindler, Valentin. *Schindleri Lexicon Pentaglotton*. Ed. William Alabaster. London: William Jones, 1635.

Sidney, Philip, and Mary Sidney Herbert. *The Psalms of Sir Philip Sidney and the Countess of Pembroke*. Ed. J. C. A. Rathmell. New York: New York University Press, 1963.

Sternhold, Thomas, and John Hopkins. *The Whole Book of Psalmes, Collected into English Meeter*. London: Richard Day, 1592.

Strong, James. *King James Bible with Strong's A Concise Dictionary of the Words in the Hebrew Bible.* Online edition, 2001–02, ed. John Hurt. Available at http://www.sacrednamebible.com/kjvstrongs; accessed December 4, 2007.

Tanakh: The Holy Scriptures. The New JPS Translation according to the Traditional Hebrew Text. Philadelphia: The Jewish Publication Society, 1985.

A Time of Healing Prayer Service. April 23, 1995. Available at http://www.oklaosf.state.ok.us/ofsdocs/gov.html; accessed September 27, 1995.

Tyndale, William. *The Obedience of a Christen Man.* Antwerp: Hans Luft [Johan Hoochstraten], 1528.

———. *The Obedience of a Christian Man.* Ed. David Daniell. London: Penguin, 2000.

———. *The Pentateuch.* Antwerp: Hans Luft [Johan Hoochstraten], 1530.

———. "The Practice of Prelates." In *Expositions and Notes on Sundry Portions of the Holy Scriptures together with The Practice of Prelates,* ed. Henry Walter, for the Parker Society, 237–344. Eugene, Oreg.: Wipf & Stock, 2004.

Udall, John. "A Brief Abridgment of the Hebrue Dictionaire." In *Mafteah Lashon Ha-Kodesh: That Is the Key of the Holy Tongue,* 1–174. Leiden: Francis Raphelengius, 1593.

———. "Hebrue Grammar." 2 books. In *Mafteah Lashon Ha-Kodesh: That Is the Key of the Holy Tongue,* 2–204. Leiden: Francis Raphelengius, 1593.

The Vulgate Bible. Trans. Saint Jerome. Available at http://www.speed-bible.com/vulgate; accessed August 5, 2006.

Wakefield, Robert. *On the Three Languages [1524].* Ed. and trans. G. Lloyd Jones. Binghamton, N.Y.: Medieval & Renaissance Texts & Studies and The Renaissance Society of America, 1989.

Critical Sources

Abrahams, Israel. "Man, The Nature Of: In the Bible." In *Encyclopaedia Judaica,* vol. 13, 2nd ed., ed. Michael Berenbaum and Fred Skolnik, 446–48. Detroit: Macmillan Reference, 2007.

Adlington, Hugh. "Preaching the Holy Ghost: John Donne's Whitsunday Sermons." *John Donne Journal* 22 (2003): 203–28.

Aherne, C. "Epistle to the Galatians." In *The Catholic Encyclopedia,* vol. 6, 1909, online edition, 2003, ed. Kevin Knight. Available at http://www.newadvent.org/cathen/06336a.htm; accessed November 6, 2006.

Allen Don Cameron. "Dean Donne Sets His Text." *ELH* 10 (1943): 208–29.

———. *The Legend of Noah: Renaissance Rationalism in Art, Science, and Letters*. Urbana: University of Illinois Press, 1949.

———. "Some Theories of the Growth and Origin of Language in Milton's Age." *Philological Quarterly* 28 (1949): 5–16.

Almond, Philip C. A*dam and Eve in Seventeenth-Century Thought.* Cambridge: Cambridge University Press, 1999.

Altman, Shimon Tsevi Alexander. "Aristoteles and Judaism" [Hebrew]. In *Encyclopedia Hebraica*, 5:853–60. Jerusalem: Encyclopedia Publishing, 1953.

Anderson, B. W. "God, Names of." In *The Interpreter's Dictionary of the Bible: An Illustrated Encyclopedia*, 407–17. New York: Abingdon Press, 1962.

Anderson, Judith H. *Words That Matter: Linguistic Perception in Renaissance England*. Stanford, Calif.: Stanford University Press, 1996.

Asals, Heather. "John Donne and the Grammar of Redemption." *English Studies in Canada* 5 (1979): 125–39.

Austin, John Langshaw. *How to Do Things with Words*. Oxford: Oxford University Press, 1962.

Bainton, Roland H. "The Bible in the Reformation." In *The Cambridge History of the Bible: The West from the Reformation to the Present Day*, ed. S. L. Greenslade, 1–37. Cambridge: Cambridge University Press, 1963.

Bakhtin, Mikhail M. "Discourse in the Novel." In *The Dialogic Imagination: Four Essays*, ed. Michael Holquist, trans. Caryl Emerson and Michael Holquist, 259–422. Austin: University of Texas Press, 1981.

Bald, R. C. *John Donne: A Life*. Oxford: Clarendon Press, 1970.

Barlow, William. *The Summe and Substance of the Conference which, it pleased his Excellent Majestie to have with the Lords, Bishops and other of his Clergie*. London: Mathew Law, 1605.

Barthes, Roland. *S/Z: An Essay*. Trans. Richard Miller. New York: Hill and Wang, 1974.

Bedouelle, Guy. "The Consultations of the Universities and Scholars Concerning the 'Great Matter' of King Henry VIII." Trans. John L. Farthing. In *The Bible in the Sixteenth Century*, ed. David C. Steinmetz, 21–36. Durham, N.C.: Duke University Press, 1990.

Beitchman, Philip. *Alchemy of the Word: Cabala of the Renaissance.* Albany: State University of New York Press, 1998.

Bennett, R. E. "Donne's Letters to Severall Persons of Honour." *PMLA* 56 (1941): 120–40.

Ben Yehuda, Eliezer. *A Complete Dictionary of Ancient and Modern Hebrew* [Hebrew]. Tel-Aviv: La'am, 1948–59.

Biale, David. "Exegesis and Philosophy in the Writings of Abraham Ibn Ezra." *Comitatus* 5 (1974): 43–62.

The Bibliography of the Hebrew Book 1470–1960. Available at http://www.hebrew-bibliography.com; accessed October 18, 2007.

Blau, Joseph Leon. *The Christian Interpretation of the Cabala in the Renaissance.* Port Washington, N.Y.: Kennikat Press, 1965.

———. "The Diffusion of the Christian Interpretation of the Cabala in English Literature." *Review of Religion* 6 (1941–42): 146–68.

Boyarin, Daniel, and Moshe Zeidner. "Mene, Mene, Tekel, U-farsin." In *Encyclopaedia Judaica,* vol. 14, 2nd ed., ed. Michael Berenbaum and Fred Skolnik, 45–46. Detroit: Macmillan Reference, 2007.

Bradburn, Elizabeth, "Bodily Metaphor and Moral Agency in *A Masque*: A Cognitive Approach." In *Milton Studies,* vol. 43, ed. Albert C. Labriola, 19–34. Pittsburgh: University of Pittsburgh Press, 2004.

Brener, Ann. *Judah Halevi and His Circle of Hebrew Poets in Granada.* Leiden: Brill, 2005.

Briggs, Charles Augustus, and Emilie Grace Briggs. *A Critical and Exegetical Commentary on the Book of Psalms.* The International Critical Commentary. Vols. 1–2. New York: Charles Scribner's Sons, 1906–07.

Brooke, George. "Review: Steven. D. Fraade, *Enosh and His Generation.*" *Journal of Semitic Studies* 31 (1986): 257–61.

Brown, Piers. "'Hac ex consilio meo via progredieris': Courtly Reading and Secretarial Mediation in Donne's *The Courtier's Library.*" *Renaissance Quarterly* 61 (2008): 833–66.

Budick, Sanford. "Milton's Joban Phoenix in *Samson Agonistes.*" *Early Modern Literary Studies* 11 (2005): 5.1–15.

Burnett, Stephen G. "The Regulation of Hebrew Printing in Germany, 1555–1630: Confessional Politics and the Limits of Jewish Toleration." In *Infinite Boundaries: Order, Disorder, and Reorder in Early Modern German Culture,* ed. Max Reinhart and Thomas Robisheaux, 329–48. Kirksville, Mo: Truman State University Press, 1998.

Cain, Tom. "Donne's Political World." In *The Cambridge Companion to John Donne,* ed. Achsah Guibbory, 83–99. Cambridge: Cambridge University Press, 2006.

Caplan, Harry. "The Four Senses of Scriptural Interpretation and the Mediaeval Theory of Preaching." *Speculum* 4 (1929): 282–90.

Carey, John. *John Donne: Life, Mind and Art.* London: Faber and Faber, 1990.

Carrithers, Gale H., Jr. *Donne at Sermons: A Christian Existential World.* Albany: SUNY Press, 1972.

Casper, Bernard M. *An Introduction to Jewish Bible Commentary.* New York: Thomas Yoseloff, 1960.

Chamberlin, John S. *Increase and Multiply: Arts-of-Discourse Procedure in the Preaching of Donne.* Chapel Hill: The University of North Carolina Press, 1976.

Chomsky, William. *Hebrew: The Eternal Language.* Philadelphia: Jewish Publication Society of America, 1969.

Cleary, Gregory. "Wild, Johann." In *The Catholic Encyclopedia,* vol. 15 (1912), online edition, 2003, ed. Kevin Knight. Available at http://www.newadvent.org/cathen/15621b.htm; accessed September 28, 2006.

Cohen, Chaim. "The Biblical Institution of Levirate Marriage in Light of a New Akkadian Text: Exegetical and Literary Conclusions." In *Contextual Priority in Biblical Hebrew Philology.* Supplements to Vetus Testamentum. Leiden: Brill, forthcoming.

———. "Elements of *Peshat* in Traditional Jewish Bible Exegesis." *Immanuel* 21 (1987): 30–42.

Cohen, Joseph Y. "The Beginning of Hebrew Printing and the First Printers" [Hebrew]. *Mahanyim* 106 (1966): 96–105.

Colclough, David. "Donne, John (1572–1631)." In *Oxford Dictionary of National Biography,* ed. H. C. G. Matthew and Brian Harrison. Oxford: Oxford University Press, 2004. Available at http://www.oxforddnb.com/view/article/7819; accessed December 17, 2004.

Costley, Clare L. "David, Bathsheba, and the Penitential Psalms." *Renaissance Quarterly* 57 (2004): 1235–77.

Craigie, Peter C. *Word Biblical Commentary,* vol. 19, Psalms 1–50. Waco, Tex.: Word Books, 1983.

Crombie, Winifred. "'To Enter in these Bonds is to be Free': Semantic Relations and the Baroque Prose Style of John Donne." *Language and Style* 17 (1984): 123–38.

Cross, Claire. "Udall, John (c1560–1592/3)." In *Oxford Dictionary of National Biography,* ed. H. C. G. Matthew and Brian Harrison. Oxford: Oxford University Press, 2004. Available at http://www.oxforddnb.com/view/article/27973; accessed May 4, 2007.

Cummings, Brian. *The Literary Culture of the Reformation: Grammar and Grace*. Oxford: Oxford University Press, 2002.

Daiches, David. *The King James Version of the English Bible*. Chicago: University of Chicago Press, 1941.

Daniell, David. "Introduction." In *Tyndale's Old Testament*, ed. David Daniell, ix–xxix. New Haven: Yale University Press, 1992.

Davies, Horton. "Ten Characteristics of English Metaphysical Preaching." In *Studies of the Church in History*, ed. Horton Davies, 103–47. Allison Park, Pa.: Pickwick, 1983.

Davis, Walter R. "Meditation, Typology, and the Structure of John Donne's Sermons." In *The Eagle and the Dove: Reassessing John Donne*, ed. Claude J. Summers and Ted-Larry Pebworth, 166–88. Columbia: University of Missouri Press, 1986.

Delitzsch, Franz. *Biblical Commentary on the Psalms*. 3 vols. Trans. Francis Bolton. Grand Rapids, Mich.: Wm. B. Eerdmans, 1952.

Derovan, David, Gershom Scholem, and Moshe Idel. "Gematria." In *Encyclopaedia Judaica*, vol. 7, 2nd ed., ed. Michael Berenbaum and Fred Skolnik, 424–27. Detroit: Macmillan Reference, 2007.

Doerksen, Daniel W. "Preaching Pastor versus Custodian of Order: Donne, Andrewes, and the Jacobean Church." *Philological Quarterly* 73 (1994): 417–29.

Duffy, Eamon. *The Stripping of the Altars: Traditional Religion in England c. 1400–c. 1580*. New Haven: Yale University Press, 1992.

Dubinski, Roman. "Donne's Holy Sonnets and the Seven Penitential Psalms." *Renaissance and Reformation* 10 (1986): 201–16.

Edwards, David L. *John Donne: Man of Flesh and Spirit*. London: Continuum, 2001.

Elsky, Martin. *Authorizing Words: Speech, Writing, and Print in the English Renaissance*. Ithaca, N.Y.: Cornell University Press, 1989.

Esterhammer, Angela. "Speech Acts and World-Creation: The Dual Function of the Performative." *Canadian Review of Comparative Literature* 20 (1993): 285–304.

Ettenhuber, Katrin. "'Take heed what you hear': Re-reading Donne's Lincoln's Inn Sermons." *John Donne Journal* 26 (2007): 127–57.

Even-Shoshan, Avraham. *Dictionary of Even-Shoshan* [Hebrew]. 6 vols. Israel: Ha-Milon Ha-Hadash, 2003.

Ferrell, Lori Anne, and Peter McCullough. "Revising the Study of the English Sermon." In *The English Sermon Revised: Religion, Literature and History 1600–1750*, ed. Lori Anne Ferrell and Peter McCullough, 2–21. Manchester: Manchester University Press, 2000.

Fisch, Harold. "Hebraic Style and Motifs in *Paradise Lost.*" In *Language and Style in Milton*, ed. Ronald D. Emma and John T. Shawcross, 30–64. New York: Unger, 1967.

———. *Jerusalem and Albion: The Hebraic Factor in Seventeenth-Century Literature*. London: Routledge & Kegan Paul, 1964.

———. *Poetry with a Purpose: Biblical Poetics and Interpretation*. Bloomington: Indiana University Press, 1988.

Fletcher, Harris Francis. *Milton's Rabbinical Readings*. Urbana: University of Illinois Press, 1930.

Flinker, Noam. "Odyssean Return and Literary Theurgy in Shakespeare and Milton." In *Tradition, Heterodoxy and Religious Culture: Judaism and Christianity in the Early Modern Period*, ed. Chanita Goodblatt and Howard Kreisel, 51–74. The Goldstein-Goren Library of Jewish Thought, no. 6. Beer-Sheva, Israel: Ben-Gurion University of the Negev Press, 2006.

———. *The Song of Songs in English Renaissance Literature*. Cambridge: D. S. Brewer, 2000.

Fraade, Steven D. *Enosh and His Generation: Pre-Israelite Hero and History in Postbiblical Interpretation*. Chico, Calif.: Scholars Press, 1984.

Freccero, John. "Donne's 'Valediction: Forbidding Mourning.'" *ELH* 30 (1963): 335–76.

Freeman, Donald C. "'Catch[ing] the Nearest Way': *Macbeth* and Cognitive Metaphor." *Journal of Pragmatics* 24 (1995): 689–708.

———. "'The Rack Dislimns': Schema and Metaphorical Pattern in *Antony and Cleopatra*." *Poetics Today* 20 (1999): 443–60.

Fritze, Ronald H. "Kingsmill family (per. c. 1480–1698)." In *Oxford Dictionary of National Biography*, ed. H. C. G. Matthew and Brian Harrison. Oxford: Oxford University Press, 2004. Available at http://www.oxforddnb.com/view/article/71875; accessed July 11, 2007.

Frontain, Raymond-Jean. "'The Man Which Have Affliction Seene': Donne, Jeremiah, and the Fashioning of Lamentation." In *Centered on the Word: Literature, Scripture, and the Tudor-Stuart Middle Way*, ed. Daniel W. Doerksen and Christopher Hodgkins, 127–47. Newark: University of Delaware Press, 2004.

Gane, Erwin R. "The Exegetical Methods of Some Sixteenth-Century Anglican Preachers: Latimer, Jewel, Hooker, and Andrewes." *Andrews University Seminary Studies* 17 (1979): 23–38, 169–88.

Gardiner, Anne Barbeau. "Introduction." In *Saint John Fisher: Exposition of the Seven Penitential Psalms: In Modern English*, ed. Anne Barbeau Gardiner, ix–xxxvii. San Francisco: Ignatius Press, 1998.

Gardner, Helen. "The Historical Sense." In *The Business of Criticism*, 127– 57. Oxford: Oxford University Press, 1959.

———. "Introduction." In *The Metaphysical Poets*, ed. Helen Gardner, 15–29. Harmondsworth, U.K.: Penguin, 1972.

George, Philip Michael. "The Sacramental Art of John Donne's Sermons on the Penitential Psalms." Ph.D. diss., University of British Columbia, 1997.

Gesenius, Wilhelm. *Gesenius' Hebrew Grammar*. Ed. E. Kautzsch, trans. A. E. Cowley. Mineola, N.Y.: Dover, 2006.

Gilmore, Alec. *A Dictionary of the English Bible and its Origins*. Sheffield: Sheffield Academic Press, 2000.

Goldish, Matt. *Judaism in the Theology of Sir Isaac Newton*. Dordrecht: Kluwer, 1998.

Goodblatt, Chanita. "An Intertextual Discourse on Sin and Salvation: John Donne's Sermon on Psalm 51." *Renaissance and Reformation* 20 (1996): 23–40.

———. "Christian Hebraists." In *Reader's Guide to Judaism*, ed. Michael Terry, 110–11. Chicago: Fitzroy Dearborn, 2000.

———. "From 'Tav' to the Cross: John Donne's Protestant Exegesis and Polemics." In *John Donne and the Protestant Reformation*, ed. Mary Papazian, 221–46. Detroit: Wayne State University Press, 2003.

———. "'High Holy Muse': Christian Hebraism and Jewish Exegesis in the Sidneian *Psalmes*." In *Tradition, Heterodoxy and Religious Culture: Judaism and Christianity in the Early Modern Period*, ed. Chanita Goodblatt and Howard Kreisel, 287–309. The Goldstein-Goren Library of Jewish Thought, no. 6. Beer-Sheva, Israel: Ben-Gurion University of the Negev Press, 2006.

———. "The Presence of Abraham Ibn Ezra in Seventeenth-Century England." *ANQ* 22 (2009): 18–24.

———. "Vetus Testamentum Multiplici Lingua." In *Hebraica Veritas?* University of Pennsylvania Center for Advanced Judaic Studies Library, May 2002. Available at http://www.library.upenn.edu/cjs/exhibit; accessed April 12, 2004.

Goodblatt, Chanita, and Joseph Glicksohn. "From *Practical Criticism* to the Practice of Literary Criticism." *Poetics Today* 24 (2003): 207–36.

Goshen-Gottstein, Moshe. "Foundations of Biblical Philology in the Seventeenth Century: Christian and Jewish Dimensions." In *Jewish Thought in the Seventeenth Century*, ed. Isadore Twersky and Bernard Septimus, 77–94. Cambridge, Mass.: Harvard University Press, 1987.

Gosse, Edmund. *The Life and Letters of John Donne*. 2 vols. Gloucester, Mass.: Peter Smith, 1959.

Grafton, Anthony. "Colloquy Live: A Discussion with Anthony Grafton." *The Chronicle of Higher Education*, July 5, 2002. Available at http://chronicle.com/colloquylive/2002/07/grafton; accessed May 5, 2004.

———. *Defenders of the Text: The Traditions of Scholarship in an Age of Science, 1450–1800*. Cambridge, Mass.: Harvard University Press, 1991.

Greenblatt, Stephen. *Renaissance Self-Fashioning: From More to Shakespeare*. Chicago: University of Chicago Press, 1980.

Greenslade, S. L. "English Versions of the Bible, 1525–1611." In *The Cambridge History of the Bible: The West from the Reformation to the Present Day*, ed. S. L. Greenslade, 141–74. Cambridge: Cambridge University Press, 1963.

Greenspoon, Leonard. "Bible Translations. Greek: The Septuagint." In *Encyclopaedia Judaica*, vol. 3, 2nd ed., ed. Michael Berenbaum and Fred Skolnik, 595–98. Detroit: Macmillan Reference, 2007.

Grossfeld, Bernard, and S. David Sperling. "Bible Translations. Aramaic: The *Targumim*." In *Encyclopaedia Judaica*, vol. 3, 2nd ed., ed. Michael Berenbaum and Fred Skolnik, 588–95. Detroit: Macmillan Reference, 2007.

Grossman, Avraham. "The School of Literal Jewish Exegesis in Northern France." In *Hebrew Bible/Old Testament: The History of Its Interpretation*, vol. 1, *From the Beginnings to the Middle Ages (until 1300)*, ed. Magne Sæbø, 321–71. Gottingen: Vandenhoeck & Ruprecht, 2000.

Gruber, Mayer I. *Aspects of Nonverbal Communication in the Ancient Near East*. Rome: Biblical Institute Press, 1980.

———. "Solomon ben Isaac." In *Reader's Guide to Judaism*, ed. Michael Terry, 565–68. Chicago: Fitzroy Dearborn, 2000.

Grünbaum, Max. *Neue Beiträge zur semitischen Sagenkunde*. Leiden: E. J. Brill, 1893.

Guibbory, Achsah. "Donne's Religion: Montague, Arminiansim and Donne's Sermons, 1624–1630." *ELH* 31 (2001): 412–39.

Guy, John. "Thomas Cromwell and the Henrician Revolution." In *Reassessing the Henrician Age: Humanism, Politics and Reform 1500–1550*, ed. Alistair Fox and John Guy, 151–78. Oxford: Basil Blackwell, 1986.

Hailperin, Herman. *Rashi and the Christian Scholars*. Pittsburgh: University of Pittsburgh Press, 1963.

Hall, Basil. "Biblical Scholarship: Editions and Commentaries." In *The Cambridge History of the Bible: The West from the Reformation to the Present Day,* ed. S. L. Greenslade, 38–93. Cambridge: Cambridge University Press, 1963.

Hall, Michael. "Searching and Not Finding: The Experience of Donne's *Essays in Divinity.*" *Genre* 14 (1981): 423–40.

Hamlin, Hannibal. *Psalm Culture and Early Modern English Literature.* Cambridge: Cambridge University Press, 2004.

Hammond, Gerald. "William Tyndale's Pentateuch: Its Relation to Luther's German Bible and the Hebrew Original." *Renaissance Quarterly* 33 (1980): 351–85.

Harland, Paul W. "Donne's Political Intervention in the Parliament of 1629." *John Donne Journal* 11 (1992): 21–37.

———. "Dramatic Technique and Personae in Donne's Sermons." *ELH* 53 (1986): 709–26.

Hartman, Louis F., and S. David Sperling. "God, Names of: YHWH." In *Encyclopaedia Judaica,* vol. 7, 2nd ed., ed. Michael Berenbaum and Fred Skolnik, 675. Detroit: Macmillan Reference, 2007.

Haskin, Dayton. "John Donne and the Cultural Contradictions of Christmas." *John Donne Journal* 11 (1992): 133–57.

Hassel, R. Chris, Jr. "'Ignatius His Conclave' and the New Astronomy." *Modern Philology* 68 (1971): 329–37.

Herbert, Edward, Baron of Cherbury. *The Life and Raigne of King Henry the Eighth.* London: Thomas Whitaker, 1649.

Herr, Moshe David. "Genesis Rabbah." In *Encyclopaedia Judaica,* vol. 7, 2nd ed., ed. Michael Berenbaum and Fred Skolnik, 448–49. Detroit: Macmillan Reference, 2007.

———. "Midrash." In *Encyclopaedia Judaica,* vol. 14, 2nd ed., ed. Michael Berenbaum and Fred Skolnik, 182–85. Detroit: Macmillan Reference, 2007.

Hill, Eugene D. "John Donne's Moralized Grammar: A Study in Renaissance Christian Hebraica." In *Papers in the History of Linguistics,* ed. Hans Aarsleff, Louis G. Kelly, and Hans-Josef Niederehe, 189–98. Amsterdam: John Benjamins, 1987.

Hirsch, David A. Hedrich. "Donne's Atomies and Anatomies: Deconstructed Bodies and the Resurrection of Atomic Theory." *Studies in English Literature, 1500–1900* 31 (1991): 69–94.

Hodgson, Elizabeth M. A. *Gender and the Sacred Self in John Donne.* Newark: University of Delaware Press, 1999.

Holsinger, Bruce. "The Four Senses of Roland Barthes." In *The Premodern Condition: Medievalism and the Making of Theory,* 152–94. Chicago: University of Chicago Press, 2005.

Hurley, Ann Hollinshead. *John Donne's Poetry and Early Modern Visual Culture.* Selinsgrove, Pa.: Susquehanna University Press, 2005.

Hutt, David. "Sermon at Matins, Sunday September 28th." In *Westminster Abbey–Sermon 2003.* Available at http://www.westminster-abbey. org/voice/sermon/archives/ 030928_trinity_hutt.htm; accessed June 22, 2007.

"Ibn Ezra, Abraham: As Grammarian." Translated from the *Encyclopaedia Hebraica.* In *Encyclopaedia Judaica,* 8:1168. Jerusalem: Keter, 1971.

Jastrow, Marcus. *A Dictionary of the Targumim, the Talmud Babli and Yerushalmi, and the Midrashic Literature.* 2 vols. New York: Pardes, 1950.

Jessopp, Augustus H. *John Donne: Sometime Dean of St. Paul's, A.D. 1621–1631.* Boston: Houghton, Mifflin, 1897.

Johnson, Jeffrey. *The Theology of John Donne.* Rochester, N.Y.: D. S. Brewer, 1999.

Johnson, Samuel. *Lives of the English Poets.* Vol. 1. London: Oxford University Press, 1906.

Jones, G. Lloyd. *The Discovery of Hebrew in Tudor England: A Third Language.* Manchester: Manchester University Press, 1983.

———. "Introduction." In Robert Wakefield, *On the Three Languages [1524],* ed. and trans. G. Lloyd Jones, 1–39. Binghamton, N.Y.: Medieval & Renaissance Texts & Studies and The Renaissance Society of America, 1989.

Karpman, Dahlia M. "William Tyndale's Response to the Hebraic Tradition." *Studies in the Renaissance* 14 (1967): 110–30.

Katz, David S. "The Abendana Brothers and the Christian Hebraists of Seventeenth-Century England." *Journal of Ecclesiastical History* 40 (1989): 28–52.

———. "Babel Revers'd: The Search for a Universal Language and the Glorification of Hebrew." In *Philo-Semitism and the Readmission of the Jews to England: 1603–1655,* 43–88. Oxford: Clarendon Press, 1982.

———. "The Jewish Advocates of Henry VIII's Divorce." In *The Jews in the History of England: 1485–1850,* 15–48. Oxford: Clarendon Press, 1994.

———. "The Language of Adam in Seventeenth-Century England." In *History and Imagination: Essays in Honour of H. R. Trevor-Roper,* ed. Hugh Lloyd-Jones, Valerie Pearl, and Blair Worden, 132–45. New York: Holmes & Meier, 1981.

———. "The Prehistoric English Bible." In *God's Last Words: Reading the English Bible from the Reformation to Fundamentalism*, 1–39. New Haven: Yale University Press, 2004.

Kelley, Maurice. "Milton, Ibn Ezra, and Wollebius." *Modern Language Notes* 49 (1934): 506–07.

Keynes, Geoffrey. *A Bibliography of Dr. John Donne*. Oxford: Clarendon Press, 1973.

Kintgen, Eugene R. *Reading in Tudor England*. Pittsburgh, Pa.: University of Pittsburgh Press, 1996.

Kirsch, J. P. "Simonians." In *The Catholic Encyclopedia*, vol. 13 (1912), online edition, 2007, ed. Kevin Knight. Available at http://www.newadvent.org/cathen/13797a.htm; accessed July 27, 2007.

Klause, John. "The Two Occasions of Donne's *Lamentations of Jeremy*." *Modern Philology* 90 (1993): 337–59.

Kolatch, Alfred J. *Who's Who in the Talmud*. New York: Jonathan David, 1964.

Kristeller, Paul Oskar. *Renaissance Thought: The Classic, Scholastic, and Humanist Strains*. New York: Harper & Row, 1961.

Kristeva, Julia. *Desire in Language: A Semiotic Approach to Literature and Art*. Ed. Leon S. Roudiez, trans. Thomas Gora, Alice Jardine, and Leon. S. Roudiez. New York: Columbia University Press, 1980.

Kugel, James L. *The Idea of Biblical Poetry: Parallelism and Its History*. New Haven: Yale University Press, 1981.

Lakoff, George, and Mark Johnson. *Metaphors We Live By*. Chicago: University of Chicago Press, 1980.

Lancaster, Irene. *Deconstructing the Bible: Abraham Ibn Ezra's "Introduction to the Torah."* London: Routledge Curzon, 2003.

Lasker, Daniel J. "Karaism and Christian Hebraism: A New Document." *Renaissance Quarterly* 59 (2006): 1089–1116.

———. "Major Themes of the Jewish-Christian Debate: God, Humanity, Messiah." In *The Solomon Goldman Lectures*, vol. 8, ed. Dean Phillip Bell, 107–30. Chicago: The Spertus Institute of Jewish Studies Press, 1999.

Lasker, Daniel J., Eli Citonne, and Haggai Ben-Shammai. "Karaites." In *Encyclopaedia Judaica*, vol. 11, 2nd ed., ed. Michael Berenbaum and Fred Skolnik, 785–97. Detroit: Macmillan Reference, 2007.

Leachman, Caroline L. "Gibbens, Nicholas (*fl.* 1601–1602)." In *Oxford Dictionary of National Biography*, ed. H. C. G. Matthew and Brian

Harrison. Oxford: Oxford University Press, 2004. Available at http://www.oxforddnb.com/view/article/10591; accessed 20 December 2007.

Lein, Clayton D. "John Donne." In *British Prose Writers of the Early Seventeenth Century. Dictionary of Literary Biography*, vol. 151, ed. Clayton D. Lein, 114–39. Detroit: Gale Research, 1995.

Leslie, Elmer A. *The Psalms: Translated and Interpreted in the Light of Hebrew Life and Worship*. Nashville: Abingdon Press, 1949.

Levine, Jay Arnold. "'The Dissolution': Donne's Twofold Elegy." *ELH* 28 (1961): 301–15.

Lewalski, Barbara Kiefer. "The Protestant Paradigm of Salvation." *Protestant Poetics and the Seventeenth-Century Religious Lyric*, 13–27. Princeton, N.J.: Princeton University Press, 1979.

Limor, Ora, and Amnon Raz-Krakozkin. *Jews and Christians in Western Europe: Encounters between Cultures in the Middle Ages and the Renaissance*. [Hebrew]. Unit 6. Tel-Aviv: Open University Press, 1993.

Livni, Yitshak, and Moshe Kokhba. *Hebrew Grammar* [Hebrew]. 17th ed. Jerusalem: Ever, 1965.

Lotman, Yury. *Analysis of the Poetic Text*. Ed. and trans. D. Barton Johnson. Ann Arbor: Ardis, 1972.

Lunderberg, Marla Hoffman. "John Donne's Strategies for Discreet Preaching." *SEL* 44 (2004): 97–119.

Mann, Lindsay A. "Misogyny and Libertinism: Donne's Marriage Sermons." *John Donne Journal* 11 (1992): 111–32.

Manuel, Frank E. *The Broken Staff: Judaism through Christian Eyes*. Cambridge, Mass.: Harvard University Press, 1992.

Marcus, Leah S. "Renaissance/Early Modern Studies." In *Redrawing the Boundaries: The Transformation of English and American Literary Studies*, ed. Stephen Greenblatt and Giles Gunn, 41–63. New York: The Modern Language Association of America, 1992.

Marotti, Arthur F. *John Donne, Coterie Poet*. Madison: University of Wisconsin Press, 1986.

Martin, Catherine Gimelli. "*The Advancement of Learning* and the Decay of the World: A New Reading of Donne's *First Anniversary*." *John Donne Journal* 19 (2000): 163–203.

Maxwell-Stuart, P. G. "De Verbo Mirifico: Johannes Reuchlin and the Royal Arch." *Ars Quatuor Coronatorum* 99 (1986): 206–09.

McCullough, Peter. "Andrewes, Lancelot (1555–1626)." In *Oxford Dictionary of National Biography*, ed. H. C. G. Matthew and Brian Harrison. Oxford: Oxford University Press, 2004. Available at http://www.oxforddnb.com/view/article/520; accessed June 27, 2007.

———. "Donne and Andrewes." *John Donne Journal* 22 (2003): 165–201.

———. "Donne as Preacher at Court: Precarious 'Inthronization.'" In *John Donne's Professional Lives*, ed. David Colclough, 179–204. Cambridge: D. S. Brewer, 2003.

———. "Introduction." In *Selected Sermons and Lectures*, ed. Peter McCullough, xi–lvii. Oxford: Oxford University Press, 2005.

———. "Lancelot Andrewes and Language." *Anglican Theological Review* 74 (1992): 304–16.

———. *Sermons at Court: Politics and Religion in Elizabethan and Jacobean Preaching*. Cambridge: Cambridge University Press, 1998.

Moody, Michael E. "Ainsworth, Henry (1569–1622)." In *Oxford Dictionary of National Biography*, ed. H. C. G. Matthew and Brian Harrison. Oxford: Oxford University Press, 2004. Available at http://www.oxforddnb.com/view/article/240; accessed January 7, 2007.

Mueller, Janel M. "Introduction." In *Donne's Prebend Sermons*, ed. Janel M. Mueller, 1–70. Cambridge, Mass.: Harvard University Press, 1971.

———. "Preface." In *Donne's Prebend Sermons*, ed. Janel M. Mueller, vii–xi. Cambridge, Mass.: Harvard University Press, 1971.

Mueller, William R. *John Donne: Preacher*. Princeton, N.J.: Princeton University Press, 1962.

Murphy, Virigina. "Introduction." In *The Divorce Tracts of Henry VIII*, ed. Edward Surtz and Virginia Murphy, i–xliv. Angers: Moreana, 1988.

Nelson, Brent. *Holy Ambition: Rhetoric, Courtship, and Devotion in the Sermons of John Donne*. Tempe: Arizona Center for Medieval and Renaissance Studies, 2005.

Neusner, Jacob, trans. and ed. *Genesis and Judaism: The Perspective of Genesis Rabbah. An Analytical Anthology*. Atlanta: Scholars Press, 1985.

Newman, Beth S. "John Donne and the Cabala." *The Jewish Quarterly* 23 (1975): 31–36.

Newman, Louis Israel. *Jewish Influence on Christian Reform Movements*. New York: AMS Press, 1966.

Ní Chuilleanáin, Eiléan. "Time, Place and the Congregation in Donne's Sermons." In *Literature and Learning in Medieval and Renaissance England: Essays Presented to Fitzroy Pyle*, ed. John Scattergood, 197–215. Blackrock, County Dublin: Irish Academic Press, 1984.

Oberman, Heiko A. "Reuchlin and the Jews: Obstacles on the Path to Emancipation." In *The Challenge of Periodization: Old Paradigms and New Perspectives*, ed. Lawrence Besserman, 67–93. New York: Garland, 1996.

Oxford English Dictionary. 2nd ed. Oxford: Clarendon Press, 1989. Available at http://dictionary.oed.com.

Patterson, Annabel. *Censorship and Interpretation: The Conditions of Writing and Reading in Early Modern England*. Madison: The University of Wisconsin Press, 1984.

Pebworth, Ted-Larry. "John Donne's 'Lamentations' and Christopher Fetherstone's *Lamentations...in prose and meeter* (1587)." In *Wrestling with God: Literature and Theology in the English Renaissance. Essays to Honour Paul Grant Stanwood*, ed. Mary Ellen Henley and W. Speed Hill, with the assistance of R. G. Siemens, 85–98. Vancouver: M. E. Henley, 2001.

Pelikan, Jaroslav. *The Reformation of the Bible: The Bible of the Reformation*. Catalog of the Exhibition by Valerie R. Hotchkiss and David Price. New Haven: Yale University Press, 1996.

Pollard, Alfred W. *Records of the English Bible: The Documents Relating to the Translation and Publication of the Bible in English, 1525–1611*. London: Henry Frowde and Oxford University Press, 1911.

Potter, George Reuben. "Explanatory Notes." In *A Sermon Preached at Lincoln's Inn by John Donne*, ed. George Reuben Potter, 64–71. Stanford: Stanford University Press, 1946.

Quinn, Dennis B. "Donne's Christian Eloquence." *Journal of English Literary History* 27 (1960): 276–97.

———. "John Donne's Principles of Biblical Exegesis." *Journal of English and German Philology* 61 (1962): 313–29.

Rainey, Anson. "Chaldea, Chaldeans." In *Encyclopaedia Judaica*, vol. 4, 2nd ed., ed. Michael Berenbaum and Fred Skolnik, 561–62. Detroit: Macmillan Reference, 2007.

Raspa, Anthony. "Introduction." In *Essayes in Divinity*, ed. Anthony Raspa, xiii–lxxix. Montreal: McGill-Queen's University Press, 2001.

Raspa, Anthony, and Judith Scherer Herz. "Response." *Renaissance and Reformation* 20 (1996): 97–98.

Reeves, Troy D. *Index to the Sermons of John Donne.* 3 vols. Salzburg, Austria: Institut für Anglistik und Amerikanistik, Universität Salzburg, 1979–81.

Reichert, Victor E. *Job.* Hebrew Text and English translation, with an introduction and commentary. Hindhead, Surrey: Soncino Press, 1946.

Reisner, Noam. "Textual Sacraments: Capturing the Numinous in the Sermons of Lancelot Andrewes." *Renaissance Studies* 21 (2007): 662–78.

Rex, Richard. "The Controversy over Henry VII's First Marriage." *The Theology of John Fisher,* 162–83. Cambridge: Cambridge University Press, 1991.

Rhodus, Tim. "Mattioli, Pier Andrea (Matthiolus). In *History of Horticulture.* Available at http://www.hcs.osu.edu/hort/history/035. html; accessed January 21, 2007.

Richardson, Anne. "Scripture as Evidence in Tyndale's *The Obedience of a Christian Man.*" *Moreana* 28 (1991): 83–104.

Roebuck, Graham. "Donne's *Lamentations of Jeremy* Reconsidered." *John Donne Journal* (10): 1991: 37–44.

Rooney, William J. J. "John Donne's 'Second Prebend Sermon'–A Stylistic Analysis." *Texas Studies in Literature and Language* 4 (1962): 24–34.

Rosenblatt, Jason P. "*Hamlet,* Henry, *Epicoene,* and Hebraica: Marriage Questions." In *Renaissance England's Chief Rabbi: John Selden's Cultural Influence,* 14–53. Oxford: Oxford University Press, 2006.

———. *Torah and Law in "Paradise Lost."* Princeton, N.J.: Princeton University Press, 1994.

Rosenthal, Erwin I. J. "Rashi and the English Bible." *Bulletin of the John Rylands Library* 24 (1940): 138–67.

Rosier, James L. "The Source and Methods of Minsheu's *Guide into the Tongues.*" *Philological Quarterly* 40 (1961): 68–76.

Rummel, Erika. *The Case against Johann Reuchlin: Religious and Social Controversy in Sixteenth-Century Germany.* Toronto: University of Toronto Press, 2002.

Sáenz-Badillos, Angel. "Early Hebraists in Spain: Menahem ben Saruq and Dunash ben Labrat." In *Hebrew Bible/Old Testament: The History of Its Interpretation,* Vol. 1, *From the Beginnings to the Middle Ages (until 1300),* ed. Magne Sæbø, 96–109. Göttingen: Vandenhoeck & Ruprecht, 2000.

Salenius, Maria. "True Purification: Donne's Art of Rhetoric in Two Candlemas Sermons." In *John Donne and the Protestant Reformation,* ed. Mary Papazian, 314–34. Detroit, Michigan: Wayne State University Press, 2003.

Sampson, Geoffrey. *Schools of Linguistics.* Stanford: Stanford University Press, 1980.

Scarisbrick, J. J. *Henry VIII.* Berkeley: University of California Press, 1968.

Schäfer, Jürgen. "John Minsheu: Scholar or Charlatan?" *Renaissance Quarterly* 26 (1973): 23–35.

Schleiner, Winfried. *The Imagery of John Donne's Sermons.* Providence, R.I.: Brown University Press, 1970.

Scholem, Gershom, Jonathan Garb, and Moshe Idel. "Kabbalah." In *Encyclopaedia Judaica,* vol. 11, 2nd ed., ed. Michael Berenbaum and Fred Skolnik, 586–692. Detroit: Macmillan Reference, 2007.

Schwarz, W. "The Philological View: Reuchlin." *Principles and Problems of Biblical Translation: Some Reformation Controversies and Their Background,* 61–91. Cambridge: Cambridge University Press, 1955.

Scodel, Joshua. "John Donne and the Religious Politics of the Mean." In *John Donne's Religious Imagination: Essays in Honor of John T. Shawcross,* ed. Raymond-Jean Frontain and Frances M. Malpezzi, 45–80. Conway, Ark.: University of Central Arkansas Press, 1995.

Searle, John R. *Speech Acts: An Essay in the Philosophy of Language.* Cambridge: Cambridge University Press, 1969.

Shami, Jeanne M. "Anatomy and Progress: The Drama of Conversion in Donne's Men of a 'Middle Nature.'" *University of Toronto Quarterly* 53 (1983–84): 221–35.

———. "Donne, Anti-Jewish Rhetoric and the English Church in 1621." In *Tradition, Heterodoxy and Religious Culture: Judaism and Christianity in the Early Modern Period,* ed. Chanita Goodblatt and Howard Kreisel, 29–50. The Goldstein-Goren Library of Jewish Thought, no. 6. Beer-Sheva, Israel: Ben-Gurion University of the Negev Press, 2006.

———. "Donne's Sermons and the Absolutist Politics of Quotation." In *John Donne's Religious Imagination: Essays in Honor of John T. Shawcross,* ed. Raymond-Jean Frontain and Frances M. Malpezzi, 380–412. Conway, Ark.: University of Central Arkansas Press, 1995.

———. *John Donne and Conformity in Crisis in the Late Jacobean Pulpit.* Cambridge: D. S. Brewer, 2003.

————. "Labels, Controversy, and the Language of Inclusion in Donne's Sermons." In *John Donne's Professional Lives*, ed. David Colclough, 135–57. Suffolk: D. S. Brewer, 2003.

————. "Squint-Eyed, Left-Handed, Half-Deaf: *Imperfect Senses* and John Donne's Interpretive Middle Way." In *Centered on the Word: Literature, Scripture, and the Tudor-Stuart Middle Way*, ed. Daniel W. Doerksen and Christopher Hodgkins, 173–92. Newark: University of Delaware Press, 2004.

————. "Troy D. Reeves. "*Index to the Sermons of John Donne*." *Renaissance and Reformation* 8 (1984): 59–62.

Shapiro, Isaac Avi. "John Burley's Notes on Donne's Sermons." *Review of English Studies*, n.s. 30 (1979): 194.

————. "Donne's Sermon Dates." *Review of English Studies*, n.s. 31 (1980): 54–56.

Shapiro, James. *Shakespeare and the Jews*. New York: Columbia University Press, 1996.

Shillingsburg, Peter L. *Scholarly Editing in the Computer Age: Theory and Practice*. 3rd ed. Ann Arbor: University of Michigan Press, 1996.

Shoulson, Jeffrey S. *Milton and the Rabbis: Hebraism, Hellenism, and Christianity*. New York: Columbia University Press, 2001.

————."'Proprietie in this Hebrew Poesy': George Wither, Judaism, and the Formation of English National Identity." *JEGP* 98 (1999): 354–72.

Shuger, Debora Kuller. "Absolutist Theology: *The Sermons of John Donne*." In *Habits of Thought in the English Renaissance: Religion, Politics and the Dominant Culture*, 115–35. Toronto: University of Toronto Press 1997.

————. *The Renaissance Bible: Scholarship, Sacrifice, and Subjectivity*. Berkeley: University of California Press, 1994.

Silverman, Godfrey Edmond, and Gershom Scholem. "Reuchlin, Johannes." In *Encyclopaedia Judaica*, vol. 17, 2nd ed., ed. Michael Berenbaum and Fred Skolnik, 247–49. Detroit: Macmillan Reference, 2007.

Simon, Uriel. "Abraham Ibn Ezra." In *Hebrew Bible/Old Testament: The History of Its Interpretation*, Vol. 1, *From the Beginnings to the MiddleAges (until 1300)*, ed. Magne Sæbø, 110–28, 377–87. Göttingen: Vandenhoeck & Ruprecht, 2000.

Simpson, Evelyn. "The Biographical Value of Donne's Sermons." *Review of English Studies* 2 (1951): 339–57.

————. "Donne's Spanish Authors." *Modern Language Review* 43 (1948): 182–85.

———. *A Study of the Prose Works of John Donne*. Oxford: Clarendon Press, 1924.

———. *A Study of the Prose Works of John Donne*. 2nd ed. Oxford: Clarendon Press, 1948.

Skinner, John. *A Critical and Exegetical Commentary on Genesis*. The International Critical Commentary. 2nd ed. Edinburgh: T. & T. Clark, 1930.

Smalley, Beryl D. *The Study of the Bible in the Middle Ages*. 3rd ed. Notre Dame, Ind.: University of Notre Dame Press, 1982.

Smith, Alan G. R. *The Emergence of a Nation State: The Commonwealth of England 1529–1660*. London: Longman, 1984.

Snyder, Susan. "The Left Hand of God: Despair in Medieval and Renaissance Tradition." *Studies in the Renaissance* 12 (1965): 18–59.

Sparrow, John. "John Donne and Contemporary Preachers." *Essays and Studies* 16 (1930): 144–78.

Spearing, Evelyn M. "A Chronological Arrangement of Donne's Sermons." *Modern Language Review* 8 (1913): 468–83.

———. "Donne's Sermons, and Their Relation to His Poetry." *Modern Language Review* 7 (1912): 40–53.

Staley, Lynn. "The Penitential Psalms: Conversion and the Limits of Lordship." *Journal of Medieval and Early Modern Studies* 37 (2007): 221–69.

Stanwood, Paul G. "Donne's Earliest Sermons and the Penitential Tradition." In *John Donne's Religious Imagination: Essays in Honor of John T. Shawcross*, ed. Raymond-Jean Frontain and Frances M. Malpezzi, 366–79. Conway, Ark.: University of Central Arkansas Press, 1995.

———. "John Donne's Sermon Notes." In *The Sempiternal Season: Studies in Seventeenth-Century Devotional Writing*, 74–83. New York: Peter Lang, 1992.

———. "Word and Sacrament in Donne's Sermons." In *The Sempiternal Season: Studies in Seventeenth-Century Devotional Writing*, 43–54. New York: Peter Lang, 1992.

Steinberg, Theodore L. "The Sidneys and the Psalms." *Studies in Philology* 92 (1995): 1–17.

Stevens, Timothy Scott. "Things that Belong to the Way: John Donne's Sermons on the Penitential Psalms." Ph.D. diss., Northwestern University, 1990.

Sullivan, Ceri. "The Art of Listening in the Seventeenth Century." *Modern Philology* 104 (2006): 34–71.

Talmage, Frank Ephraim. "Apples of Gold: The Inner Meaning of Sacred Texts in Medieval Judaism." In *Apples of Gold in Settings of Silver: Studies in Medieval Jewish Exegesis and Polemics,* ed. Barry Dov Walfish, 108–50. Toronto: Pontifical Institute of Mediaeval Studies, 1999.

Teugels, G. M. G. "The Creation of the Human in Rabbinic Interpretation." In *The Creation of Man and Woman: Interpretations of the Biblical Narratives in Jewish and Christian Traditions,* ed. Gerard P. Luttikhuizen, 107–27. Leiden: Brill, 2000.

"Texas Christian University Acquires Noted Jewish Scholar's Library of Judaica." *Religion News Service,* January 15, 2002. Available at http://www.religionnews.com/press02/0115_3.html; accessed March 8, 2005.

Touati, Charles, and Bernard Goldstein. "Levi Ben Gershom." In *Encyclopaedia Judaica,* vol. 12, 2nd ed., ed. Michael Berenbaum and Fred Skolnik, 698–702. Detroit: Macmillan Reference, 2007.

Touitou, Elazar. "The Exegetical Method of Rashbam against the Background of the Historical Reality of His Time" [Hebrew]. In *Studies in Rabbinic Literature, Bible and Jewish History,* ed. Y. Gilat, Ch. Levine, and Z. Rabinowitz, 48–74. Ramat-Gan: Bar-Ilan University Press, 1982.

Tribble, Evelyn B. *Margins and Marginality: The Printed Page in Early Modern England.* Charlottesville: University Press of Virginia, 1993.

Turner, Mark, and Giles Fauconnier. "A Mechanism of Creativity." *Poetics Today* 20 (1999): 397–418.

Twersky, Isadore [Isaac]. "The Figure of Maimonides: An Essay on His Special Place in Jewish History." In *Asufot: Annual for Jewish Studies* 10 (1995): 9–35.

Umbach, Herbert H. "The Rhetoric of Donne's Sermons." *PMLA* 52 (1937): 354–58.

Vessey, Mark. "Consulting the Fathers: Invention and Meditation in Donne's Sermon on Psalm 51:7." *John Donne Journal* 11 (1992): 99–110.

Wallerstein, Ruth. *Studies in Seventeenth-Century Poetic.* Madison: University of Wisconsin Press, 1965.

Walton, Izaak. *The Life of Dr. John Donne, Dr. in Divinity, and Late Dean of Saint Pauls Church London.* London: R. Marriot, 1658.

Webber, Joan. "Celebration of Word and World in Lancelot Andrewes' Style." *Journal of English and Germanic Philology* 64 (1965): 255–69.

———. *Contrary Music: The Prose Style of John Donne.* Madison: The University of Wisconsin Press, 1963.

Weber, N. A. "Anabaptists." In *The Catholic Encyclopedia*, vol. 1 (1907), online edition, 2007, ed. Kevin Knight. Available at http://www. newadvent.org/cathen/01445b.htm; accessed July 27, 2007.

———. "Waldenses." In *The Catholic Encyclopedia*, vol. 15 (1912), online edition, 2006, ed. Kevin Knight. Available at http://www.newadvent. org/cathen/15527b.htm; accessed August 20, 2007.

Weiner, Seth. "Sidney and the Rabbis: A Note on the Psalms of David and Renaissance Hebraica." In *Sir Philip Sidney's Achievements*, ed. M. J. B. Allen, Dominic Baker-Smith, Arthur F. Kinney, and Margaret Sullivan, 157–62. New York: AMS Press, 1990.

Wenzel, Siegfried. "Reflections on (New) Philology." *Speculum* 65 (1990): 11–18.

Werman, Golda. *Milton and Midrash*. Washington, D.C.: Catholic University of America Press, 1995.

Whalen, Robert. "Sacramentalizing the Word: Donne's 1626 Christmas Sermon." In *Centered on the Word: Literature, Scripture, and the Tudor-Stuart Middle Way*, ed. Daniel Doerksen and Christopher Hodgkins, 193–223. Newark: University of Delaware Press, 2004.

Williams, Arnold. *The Common Expositor: An Account of the Commentaries on Genesis 1527–1633*. Chapel Hill: The University of North Carolina Press, 1948.

Woodhead, Abraham. *Church-Government Part V: A Relation of the English Reformation*. Oxford, 1687.

Wynne, John J. "Asperges." In *The Catholic Encyclopedia*, vol. 1 (1907), online edition, 2006, ed. Kevin Knight. Available at http://www. newadvent.org/cathen/01793a.htm; accessed January 6, 2007.

Yates, Frances A. *The Occult Philosophy in the Elizabethan Age*. London: Routledge & Kegan Paul, 1979.

Zakai, Avihu. "'All Coherence Gone': Donne and the 'New Philosophy' of Nature." In *Jonathan Edwards's Philosophy of Nature: The Re-Enchantment of the World in the Age of Scientific Reasoning*. London: T & T Clark, forthcoming.

———. "From Judgment to Salvation: The Image of the Jews in the English Renaissance." *Westminster Theological Journal* 59 (1997): 213–30.

Zim, Rivkah. *English Metrical Psalms: Poetry as Praise and Prayer 1535–1601*. Cambridge: Cambridge University Press, 1987.

———. "The Reformation: The Trial of God's Word." In *Reading the Text: Biblical Criticism and Literary Theory*, ed. Stephen Prickett, 64–135. Oxford: Basil Blackwell, 1991.

INDEX

Page references in italics signify illustrations.